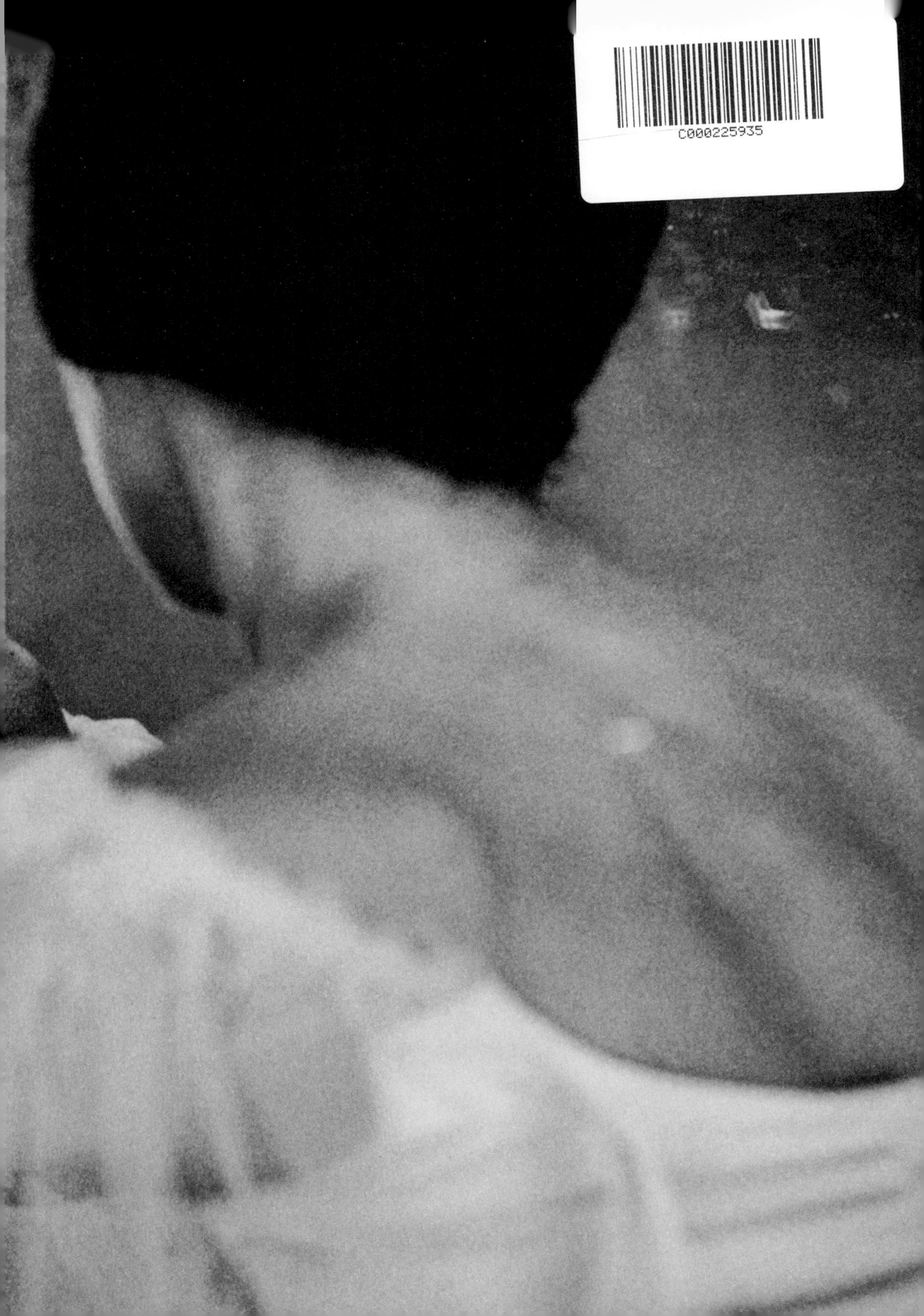
C000225935

AN ARTIST'S LIFE

BY
ELEANORA
ANTINOVA

for David forever

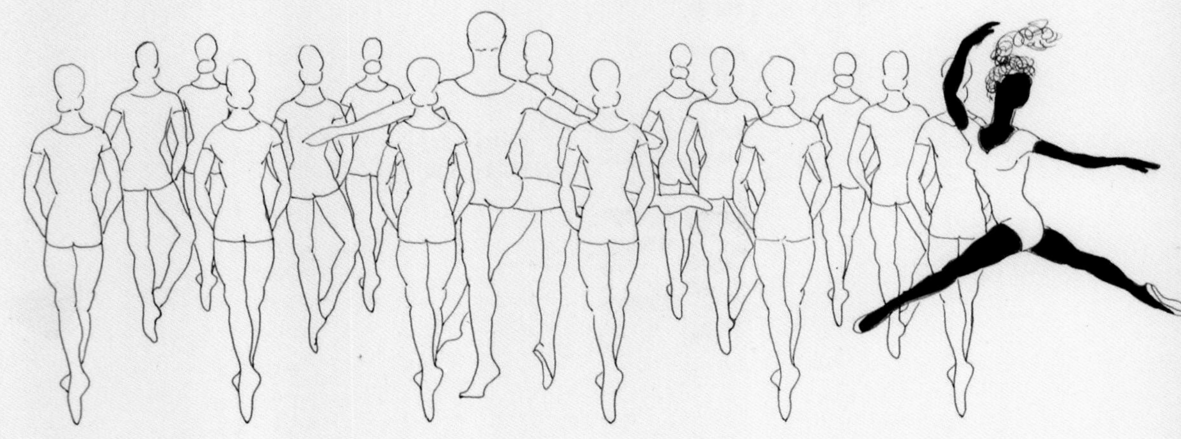

ELEANOR ANTIN

AN ARTIST'S LIFE

BY
ELEANORA
ANTINOVA

HIRMER

115

BEING ANTINOVA

PREFACE

ELEANOR ANTIN
San Diego, California
June 2014

Years ago, while still in college, the young artist Eleanor Antin worked in a coffee shop on Broadway in Upper Manhattan, around 103rd Street. In those days when everybody smoked, the dimly lit, pleasant coffee shop catering to college students and neighborhood people wanting to cool off from a busy day, had a friendly smell of coffee beans, though smoke hung over it like a cloud and her eyes were often irritated and she rubbed them a lot. But as she wryly observed, she smoked one cigarette after another too, so she could hardly complain. She had the night shift and it was an easy job except that the place closed at 3 AM and she had to hang around even when there were no customers, before walking home the several blocks to where she lived on 109th Street between Broadway and Amsterdam. But she liked the quiet walk, Broadway was so peaceful at night, and sometimes she felt like she was so tired she was gliding along in her sleep. The boss was a nice enough guy who spent all day and night, reading comic books from a pile on the table in front of him. Sometimes, when there were no customers during the night, Eleanor joined him. She had a passion for Wonder Woman because at the end of the stories, Wonder Woman often visited her mother who was queen of a Greek isle and her noble ladies wore Grecian robes. Unfortunately, Greg didn't have too many issues of *Wonder Woman* and Batman and Robin were pretty boring so she usually read or did her homework.

Several times a week, a little old lady would come in after midnight and go directly to the same corner table, carefully placing her old fur coat over a chair. While nursing a single cappuccino until closing time, she spent several hours writing in a beautiful red leather notebook. When the boss wasn't looking, Eleanor poured some fresh hot coffee into the woman's cup but she was so intent on her writing that she rarely looked up. Though when she did, her lightly brown, wrinkled face lit up with a conspiratorial smile before looking down and continuing to write. Eleanor tried to read the writing while she poured the extra coffee but the text was written with a thin pen that had to be refilled very often from a small bottle of ink. They were tiny, very florid letters and she couldn't make out any of it.

One rainy night, when the lady writing in the corner was the only customer, even Greg had to admit nobody else would be coming in and they should close an hour early. Eleanor apologized to her. "I'm sorry," she said, "but we're closing early tonight." The woman immediately closed her book and wiped her pen with a kleenex. Eleanor helped her on with her coat which she noticed for the first time was missing most of its lining. "Do you have an umbrella?" she asked. "No dear," the woman smiled. "I've lived through much worse weather than this, in my time." Eleanor closed the door after her and watched her slowly walk down the wet street. Those were pretty high heels. "I hope she doesn't fall," she thought. The streets looked very slippery. It had been raining for hours. "She probably lives around the corner on West End." But when she began cleaning up she realized the old woman had forgotten her book. She couldn't resist flipping through it but again was put off by the tiny letters. Not something you could glance at, for sure, you'd have to sit down and read it. She wrapped it in a napkin to protect it from the rain and went back to the door planning to run after the woman and return her book. But Broadway was empty in both directions. The wet streets shimmered in the yellow light from the lampposts. An occasional car swished by, but otherwise there wasn't a person in sight. She must have turned off to West End already, Eleanor thought, so she tucked the book in the cubby behind the counter until the woman returned.

Only she never did. Eleanor never saw her again. Though sometimes she felt somebody was there at the table she used to sit at, but when she turned around it was empty. For some unknown reason nobody else ever sat at that table again, except perhaps when it was crowded which was very rare. She soon forgot about the book — until Greg decided to close the shop for good and open one downtown where the trade was better. When she was collecting her things on the last night she found the book at the back of the cubby where she'd stuck it so many weeks before. She took it home along with her sweater and notebooks and put it away in her bookcase which was so packed with books, she could never find the right book when she needed it.

Years later, she moved to San Diego with her husband, the poet David Antin, and their one-year-old son, Blaise. They drove in an ancient Cadillac filled with the books they had hoped to give away but found they couldn't. Who knew when they'd want to reread *The Brothers Karamazov* or Casanova's memoirs? "But of course we can always get those books anywhere," she said to David. "It's not as if these are the only editions." But they just looked at each other. "Fuck it," she said. "Let's go to the market and get some boxes."

Later, unpacking the boxes in Solana Beach, the first place where they lived in Southern California, David found a red leather notebook. "What's this?" he asked. "It can't be yours. Your handwriting is unreadable." Eleanor flipped through the pages. "This handwriting is worse than mine," she said. "Can you read it?" He looked over her shoulder. "Nope," he said, losing interest. But she sat down on the couch and began to read. It was slow going. At first she couldn't figure out what it was that the little old lady of so many years ago was writing. "Oh my God," she realized suddenly. "It's an autobiography. Of a ballerina." "You're kidding," David said. "It's in longhand. Who wrote it?" "Don't talk to me now," she said. "I'm reading." "But we have to unpack," David protested. But she didn't answer. She was far away. Even the difficulty of reading that tiny flourishing hand was a pleasure. It made it all so much realer. History isn't a grocery list. The little old lady in the ratty fur coat was writing to her from so far away. Of course, she was dead now. "Jesus, why didn't I sit down and talk with her? What an asshole I am. There was a ballerina who danced with Diaghilev and all I could do was pour her some fucking coffee."

But when she went to the university library and looked up Diaghilev and histories of modern ballet, there was never any mention of Antinova in the indexes. After a while, she stopped looking. She wasn't there. History had forgotten her. But Eleanora was tough. Wasn't she correcting History's mistake by writing her own?

So here's her story. The glory days with the *Ballets Russes* and the lonely years traveling the American wasteland in broken old vaudeville theatres. Poor Eleanora, like all artists she kept reaching for the stars only to be washed away in the inexorable tsunami of history. As she says in her memoir, "Art is not kind to her children."

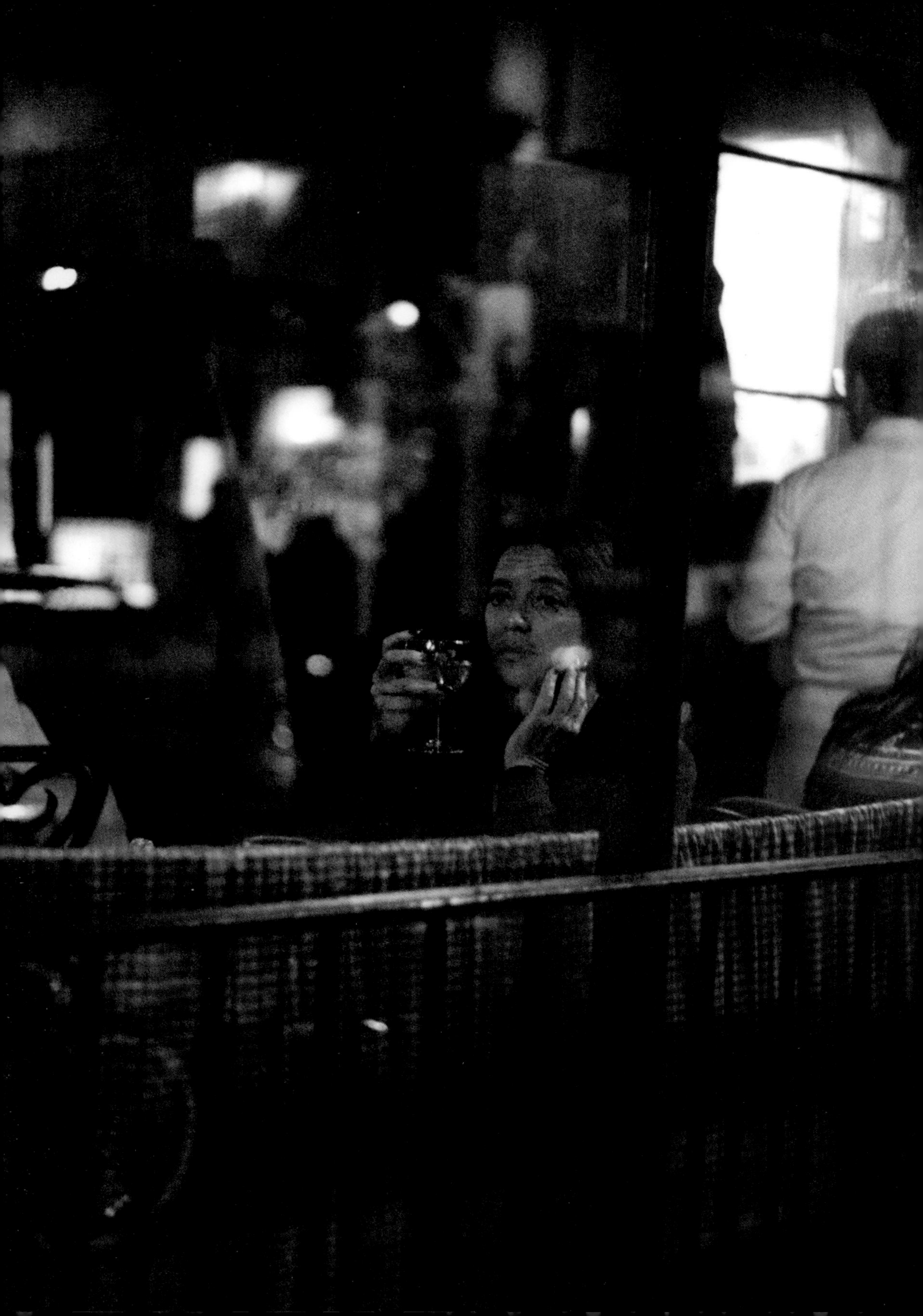

ELEANORA ANTINOVA'S

AN ARTIST'S LIFE

Chapter 1

My Life Begins

You want me to begin at the beginning?

Life never begins at the beginning. One day you find you are someplace like Paris but how you got there is not easy to say.

One can always say on a boat. Yes, I came to Paris on a boat. In steerage, don't you know. With Galician workers returning home from the Burlington Mills. The food was terrible, the old people died of ptomaine poisoning. It was a Brazilian boat, you see, not very high class. It smelled of sardines.

The sailors, though, were all nice boys. They were my age and felt sorry for me cooped up with seasick peasants. When it got dark they let me sneak through the gate to the upper decks where I could breathe again. They were always tired, poor things. The captain made them sit all night on campstools outside the cabins of the single women. He was very strict about that, very Spanish. They told me he wouldn't let the women smoke or dance the tango—these were first class passengers! But he didn't think anything of giving the poorer passengers spoiled food. So they nearly died!

Nothing could kill me, though. The world was at my feet. From the moment my mother kissed me good-bye at the dock, I was free. Naturally she told me again how much she was sacrificing for me. It was true she was. She wasn't a rich woman. She didn't sell insurance.

My father had a small upholstery establishment and wasn't very good at it. Everything he sewed was always off by a few inches. Luckily the people in North Branch were so old they couldn't see well anymore, and besides he never had to make anything new, just repair worn out furniture. Mother had an inn in North Branch but nobody ever came; so she didn't do well either. There was no reason for anybody to come to North Branch. People left from there but no one ever arrived. The population got smaller by two every year because somebody hung himself on the back porch in the fall before the long winter, and somebody else hung himself in the spring after the long winter.

But that sounds Russian, doesn't it? I always said my mother had a Russian soul. That's why I understood the Russian dance so well. You'd think I wouldn't fit in, being American, being black —of course, we weren't black then, we were Negroes. But they sounded like my mother, those Russians. For one thing, she was always shouting at life for dealing her so many blows. When the dancers jumped up and down with clenched fists, I grew calm as a cucumber. I knew they would stop, you see, my mother always did.

Afterwards, they fell all over me, kissing my hands, my ears. "Eleanora, you are an angel, an inspiration. You are strong. In your tiny body is the strength of 10." I got a reputation for being wise. People would confide in me. I had such a solemn expression on my face. "Little owl," Natasha Vitushnyeva used to call me.

I know so many secrets!

But what can one do with secrets? They burn a hole in your head, if you think about them. Better not to think about them. Easy come, easy go. I never asked to know such things. All I wanted to do was dance, but all they wanted to do was talk. Or do great things. They were always dreaming of great things.

My mother was that way. When the bank sent her a small sum to correct an error, she was sure someone had died and left her money in his will. "But mother," I would insist, "you have to be notified by a lawyer of such things." She would look at me scornfully. "You are a child. You know nothing. Such things must be done incognito. My benefactor does not want his family to make trouble. They are nasty people." "But mother, who are they?" But by then she was out of the room, clutching the check in her hand, dreaming of the even more generous benefactor who would appear at the inn next week. My mother had a positive mind. From her I learned hope even in the most dire circumstances.

I needed hope in those days. There I was, poor as a church mouse in a foreign city. I used to encourage myself. "Courage, Eleanora, you are free, black, and 21. Act it!" Those were good times then. The French adored *negritude.* Josephine Baker was in her heyday. People would point out Jack Johnson when he went by with his elegant white wife. The first winter I would have starved except for Jules Pascin. Jules liked black women. He always had several black mistresses around the studio and they were very elegant and knew their way around like nobody's business. They came from glamourous places like Port-au-Prince and Martinique. Once one of them asked me where I came from. "North Branch," I said. She looked at me queerly. "What is North Branch? A tree?" So they all said I came out of a tree. Dorianna, a great big Haitian woman with skin like black velvet, took me under her wing. "Poor baby," she would caress me in her generous arms, rich with the fragrance of musk and Havana cigars. "They are barbaric, the Americans. To come out of a tree. It is shameful."

Pascin wasn't a fashionable painter. He liked to paint women taking off their clothes, when modern painters were all chopping their women into squares and cubes. But whenever he sold a painting to some American tourist, he shared the good luck with us. Then we would go out to Cocteau's club, *Le Boeuf sur le Toit.* I didn't drink like the others because I was Presbyterian—always saving myself for dancing.

I wouldn't eat 2 hours before class and an hour afterwards, can you imagine? When I had several classes a day I just went without food until evening, when I ran down the hill to where the artists lived and Jules would feed me. It was just as well I didn't eat all day, I didn't have money, anyway. What with new tights, dance shoes, and the rent on the hole in the wall with the bidet that didn't work, there was little left over for food.

And that winter was cold. The worst winter Paris had seen since the 19th century, people used to say. When they met in the street people's breath steamed like in a Turkish bath. I had a fur coat that used to belong to a countess; but that was many years before, when the armpits didn't ventilate. It was so old I dropped fur whenever I got up from a chair. But it was my first fur coat. If I snuggled my face into the collar it felt soft and pretty. I couldn't see how it looked anyway when I wore it, could I? I used to sail into *Le Boeuf sur le Toit* just like the other chic ladies with their svelte hats and silky legs. The women were ravishing and everybody was in love with everybody else. Poets, musicians, dancers, art dealers, painters, journalists, pederasts, transvestites, actresses, millionaire sportsmen, anarchists.

> *Fourmillante cite, cite pleine de reves*
> *Ou le spectre, en pleine jour, raccroche la passant!*

An old black woman used to sell flowers at the tables. Our set bought some and doubled the money. "She was beautiful once," my friend Dorianna whispered, clucking her tongue in sympathy. "She was the most sought after of the models. All the painters wanted her. She worked with Renoir, Degas—the anarchist Lenin was her lover. She found him in a café starving, took him home and fed him like a stray cat. He stayed with her, but what good that was to her God only knows. They say he read books all the time and when he wasn't reading, he was writing. And dirty foreigners used to visit and make muddy tracks on her old wood floor. She couldn't even afford a rug, poor baby. They say when he went back to Russia to make the revolution she wrote asking for money. She was no longer in demand. She was old. She was hungry. He never answered her letters. It was as if he had never known her. Not a *sou* did she get from him."

"Men!" Dorianna spat on the floor. "You will not do that to me, Jules, do you hear? I will take a knife to your heart and plunge it down to your buttocks."

"Shut up, Dorianna," Jules laughed while his wife looked down her nose.

Mme. Pascin always acted as if the gorgeous women in their set were only models. I don't know how she carried it off, but she did. The funny thing was that I really was only a model, and not much of one at that, since I was in class all day, but she suspected me of the most evil intentions. I would catch her giving me the evil eye and I swear I was innocent. Yet when she looked at me I got hot all over. I felt guilty because she thought I was guilty. I, with my Presbyterian soul. I, who did not yet know men.

Perhaps she distrusted my youth. She was the type of older woman who was afraid of girls. How ridiculous! I was green, unripe, there was no flesh on me. I put my foot into everything. Jules would have been embarrassed to lay a hand on me. I was everybody's mascot. Ah yes, I led a charmed life.

But the winter could not last forever. Spring came as it always does. The snow melted and I lost my heart.

My first love was a young French poet, Jean Meunier. Perhaps you have heard of him? He had something of a vogue at one time but I don't think he is much remembered anymore. With artists it is always the same. For years one works and dreams and later there is nothing. It is almost as if those years didn't happen. Sometimes one feels as if one's memories are borrowed from a book. How can they be real if nobody else shares them?

But then I was in the morning of my life. I didn't know of such things. Jean was a poet. He was my first poet. All my life I have had a weakness for poets. He would recite to me in those dark glamourous tones the French use for poetry and I was flattered. Alas, he went on for hours. My back hurt from sitting still. Outside the sun was shining. I wanted to move through the streets of Paris. I was a dancer not a statue.

So I began to improvise as he read. Slowly at first, because I didn't know how to move to language. I was used to the regular beat of the studio pianos, you see. In class each variation is played twice. The steps must be danced exactly the same way from both the right and left sides. It was very awkward at first. I was ashamed for him to see how inept I was—so I danced with my back to him.

The room was very small. There were perhaps a dozen feet of space between the bed and the window. I looked outside at the brilliant streets of Paris and moved to the rhythms of the fierce, violent voice behind me. You see, Jean had a *folie.* He believed that in a previous life he had been

Baudelaire. So the only poetry he read was from *Les Fleurs du Mal.* It had a stately classical sound but it was ruptured by violence. Jean perhaps erred in favor of violence. He was young and passionate. He began to believe I was Jeanne Duval, Baudelaire's dusky mistress from Martinique and the inspiration for the Black Venus poems.

Je pense à la négresse, amaigrie et physique
Piétinant dans le boue, et cherchant, l'oeil haggard,
Les cocotiers absents de la superbe Afrique.

Hers really was a sad story. I have seen many terrible things in my long life, and I can tell you some of the worst have been done in the name of love. Baudelaire hid behind his name when he stole the young actress Jeanne Duval away from the stage. He locked her in a small apartment in a side street of Paris where nothing would ever happen to her again. Except of course for his visits, which indulged what the French call "complicated tastes." The inevitable happened. The poor girl turned to drink to keep her company. He already had his drugs.

But could her prison have been any smaller than the room where Jean's insistent voice compelled me to dance? The only place I could leap was out the window, which I assure you never occurred to me for a moment. But dance is movement. Where could I move in such a narrow space?

From side to side, of course.

Up and down!

I attached chains to my wrists and crouched facing stage right. With painful slowness I turned 180 degrees to face stage left. I drew out what was little more than a stage direction until it turned into a scream. I did this by liberating the individual parts of my body so they could move independently—head, shoulders, chest, arms and hands, hips, legs, knees even—till I quite forgot I was moving everything but my feet. The insanity of my concentration on the most minimal gestures liberated me from the immobility of my position.

How preposterous!

I was the only dancer in the world to dance a stationary dance.

But there was a poetry to it. Didn't poor Jeanne have only a narrow space in which to move? The constrictions of her life became the restrictions of my dance.

One day, Jean shouted out behind me. "You are magnificent. We must show our creation to the world." I whirled around. I had forgotten all about him. He was jumping up and down, snapping his fingers like a Spanish dancer. I was mortified. How could I bare my secret thoughts to the cynical eyes of Paris? He cajoled. He shouted. Finally, he went to a little café in Montparnasse frequented by the younger, poorer artists, and arranged for us to do our piece without telling me.

I was outraged. How dare he do this. I packed my clothes. I would leave him. I would go back to Pascin. His ladies would look after me. At Madame's they were already whispering that I was missing classes. My work was losing its crispness. I was becoming careless.

He opened the door. "Leave at once," he said in a cold, miserable voice, as if I were lower than the ants. "How could I waste my time with such a coward?"

"I am not a coward," I sobbed. "I'm just afraid." He glared at me. I collapsed in a heap. "Do what you want," I moaned. "Only don't shout at me. You are making me deaf."

So "L'Esclave" debuted at a miserable little café whose name I no longer remember. I may never have known it. It was dark and dismal. But we struck a chord in the hearts of those artists. They adored me. They came back every night. I was the toast of Montparnasse. Invitations began to appear from the more advanced salons. Jean bought a new cape and velvet pants. I thought he looked ridiculous, like a monkey.

"I like you better in your laborer's smock and the old beret," I said.

"Bah," he shouted. "We must make an impression. We are artists, not beggars."

But I didn't worry too much about him. Performing in the elegant salons, where we were sometimes invited to mingle after the performance, my eyes were opened to the great world. It no longer troubled me that my piece was incorrectly understood and poor Jeanne was ignored by everybody. It was what the artists call "the self-referential ironies" of my work that people talked about. The newspapers even wrote about the "dark little dancer and her attendant poet." Those were wonderful days, but again, they too were numbered.

The fashionable Misia Sert invited us to dance at her salon. Misia Sert! The great friend of Diaghilev and the Russian dancers! Isadora had danced for her guests! The writers of Paris sat at her feet!

But she was charming, unaffected by fame. "Coco Chanel is here tonight," she whispered. "If you please her she will design a costume for you. Africa excites her. Your fortune will be made."

I don't know if Chanel liked my dance or not. After the performance I went to feed myself from the great table of delicacies I had noticed earlier. A giant of a man with a white streak running through his hair studied me through his monocle. It was the Silver Fox himself—Sergei Pavlovitch Diaghilev! What did I care about Coco Chanel! That was the evening I met Diaghilev and he invited me to join the *Ballets Russes.*

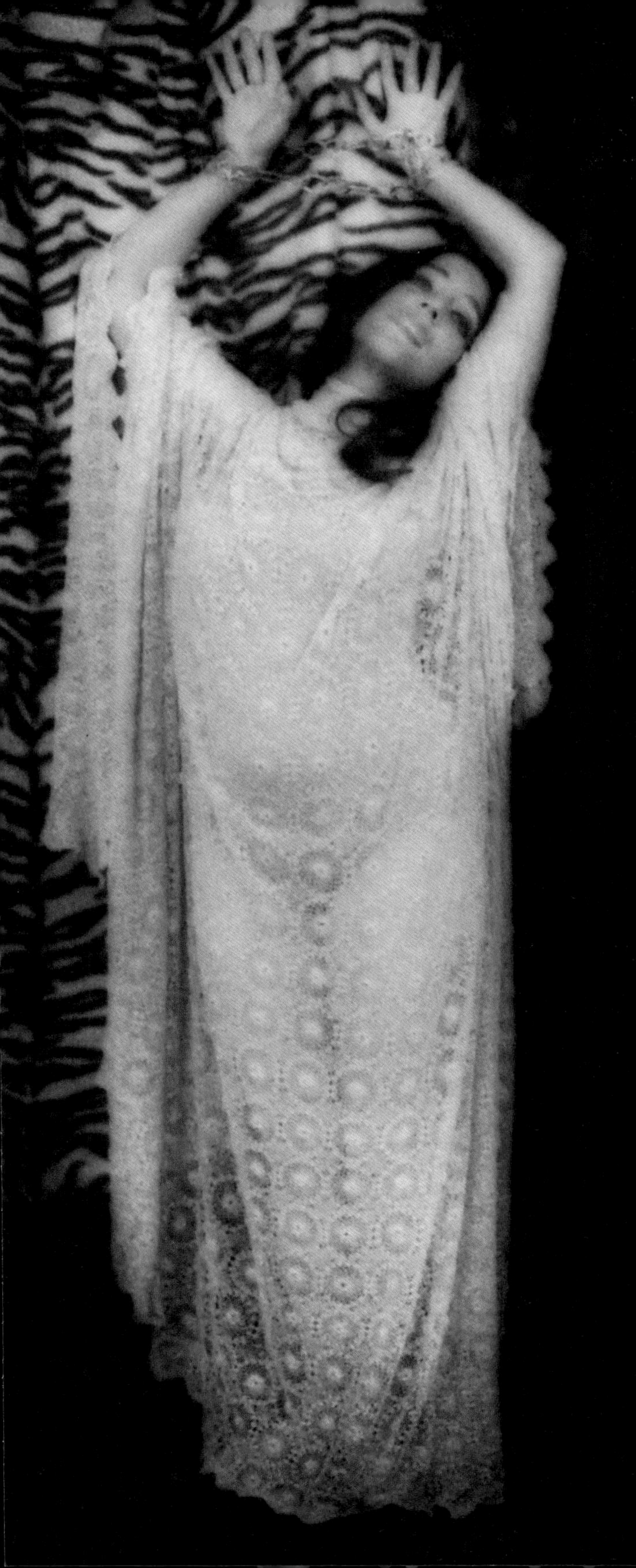

Eleanora Antinova in *L'Esclave*

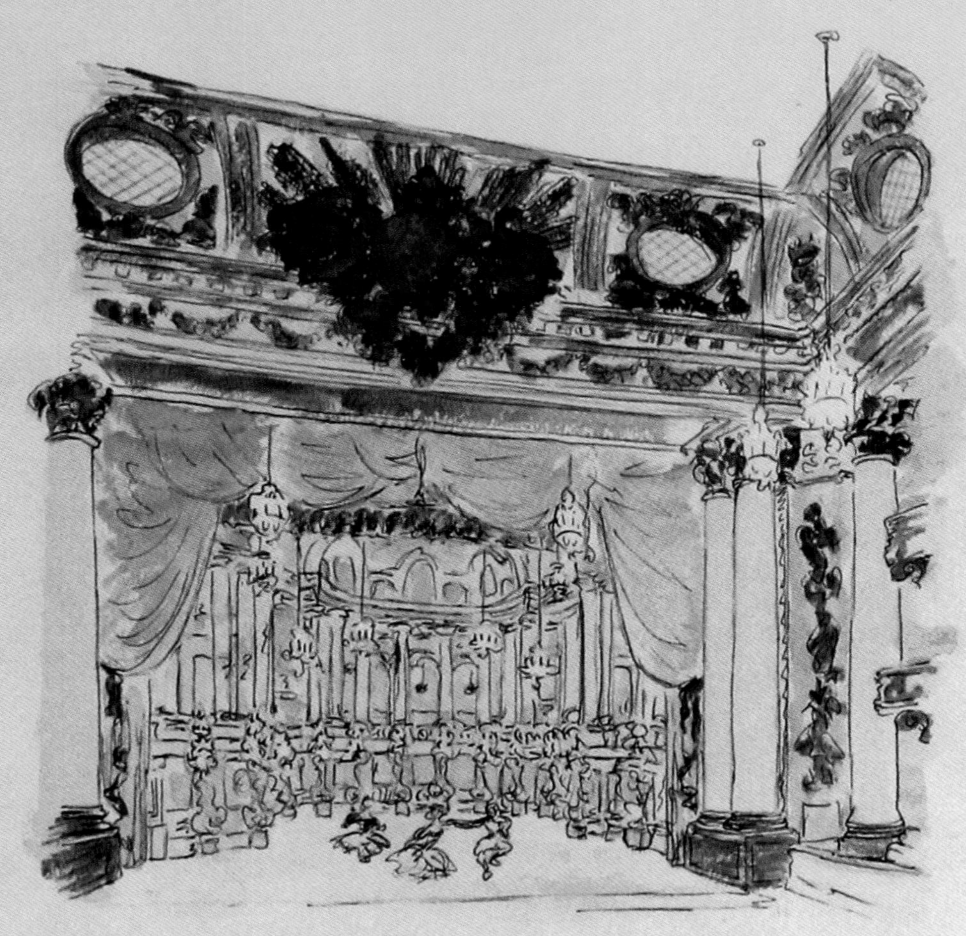

"It was always as though we were acting in a play someone else had written. Each of us — as well as the audience — knew the ending too well."

Later that night, Jean raged at me. How could I leave our artistic collaboration for a decadent ballet company?

"They are Czarists," he shouted. "Aristocrats! Would you leave me for a Grand Duke?" He was shocked at the thought.

"Jean," I said, packing my bags. "I am leaving you for the world."

I walked out the door and never looked back.

But, my dear, that is a whole other story, isn't it?

Chapter 2

My Life in the Corps

The best times were between seasons in Monte Carlo, when we rehearsed the new ballets. Afterwards we would spend our free time on the boardwalk. The costumes were amazing. We saw the most advanced designs before they reached the boulevards of Paris. True, many ladies still floated by with heads wrapped in furry chignons, sparkling with diamonds and pearls, long lacy hems and scarves trailing behind them.

"Reactionaries," Katya spat in contempt. "When will they enter the 20th century?" We dancers adored the sleek heads of the modernist party, their skinny bodies defiantly devoid of curves, blood red fingernails bringing onyx cigarette holders to matching lips in short defiant jerks. Bored eyes said no man will weigh me down. Life is beneath contempt . . .

The notorious Contessa de Chevigne, rumored to have been the lover of the mysterious Ida Rubenstein, was always followed by a tall African holding 2 leopards on a leash. "Where is he from?" the girls whispered to me. "Why do you not speak to him?" "Don't be ridiculous," I hissed at them. "He is an Ethiopian for sure. I do not know Ethiopian." "How do you know he is Ethiopian?" Katya asked suspiciously. "He looks Nubian to me." "Because she is Italian, that's why," I explained angrily. "He is a slave." The girls were shocked. "Is that why his head is shaved?" someone asked in a hushed voice. "Poor man," Tanya said, crossing herself. "The Contessa is very wicked. Perhaps she feeds the ugly ones to the leopards." "Don't be absurd," I said. "This is not a Fokine ballet. It is life."

One warm day in May, we were unwilling witnesses to one of the scandals of the season, when two identical frocks of the modern mode encountered each other. As it turned out none of us actually saw it since, as we learned later discussing the event in hushed tones, we had all been looking in the opposite direction.

It was Natalya who pointed us to where her sharp eyes had already observed the approach of the elegant Contessa de Beaumont, her long thin body wrapped in satin folds of orange, black, and silver rectangles. At the same time, gliding towards her was the Contessa de Chevigne. "Oh sweet Jesus," Tanya crossed herself, she was always crossing herself. "Hold me up, my darlings. I am faint." Two identical frocks of the modern mode were preparing to encounter each other on the boardwalk.

A hush fell upon the crowd. Waiters stopped in their tracks, trays poised dangerously in the air. Only the principals seemed not to notice—except the young Contessa stopped moving. Her legs appeared to levitate in a miraculous manner until one noticed the tight grip upon her arm maintained by her escort who had a stiff upper lip in the English manner and looked neither to the right nor the left. The Contessa de Chevigne turned a high color.

"She is having a stroke," Katya whispered.

"But she is smiling," an indignant voice protested. "Shameless woman."

The daily costume represented the wearer's soul and aspirations. For two persons to display the same soul was an intense personal embarrassment for everybody. That they should be modernist souls was a severe loss of face for our group, and sure enough, shortly after the event, the old man and Kochno, deep in animated conversation, hurried past us in the direction of the theatre.

I learned later one of the unfortunates, the Contessa de Beaumont, on her arrival home was overcome by such a melancholy frame of mind that her family removed her to a Swiss hospital for the remainder of the season. The Contessa de Chevigne, on the other hand, was older and of a severe character. She maintained a fixed smile for several hours but was forever after unable to remove it, and her mouth continued to turn up at the corners irrespective of whether the poor lady found herself at a wedding or a funeral.

"And the last shall be first," Carla whispered, crossing herself in the Italian manner.

Pavel, our resident Bolshevik, laughed. "We shall see what we shall see," he warned all who would listen.

"What shall we see, idiot?" Katya demanded.

He laughed and rolled his eyes. They bulged a little and were not pleasant to look at even in the best of times.

Katya turned away. "You are disgusting," she said.

"When the worm turns you will speak differently of Comrade Pavel," he shouted, waving a fist in the air.

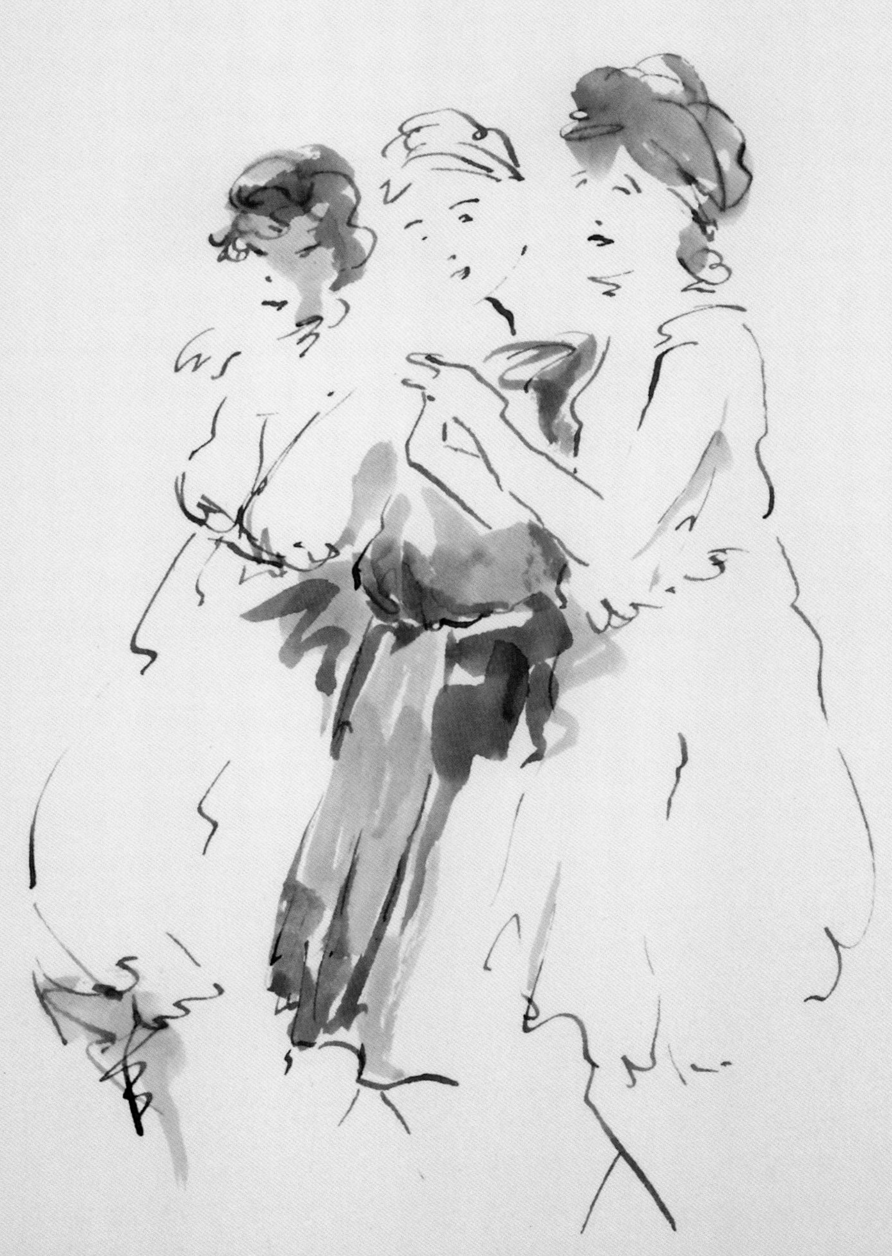

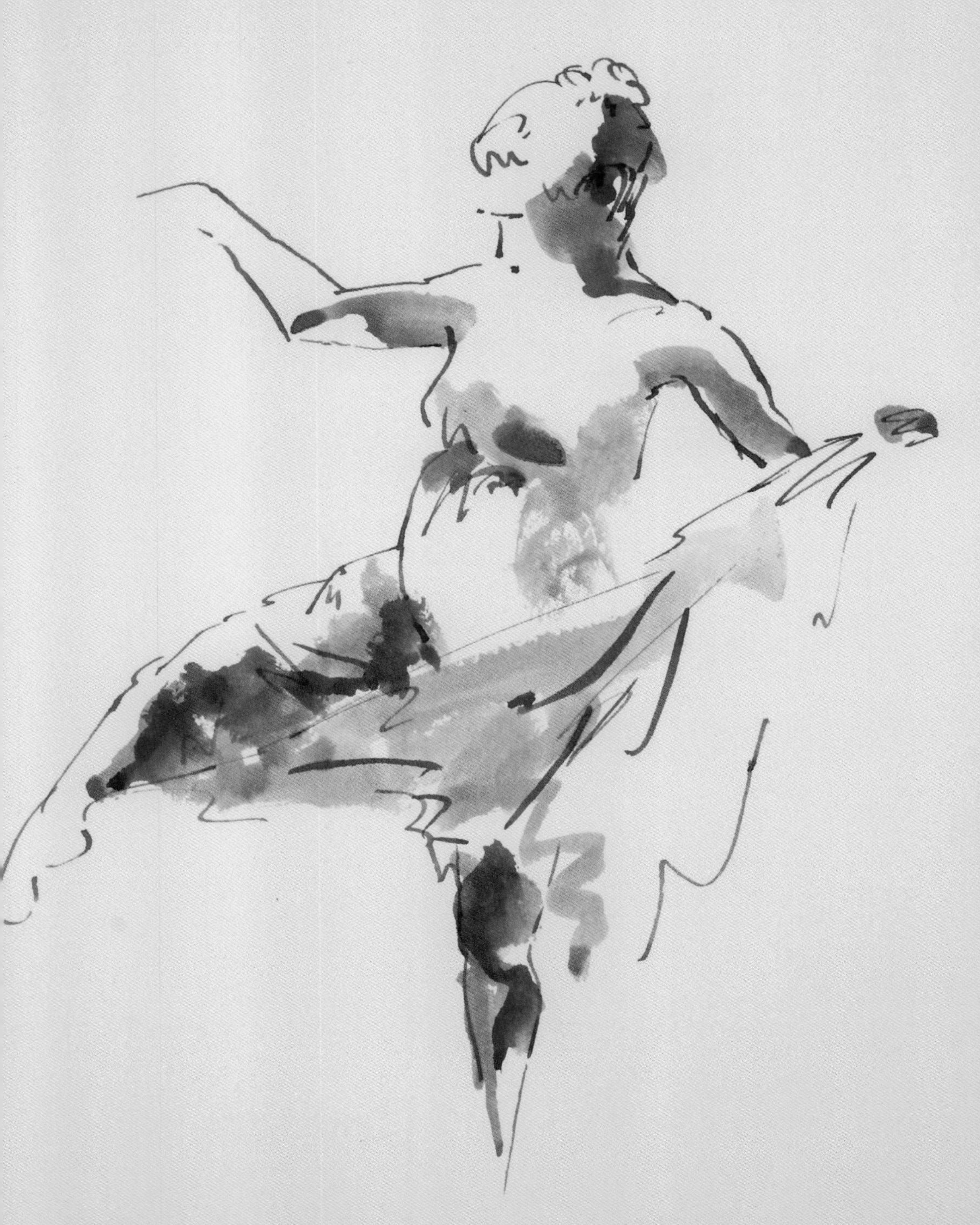

“Careful,” I warned. “He is vengeful. He may partner you one day.”

“Have no fear,” she sighed. “The pig will act the rooster. Is the red so different from the white?”

“What is the use?” Tanya said.

“You are like my father,” Carla shouted. “We were depressed to look at him. ‘Is that how it is, then?’ he asks me. ‘Is that how what is, papa?’ ‘You know little button,’ he winks and pinches my bottom.”

“What did you know, Carla?” Natalya asked.

“What is there to know?” Carla shrugged. “He fell into a quarry and died and poor mama is so old she does not remember her daughter.”

“Still, what is the use,” Tanya insisted, “when one fine day without any warning, and for no reason, one is made to feel a fool.”

“One must always remember one *is* a fool. Then one cannot be too surprised when it is made public.”

“It is terrible to be a fool in public. In private, one can keep oneself busy and not think about it.”

“All men are fools.”

“We are not men, simpleton.”

“We are fools,” Katya said, “because we sit here at *Chez Pasquier* where they forget to wash the tablecloths while the old man sits at the *Café Paris* with a silk hat.”

“But, Katya, it is terrible there. It costs 10 francs for a bottle of mineral water.”

“Yes, and why can I not afford to pay it?” she demanded.

“But only a fool would pay such an outrageous sum.” Natalya was appalled.

“You do not understand. It is a hypothetical question.”

“So ask a real question,” Carla shouted.

“Yes. One with an answer,” Natalya agreed.

"How can there be an answer," Tanya said mournfully. "How can there be an answer when you do everything right and you are still a fool."

Later that week, the waiter at *Chez Pasquier* leaned over and whispered the price of *pirozhki* was going up 2 francs. "What?" Tanya shouted, shoving her daily allotment of 6 francs for 2 *pirozhki* at him. She was on a tight budget. Every week she sent money to a farmer in Brittany who boarded her young son.

The waiter shrugged. "I, too, must pay," he said.

"You?" Katya was appalled. "You who work here in this miserable place?"

"It is the proprietor. He is a miser. A skinflint. He would charge for an open bottle of mineral water."

"Had we known we would never patronize such a beast."

"Perhaps," the waiter smiled. "But where else would the Russian dancers go? This is hardly *Montparnasse*." He was right, of course. With the rapidly rising prices *Chez Pasquier* was the only establishment on the boardwalk we could afford. The others didn't sell *pirozhki*. What would the elegant bistros and cafés do with little meat pasties invented by Polish peasants?

I looked at the waiter for the first time. He was not old but already had a hump on his back as big as a dwarf. He was too tall to be a waiter. Even now, when he didn't need to, he stooped over us. "Stand up straight," I said. "Why do you stoop?" He bent yet further over me, smelling of peppers and onions. "Shall I sit beside you, *Mademoiselle?* Would that be to your liking?" The poor man was awful! There was nothing to be done for it. We ordered a *pirozhki* each with mineral water. "Still, it is outrageous," Katya announced to his departing back.

"And what is there to do about it, Excellency?" Carla snapped.

"Go down on our knees and thank God for our good fortune. You, who have never been to the University. What are you, an educated woman?"

"It would be better to be a cashier. You do not get so hungry," Natalya said.

Carla snorted. "Yes, and grow fat like a sausage."

"At least we do not get water in our legs," Natalya agreed.

Lizavetta began to whimper. "I have a dream. I will grow old. I will be a *concierge*."

Katya shook her head.

"We will merely be a little hungrier, my friends, *n'est-ce pas*?"

The mineral water arrived.

"Prosit!"

Olga and her new painter joined us for an aperitif after rehearsal. The little Spaniard rubbed his nose into her ear under the large straw hat she always wore.

"He is smelling me, the scoundrel." She stuck her fingers into his nostrils. "Stop that, pig! Stop at once!"

"They say you are a painter but you are a puppy dog," I teased him.

"He is a bulldog like the English." Olga tweaked his nose, showing him off affectionately. "Look, look, Eleanora. What kind of nose is that?"

"An insignificant nose," I giggled.

"A negligible nose." She shook her head severely. "Alas, poor Pablito. You will never get anywhere in this world with a nose like that."

"Yes," I agreed. "It is a timid nose."

"A puny nose. It is absurd. It is invisible, that nose," she shouted, tugging at it mercilessly.

He bit her cruel fingers with his teeth, coming down hard. She screamed.

"Miserable fauve."

They struggled but he wouldn't release her fingers from his mouth. She began to shout and curse in Russian.

"Look, look, over there." She rolled her eyes desperately. "Now there is a real man. Such a nose!"

He turned to look and she pulled her fingers away, moaning softly as she licked each one gently. The teeth marks were still there.

He stared at the rival nose.

"It is certainly a nose of substance," he agreed.

"It is coming this way," I whispered.

And sure enough, a dark lugubrious man with a serious nose was bowing and introducing himself to Olga.

"You are a friend to my family," he said, "for you make love to my cousin, the Count Sylvestre."

She smiled sweetly, blowing on her bruised fingers with her lips.

"My dear man, it is all the same to me. I have made love to all of your cousins, but, alas, I do not like you any the better for it."

Sure enough, she surprised everyone by marrying her little Spaniard soon after. But he was already rich from his paintings even then and it wasn't long before she left us.

On the way back to my room after rehearsal, I tried not to look directly at the wretched little pile on the ground. The night sweeper from the casino passed the letter to me. He was an old hand and didn't appear impressed.

> *My Dear Mother,*
> *All my hopes have been ruined. I fancied myself a man of genius. The reality has proved me to be a fool. I die, because life is no longer to be supported. Look charitably on this last action of my life.*
> *Adieu . . .*

"No name?" I asked the sweeper.

"He is Albanian," he shrugged.

"Yes, I know. I have heard."

I went back to Tanya and Hilda.

"The poor woman," I said, sitting down on the bench.

"He was demented," Tanya answered. "'His mother it seems has been dead for many years and it is his wife with whom he has been traveling. She, on the other hand, wants no part of him and refuses to receive the body."

"Who will get the suit? It is a good one."

"She is mad. She will not accept the suit. She will not even speak to the inspector. She threw her clothes at him. She tore up her passport in his face and then tried to eat the pieces. She is very angry at the French."

"The inspector is not French."

"She does not know the difference."

"Perhaps she is right. There is really not much of a difference."

"This is a terrible place," Hilda said.

"What will they do with him?"

"They are trying to learn if he was Catholic or Orthodox."

We stared silently at the flourishing garden. Exotic flowers rioted along the walls. Overhead, the sky was a clear blue, almost white.

"It will be hot today and we have much to do," Tanya sighed, getting up. She was always practical. We used to say, when the angels came for Tanya she would ask to see their papers. She was more French than Russian. "The Duke of Connaught will be in the audience tonight. The old man hopes he will pay for a new ballet."

"I have certainly lost my *pirouettes* now," Hilda sighed. "It will be a bad day, for sure."

I was always the last to leave after the evening performance. I liked the silence of the deserted theatre. It was a good time to take stock of things. One night, I was alone in the dressing room darning a pair of rehearsal tights with more holes than threads, when one of the supers shuffled in.

"A gentleman is here and wishes to see you."

"Please send him away."

Half an hour later the super shuffles back.

"The gentleman is waiting for you. He asks what you would like to drink."

"What would *you* like to drink?" I asked.

He gave me a broad toothless smile.

"Champagne."

"Tell him champagne and go drink it yourself."

"And make sure he sees you," I called after him.

The small round gentleman with the cane limped towards me out of the shadows. For several weeks we had observed him in faultless evening clothes standing apart from the usual motley crowd of friends and family waiting at the stage door. "He has a history, that one," the girls agreed, wondering who had excited the interest of such a distinguished "and rich" gentleman. Franca, who was part Italian and very daring, grew impatient and threatened to speak to him. "But what is he then, a deaf mute? We shall grow old. He must declare himself."

"I am sorry about the champagne," he murmured.

"I'm tired," I explained sharply. "I have been working since 8 o'clock this morning. It is now almost midnight."

"But I thought perhaps a *chocolat* at *Chez Pasquier*. I have seen many of the Russian dancers there."

"Do you not understand? I must be back in class again tomorrow morning at 8 o'clock."

He gripped my arm with the surprising strength lame men often have. "It has taken me two weeks to get up the nerve to speak with you. Tonight, I am mad with courage. It will be gone tomorrow. I beg of you . . . "

"It is your problem."

"You are cruel . . . you . . . an *artiste* . . . "

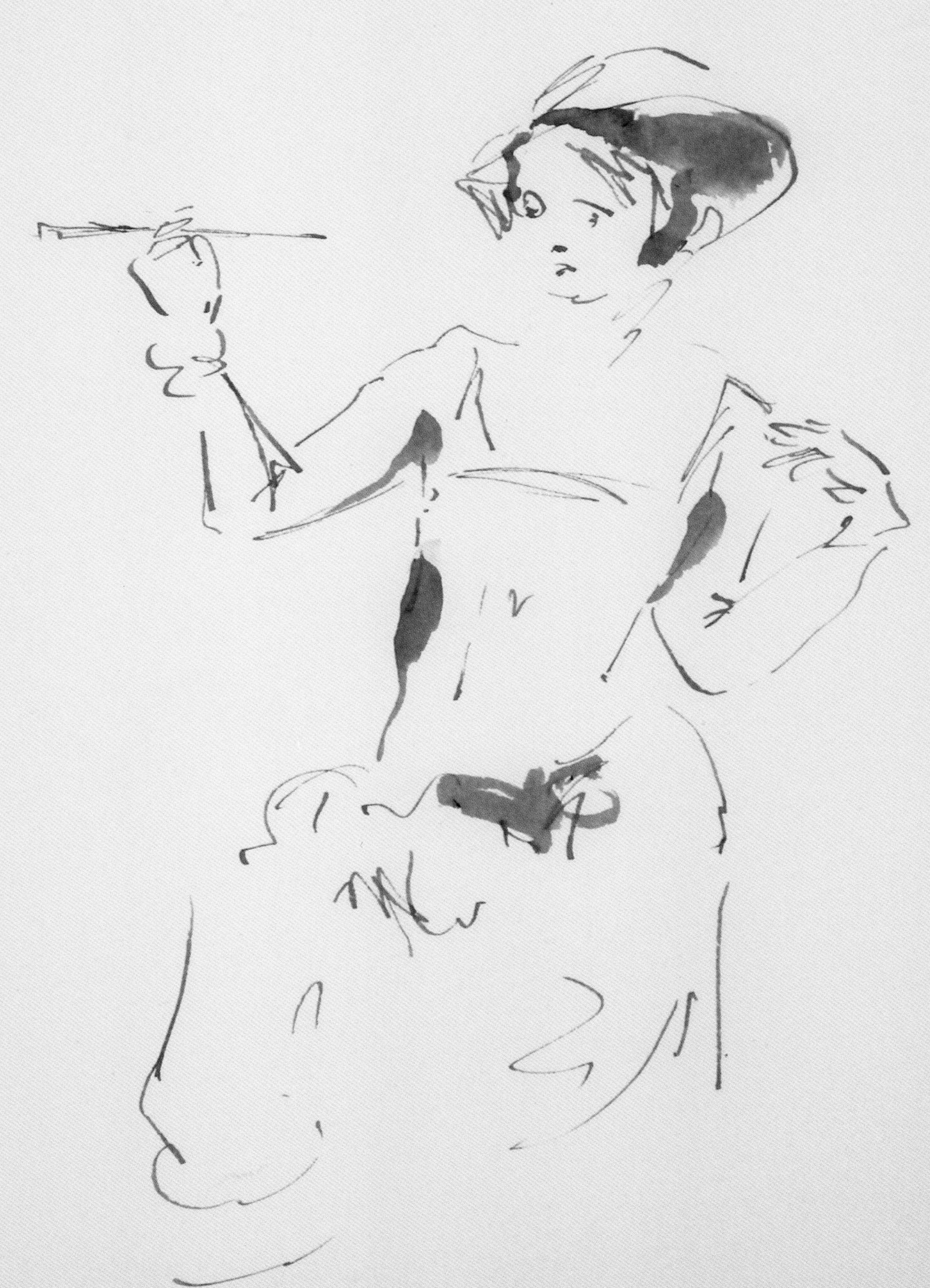

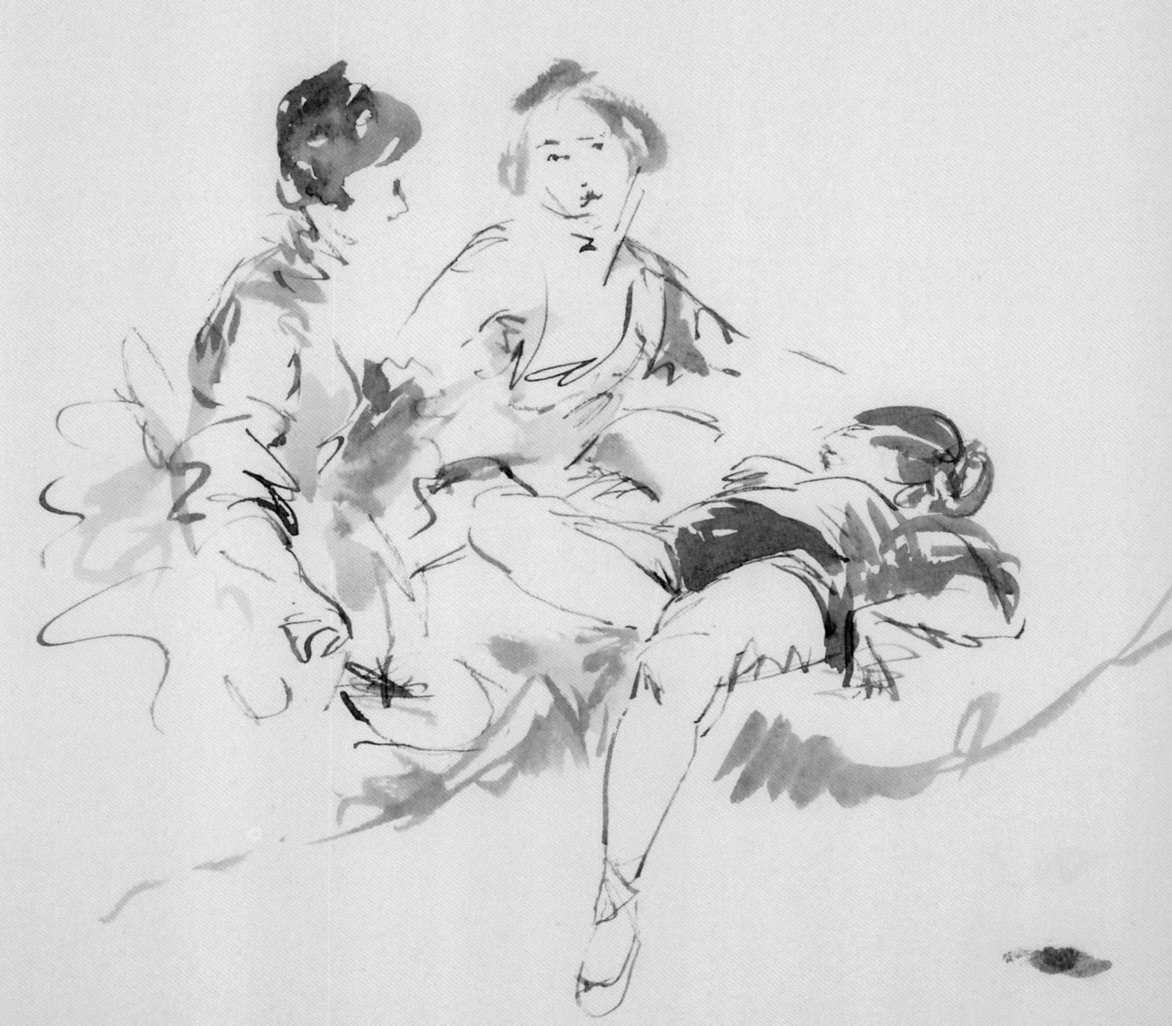

“Art is cruel.”

“And love?”

I looked into his large dark eyes. He was short like me and they were on a level with my own.

“No,” I relented. “Love is not cruel. It has no class at 8 o’clock in the morning.”

There were few people still up at that hour and we easily found a corner table out on the terrace where we could listen to the distant sounds of waltzes from the casino orchestra. Since I was a guest I ordered *tartlette, gateau anglais, tablette de chocolat,* and a tray full of *biscuit des fourges.* “I am a Scot.” He introduced himself in English. “Bobby Duff, 8th Earl of Fife. They call me Grey Bobby. I have lived a very lonely life.”

He began escorting me home every night. We fell into the habit of first stopping at *Chez Pasquier.* My boorishness amused him and he encouraged me to wolf down successive quantities of *gateaux, crèmes, petits fours, chocolats, glaces* . . . “I am like an old woman who has lost all other pleasures in life,” I confessed to Tanya. “I am ashamed.” Whereupon she exclaimed *“Quest-ce que vous voulez, ma petite? On se volupte comme on peut.”* No doubt about it, my voluptuous life was beginning to tell. Mitya took to pinching me when I passed close to him. “Like grape-fruits,” he shouted, lunging for my breasts.

Only my patron took no notice of the changes in me. It was enough for him to enjoy the pleasures of feeding me while sharing the experiences of my day. He reveled in backstage intrigue, pestering me to remember facial expressions, pondering the meaning behind simple words. “And what do you suppose she means by that?” he would often say. “Not much, I expect, Russians have bad memories. They forget tomorrow what they raved about today.” But he was a Scotsman and wasted nothing. He spent hours trying to convince me of the depths lurking beneath the simplest events. A shrug of a shoulder was enough to set him fabricating for the rest of the night. His connections were very ingenious. Fortunately, they weren’t true, but I don’t think truth had anything to do with it.“It *could* be the case,” he insisted.

“It *could* be, Grey Bobby, but it *isn’t.*”

He shook his head sadly. “Poor Eleanora. A lamb among wolves. You will never get anywhere in this world.”

“You have taken my advice. You have a patron,” the old man nodded approvingly. “They say he is a Scottish Earl. The Scots are all rich. It is a well-known fact. He must give you many presents.”

"Look at my new diamond!"

The girls buzzed admiringly around Choura, trying to touch the sparkling stone on her short stubby fingers.

"Who gave it to you, you little demon? The one with the fat nose or the little red one?" They pestered her with questions. "Will you keep it or sell it?"

"I would keep it . . . even if I were starving, I would keep it . . ."

"Me, I would rather have filet every night for a year. For that I would sell my diamond."

"You do not have a diamond. With your common character, you never will."

"What do you know? I have had 10 diamonds in my time. But I preferred a good meal, a good bed . . ."

"I won't argue that one!"

Giggling and backslaps . . .

That night for the first time I noticed Grey Bobby's hands. "You don't wear many rings," I said. "The gentlemen in Sergei Pavlovitch's circle wear many rings. It's the thing."

His voice was brusque, angry. "What with so many thieves running around looking like gentlemen?"

But at the theatre the next night he carried a large box with a silver wrapper. "A present." He blushed. It looked awfully big for a ring.

Could it be a fur coat? Lydia always swore they were the best. "With a cold finger you can dance, *ma petite*. But with a cold *cul*?"

At our table at *Chez Pasquier* he drank a toast to my future and I unwrapped my present. It was a red wool sweater. "From my factory," he beamed proudly. "The neck, the sleeves, are hand fashioned." It really was a nice sweater. I put it on and puffed out my chest. He applauded, ordered more wine and cried with pleasure at his success.

"What's that?" Mitya muttered sourly when I pranced in. "You look like a *concierge*."

"A present from Grey Bobby," I announced proudly.

"Well, tell him I need one, too," he growled. "It has been getting cold at night. But tell him a big size. I don't want to wear a glove around my neck."

The next night I told Grey Bobby of Mitya's request.

"But, of course, I love poets, too. I would like nothing better than to present him with a token of my handiwork. Perhaps he could present me one of his as well? An autographed copy of his book? Do you think it is possible?" His voice sounded wistful.

Naturally, Mitya agreed. He had hundreds of copies of his book stacked under the bed. They held up the sagging mattress.

"And tell the old capon he can have copies of my other books as well. One for each sweater. I'll send them back home. That will give them something to howl about all right."

Soon I was requesting sweaters for everybody. The studios were filled with sweaters of all colors and sizes. It looked like all of Russia would be warmed by Scottish wool, since after getting several for themselves the requests came in for a poor old mother freezing in Moscow, a younger sister without a stitch for her trousseau, the old dancer with crippling arthritis freezing in the bed he would never leave.

"But, of course, poor things. Dear, dear people. Of course I am honoured to help the Russian dancers. Such great *artistes.* Perhaps in return an old slipper? The discarded costume from *Les Biches*? May I be the fortunate recipient of these glories?"

Soon dancers were running up to ask whether I thought "his Lordship" would prefer a torn slipper or a shredded *tutu.* These were always in terrible shape since we continued to repair and mend our worn dance clothes until there was no fabric left to sew two torn parts together. It was unimaginable that anybody would want them and certainly not in exchange for new wool sweaters. Once I came upon the girls talking about a man who collected the cut hair from dancers' heads and at night did something with the strands, but I didn't catch what it was because when they saw me they changed the subject. When we met any of them in cafés or on the boardwalk wearing their new sweaters, they would stroke their brightly clad breasts with one hand and giggle behind the other like peasants.

"*Charmante, charmante,*" Grey Bobby would murmur, doffing his hat and bowing. Once I stuck out my tongue at the false Grushenkas behind his back and they cracked up with laughter. Katya wondered whether "his Lordship" would be interested in some snapshots she had collected over the years. She had a very "artistic" one of herself and Sokolova doing arabesques on Idzikowski's shoulder on the beach at Cannes, and several unfortunately blurry ones of the American tour—even one of Nijinsky and Romola sitting on the deck of the boat. When it got about that she exchanged her box of photographs for 3 sweaters there was a run on old souvenirs. Virginia came up with some letters the Maestro had written to her when she was in the children's class back in London, when she would sit in his lap after class and eat chocolates while he pinched her lightly on the arms and legs. She got a yellow sweater for those.

Whether the exchange was arranged directly with him or me, Grey Bobby was very meticulous about writing my name in his careful, florid script on the gift cards. He never referred to the exchanges as anything but gifts. "You are the Lady Bountiful," he smiled graciously at me. "Now what else can they do but love you?"

"Thief! Thief!"

The unaccustomed words rang out through the dressing rooms. Doors slammed. People started running.

"It is Stefan! They say it is Stefan!"

"I have stolen nothing," shouted Stefan. "I am innocent. Call Grigoriev before it is too late. The Russians are attacking me."

"Help!" Dounia wailed. "The Russians are attacking Stefan."

"He stole my sweater, he did," Franca screamed.

"How can a man steal his own sweater? It is mine. It came this morning in a white box."

They crowded through the door into my dressing room. I surveyed them coolly from my mirror where I had been painting my lips.

"I know nothing about any sweaters," I said.

"What do you mean you know nothing? Your name is on the card. You are Antinova — the giver of sweaters. Who else if not you?" Dounia waved her finger accusingly at me.

"It is my patron. I am a miser. I do not give presents. Ask Tanya. She knows I am a miser."

"It is true," Tanya defended me. "A terrible miser."

"A man will go to jail. You must lift a finger." Dounia began to cry.

"Idiot! One does not go to jail for stealing a sweater."

"How do you know? You are not a judge. My grandfather went to Siberia."

"This is France."

"I have not stolen any sweaters. It is my property. It came in a white box."

"Stop shouting, you nasty Hungarian! Who cares about your dirty sweaters."

Every day, messengers delivered gaily wrapped boxes to the *pension.* The small rooms filled with sweaters and I began to despair of keeping the place clean. Afraid I would complain to my benefactor, Mitya took to whisking them away before I returned from the theatre. I suppose he sold them in the cafés, because I began to see bright blue and yellow sweaters on the boardwalk in the evenings. Mitya himself began to sport fancy ties, spats, a dandy straw hat, a new fountain pen. I never saw a penny from his new business. Not even a silk scarf. He could at least have bought me a silk scarf.

"How is the little capon, lately?" he asked anxiously. "You were early last night. Didn't he feed you?"

"I was tired last night, Mitya. Have you forgotten that I am dancing the new roles? I wanted to sleep."

"These aristocrats need to be led." He pulled the end of his nose. "Whet his appetite. He'll snap to, all right." He uncurled a large scented handkerchief from the breast pocket of his new silk suit and blew his nose. "Tell him I need more sweaters with turtlenecks. They are very popular."

I grabbed my practice clothes and slammed the door behind me. My only peaceful moments were in class where everybody agreed my dancing grew richer, deeper. "You are maturing," the girls said. "Your *adage* breathes, the postures melt like butter into each other. Such *epaulement!* Choura looked at you from under her eyelids today. She is worried."

"But I suffer so." I confided to Tanya. "Men are such bores. They think only of themselves."

"Alas, with women, it is always so. So long as you are not beaten you can count yourself lucky."

"Karsavina is not beaten. Pavlova is not beaten"

"But you are not Karsavina. You are not Pavlova."

"How do you know I am not? I am young yet."

"Hush! Be thankful. You are dancing principal roles. Sergei Pavlovitch has plans for you. Two men love you."

"Who needs them? One robs me and the other is so complicated! I shall collapse with weariness."

"Foolish girl! You are fortunate."

"But I do not feel fortunate," I wailed.

"You Americans are spoiled. Life is so!"

"But I don't like it!"

"Who asked your opinion? One lives the best one can. It is a bad business all around."

"Grey Bobby," I begged one night. "Please do not give us any more sweaters."

His eyes grew big like saucers. "But my product is good. I thought you appreciated my sweaters."

"I love them, dear Grey Bobby. But couldn't you give me another present? A ruby, maybe? Or a diamond? The girls say that when a diamond merchant gives a dancer diamonds she know what he wants, but when a sweater manufacturer gives her sweaters, who can know what he wants?"

"Who has said this?" He began to weep. "Who has turned you against me?"

"Oh, stop it, please. I am not against you. I am just bored with your absurd sweaters."

He pressed my fingers passionately to his lips.

"Eleanora, you are a brave, generous, passionate creature. But then you are a great artist. I, alas, am a miserable cripple, good only for carrying your shawl, your fan, running after you with scent bottles when you are faint, gazing in ecstasy at your *pirouettes*."

He thrust his arms straight up above his head.

"Whereas horse's legs have long been the ruin of my family, I wish only to devote myself to the support and well-being of yours."

“You are doing it again, Grey Bobby. Making mountains out of molehills.”

“You do not know. I am afflicted.”

Leaning over the table, our faces touching, he whispered of his hopes “this time around . . . I like to think that you alone can save me. An American. A Negress. I could lose myself. I would be born again.”

He sounded ominous. Were the girls right, after all, with their dark looks and secret whisperings?

“Now look here, Grey Bobby. This is getting out of hand. You’d better explain yourself.”

He groaned. “More than anything I would be brave, generous, passionate. That is why I love *artistes*. Have you ever heard of a stingy *artiste*? But I cannot help myself. I despise myself. Yet I suffer even more when I go against my nature.”

He began kissing my hand, my wrist, my forearm, my elbow . . .

“If I should give you a ring now . . . and how I have dreamed of this . . . your wicked little face looks mysteriously up at me. I tremble . . . your fingers move toward the pretty little Tiffany box I hold out to you . . . but my passionate dream always breaks off here. It is my disease . . .”

He hid his face in his hands.

“I cannot suffer to see you open it. 1,000 cannons pointed directly at me could not force me to look into that little box . . . We are frozen there, you and I, forever . . .”

He opened his eyes and they were filled with tears.

“My darling, if I should give you a ring now I would suffer the pangs of fierce regret and morbid miseries. I should torment you with entreaties to return it to me if but for a moment. I would cajole you to loan it to me for an evening. I would offer to repair an imperfection I had noticed in the setting and steal it away from you. There is no hope for me. Have pity . . .”

That night I wrote to my sister.

> *Dear Marcia,*
> *I am still unlucky. I have always been unlucky. Please accept this lovely green sweater as a present from your loving and very tired sister. Next week I will send you a yellow one and perhaps also a brown.*
> *Eleanora*

Chapter 3

A Romantic Interlude

There are many fantastic stories about how I became a soloist after 3 years in the back row of the Corps. How somehow I made water on stage so that when Vera Petrovna did her *fouettés* she slipped and crushed her kneecap. Or, how because my room was next to hers in the *pension*, I kept her awake all night singing love songs. Naturally, these made her cry bitterly, so that by the end of the week she was so tired she fell asleep on stage in the middle of an *adage*. It has even been said that I slipped castor oil into her vodka after a matinee and she soiled her evening *tutu* and couldn't go on.

It was the Russians who passed these stories around. They made up stories like devils. They rolled their eyes and whispered so loud you could hear them out front and they beat their chests and groaned and told you terrible things. They themselves thought nothing of scattering broken glass on the floor to steal a rival dancer's part. Everybody knows how at the Maryinsky, Kchessinka's dresser searched the floor before she went on—to make sure it was powdered with resin and not glass. They say the Grand Duke Andrei, when he was her lover, enjoyed crawling around on his hands and knees, getting resin all over his clothes and face, while she encouraged him from the wings. It was only because Sergei Pavlovitch knew what they were like and wouldn't stand for it, that we had so little of that. Still—the time the trap door opened under Bohlm during the *Polovetsian Dances* and he fell through and was out for the rest of the season . . .

It was Boris who danced the part after that!

The real story is that Vera Petrovna was 8 months pregnant and couldn't get away with dancing any longer. She took to her bed and tried peasant remedies to bring the baby out early, but nothing worked, and she had to stay put for a while. That was the day Lydia eloped with the English Lord, and Sokolova was still ill in Monte Carlo, and Alicia already had more parts than she could handle at her age.

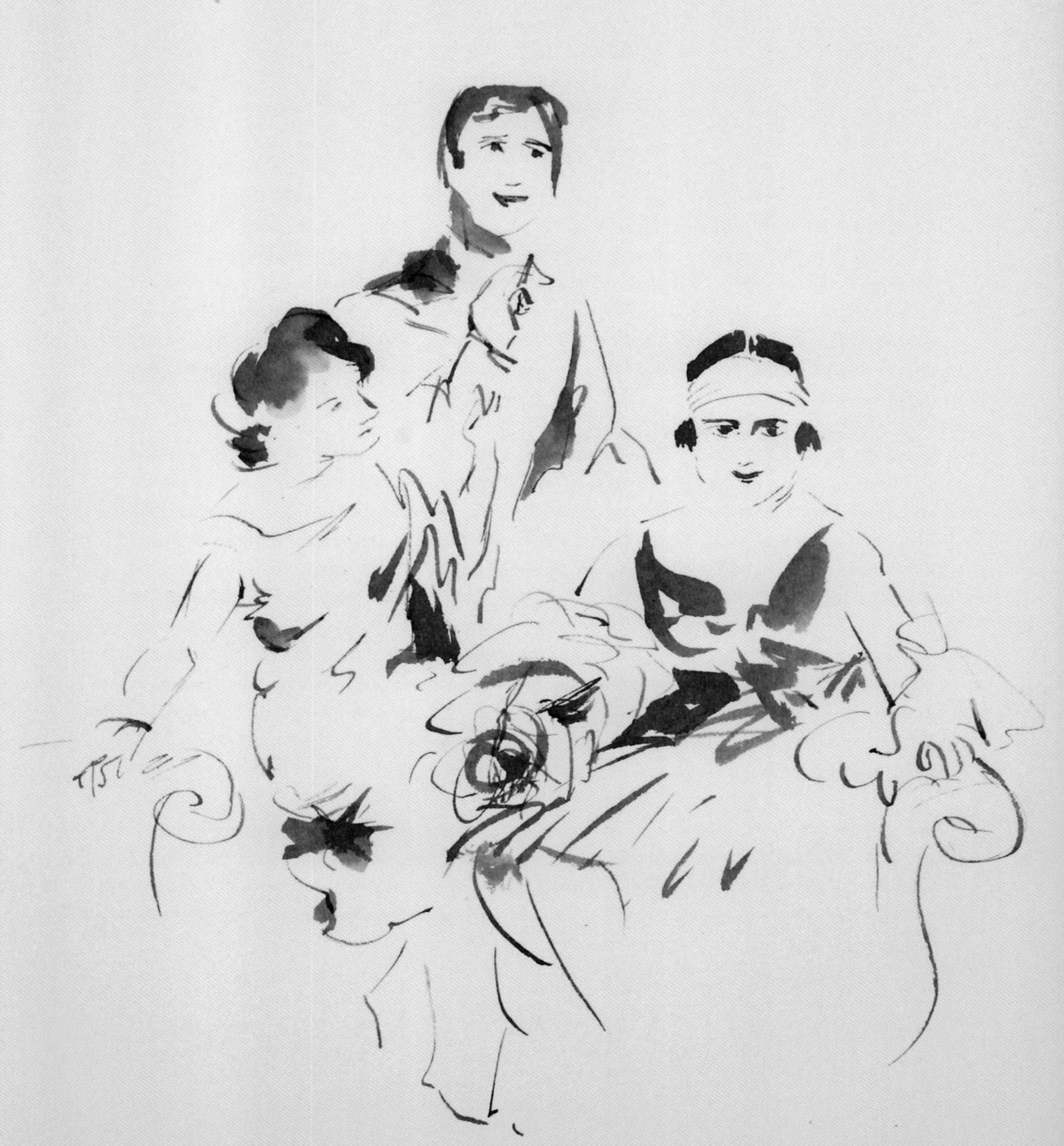

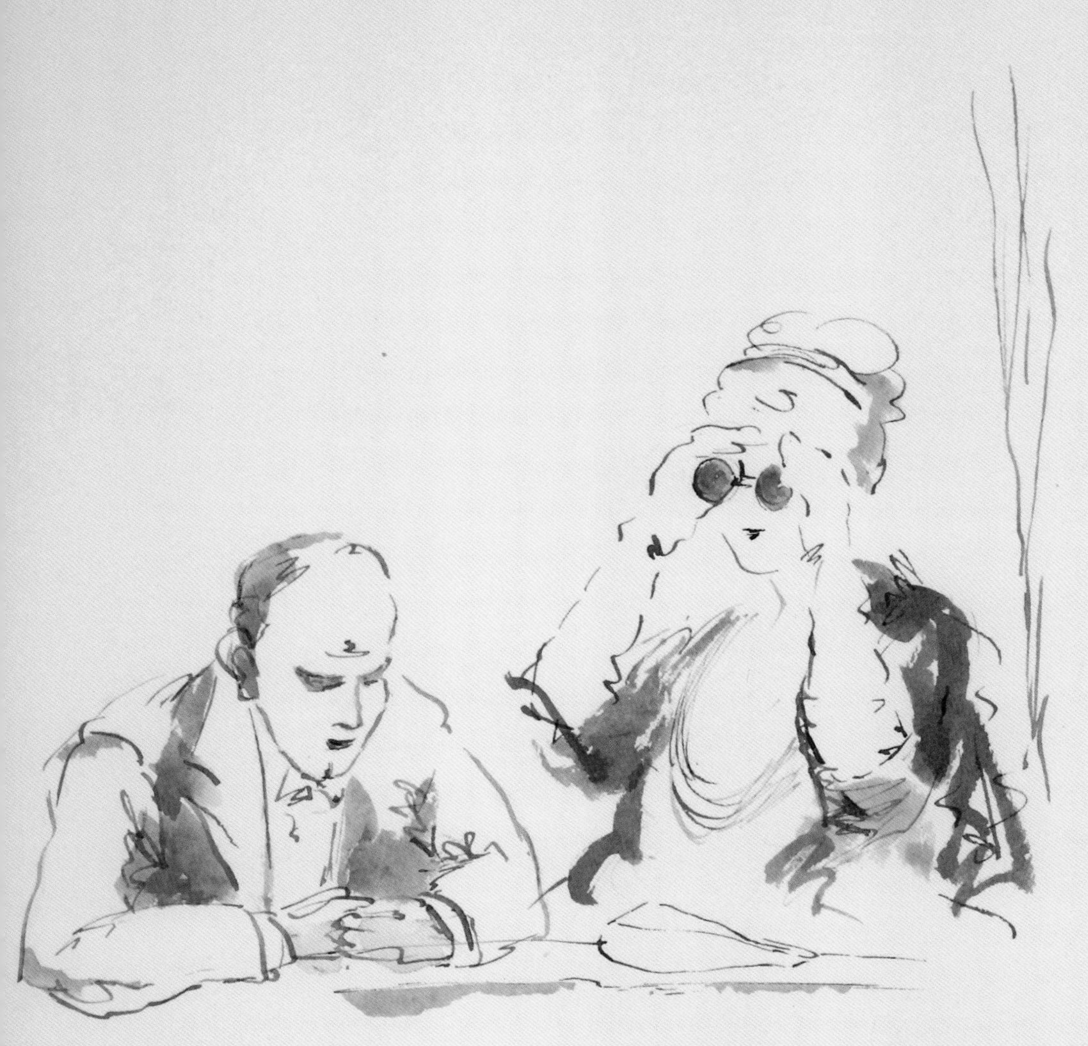

The rumors were fantastic!

Grigoriev was trying to get Karsavina back out of retirement. They even wired Pavlova in Argentina to beg her to come. As if she would even answer their cables! So Sergei Pavlovitch called us all together in the rehearsal room. He sat surrounded by the Maestro, Grigoriev, and Kochno, while we stood at the *barre* shivering with nerves. Dounia bit her lip so hard, it bled. The old man tapped his cane and stood up. He looked around the room very slowly. I, myself, was perfectly unconcerned. There was no chance for me. My luck with the company had been running bad. I was thinking of quitting and seeking my fortune in the London music halls. Surely Sergei Pavlovitch would not choose an American, and a black one at that.

It must have been 5 minutes before his eyes settled on Little Maria. He offered her his hand. She moaned softly and fell over in a faint, hitting her head on the *barre.* She was unconscious and everybody ran around in hysterics not knowing what to do, until Patrick took the Maestro's bottle of mineral water and poured it over her. She got up looking dazed, stepped forward, and fell over my foot.

I didn't ask her to fall on my foot. I was merely doing some *battements tendus* to work out a cramp in my instep. So now she had a sprained ankle and everybody got hysterical again. Kochno was jumping up and down, Katya started to scream and the Maestro began playing his violin to calm everyone down. I went up to Sergei Pavlovitch who was hunched over his cane, an unbelieving look on his face.

"Can't we have some peace and quiet, Sergei Pavlovitch?" I asked. "How can we work with such children?"

The old man looked at me as if he didn't understand what I was saying. Then he smiled. "Eleanora," he sighed. "That is what we need. A practical American." Signaling Kochno to follow, he walked to the door. "Eleanora, be at rehearsal promptly at 1:00. Grigoriev, you will begin coaching her in Vera Petrovna's roles." He paused at the door. "And fine Little Maria 2 francs for disturbing the peace!"

We broke for lunch. I ran home. "Mitya, Mitya, I am to have Vera Petrovna's roles. Our fortune is made."

There was only a crowd of fat drunken flies sucking the mouth of yesterday's wine bottle. A torn sheet, tangled tights, soiled shorts—the floor was like a memory of a day old mistral. In the blazing afternoon sun the room had the weather beaten look of barns back home. We should paper the walls. Cheer the place up. Maybe now we could move to a larger room—with a toilet perhaps . . . But I had forgotten to ask about my new salary.

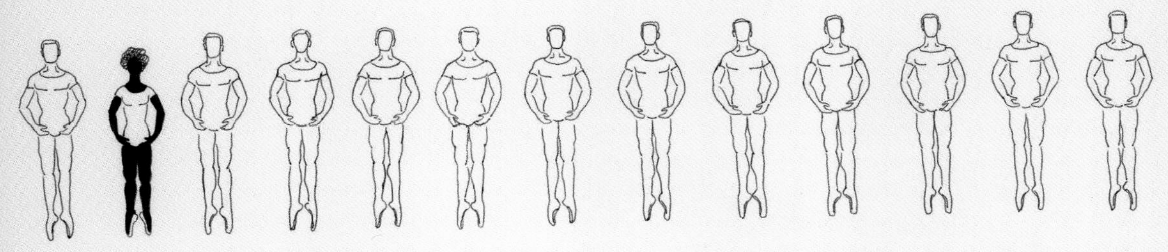

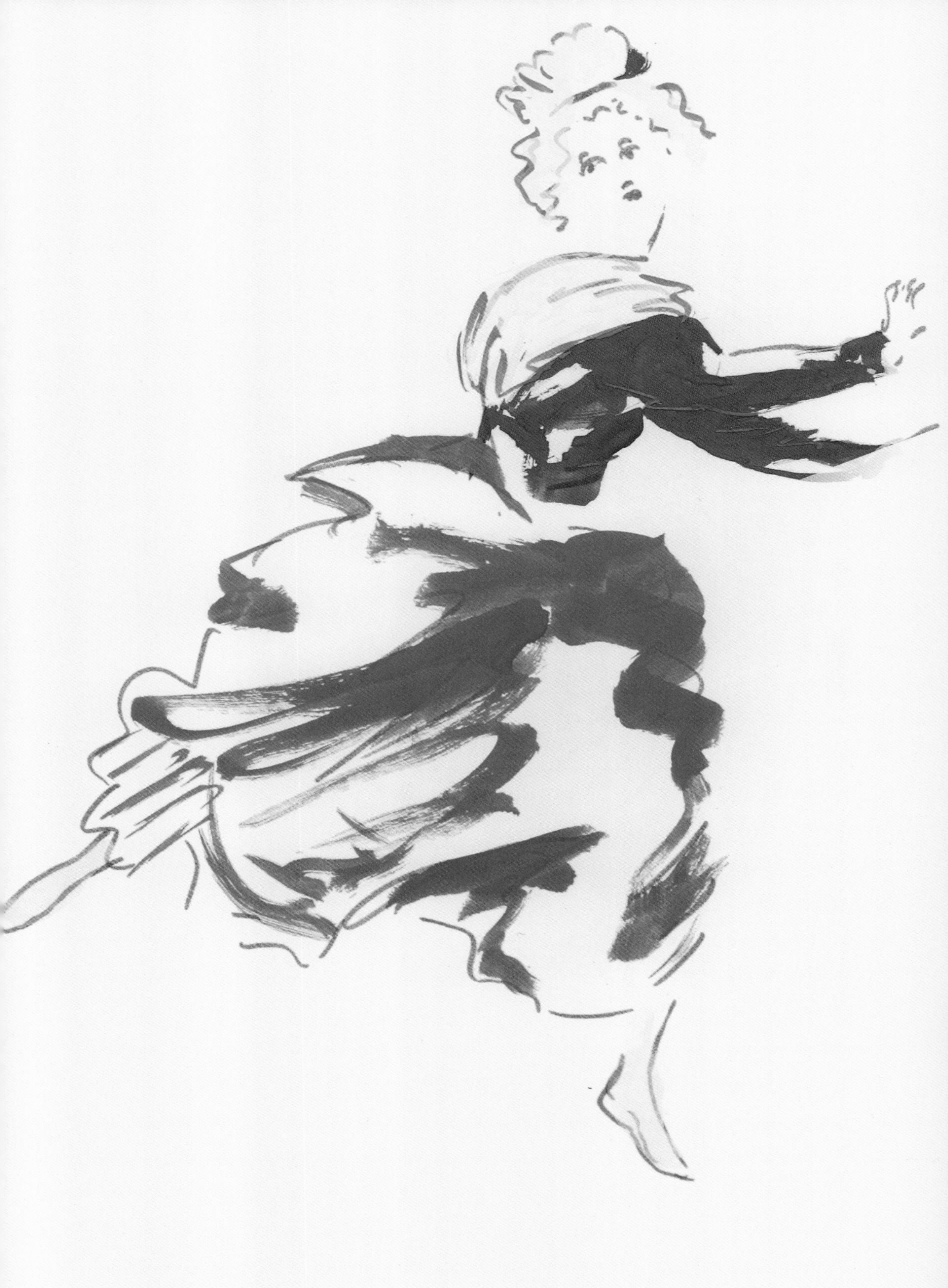

Coward! You didn't forget. You were afraid of the withering looks, the aggrieved tone.

"We have done so much for you. You are our child. We have adopted you, a poor orphan."

"I am not an orphan. I have 2 parents, 3 brothers, 1 sister . . ."

"They might as well be in Russia. They are 10,000 miles away. Here you are an orphan. If you sicken and die—God forbid!—it is we who will sit with you, pray for you."

"But it isn't fitting that a soloist of the *Ballets Russes* should wear only rags upon her back. I need a new trunk. Mine was given me by a music-hall dancer. It isn't fitting."

"Look!"

He will sit down and show me the soles of his shoes. They will have big holes in them the size of nickels.

"Is this fitting for the greatest impresario in the world? Alas, it is the price of Art. For myself, I must suffer. But you—you are young. An *artiste.* It is easy for you. Do as the others do. Find a patron. You will have a trunk with a lining of silk from the Avenue de l'Opera. You will travel like an *assoluta.*"

I thought of my old patron, the Scotsman. "No, no, I am an American. We are clumsy. We do not have the knack for such things. And I am hungry." I will stare at his portly belly. "You, at least, do not deny yourself."

Like a rug merchant from the Caucasus, his eyes narrow into slits

"So! Thus you repay me! How will it look—tell me—a mahogany Sugar Plum Fairy? Can this be Sylphides? A black face in a snowbank? The critics will denounce me. I will become a laughing-stock. Thus do you repay my sacrifices . . . but what does one expect of Americans! Savages! Half-breeds! Gangsters! Go back, go back! Capone! He will love you! Dance for Capone! He will applaud you with machine guns!"

But now time was passing. Soon I must return for the afternoon rehearsal . . . I ran down to the market without much confidence. Every morning when I left for class I would see the cooks from the big villas with immense baskets over their arms. Within an hour they would have cleaned out the stalls of the reddest cherries, the straightest asparagus, the blackest truffles. Sure enough, the locusts had come and gone. Picked the street clean. The stalls were closed.

"Here, *ma petite*, over here," a bossy voice called out. "Why do you stand there in the empty street like a plucked pullet? Take my cut of veal. It's all you will get now, God knows. Serves you right, too. Sinning all night. Sleeping all day. I shouldn't even help you, such a sinner." She began to roll a suspiciously dark cut of veal into a newspaper. "Ah, I am a fool, a fool. I have always been a fool." "It is the only calf who died of old age," I marveled. "You should frame it and place it in a museum." "What do you know? You know nothing. A good beating and it will serve you like an angel. Here. 3 francs. My feet hurt. I want to get out of this sun. I am an old woman. If I stay out any longer, I shall begin to look like you." She cackled loudly at her joke. "You are a nasty old woman," I said, giving her 2 francs. "That is all you deserve." A good pounding along with some lemon and butter, a dish of dandelion greens . . . My veal will grow young again.

"Au revoir, *ma petite*."

"Au revoir."

When I came home that night after the performance, his voice roared out from the kitchen table. "I will never show my face again. I will eat here, sleep here. I will die here. Send for my blanket, my poor torn pillow. I will live here with my chamber pot. My pen. I am a poet."

Like a distraught Ouija board, the table jumped up and down. The marinating veal was certainly having a hard time of it. "But, Mitya, dear, even poets must eat and you are endangering your dinner."

As if in answer, the dish slid off the top and crashed to the floor. I screamed and tried to save the meat, but his hand reached out and grabbed my ankle. He twisted so hard, I fell and slipped on the wet floor.

"Mitya," I begged, "please do not do this. You do not understand. We are supposed to celebrate. I am to dance Vera Petrovna's roles. I have been chosen by Sergei Pavlovitch himself."

"You should be ashamed," he shouted. "You call that dancing? For czars, that is dancing. For perverts. Neurasthenics. With water in their veins."

"We shall be rich," I lied.

"I do not need you, dark witch. Hard like a brick sidewalk . . . Ah, Maxim . . . Essenine, my beloved . . . Where are my friends? How we would drink together, eh, my beauties? We were giants then . . . Poets all . . . food of my soul . . . " His voice roared out. "Not this band of bloated fish."

I lost my temper then. "This band of bloated fish feeds you. You haven't a sou. You are helpless like a count. You can do nothing. I hate you. You are an ungrateful wretch. You have ruined my triumph."

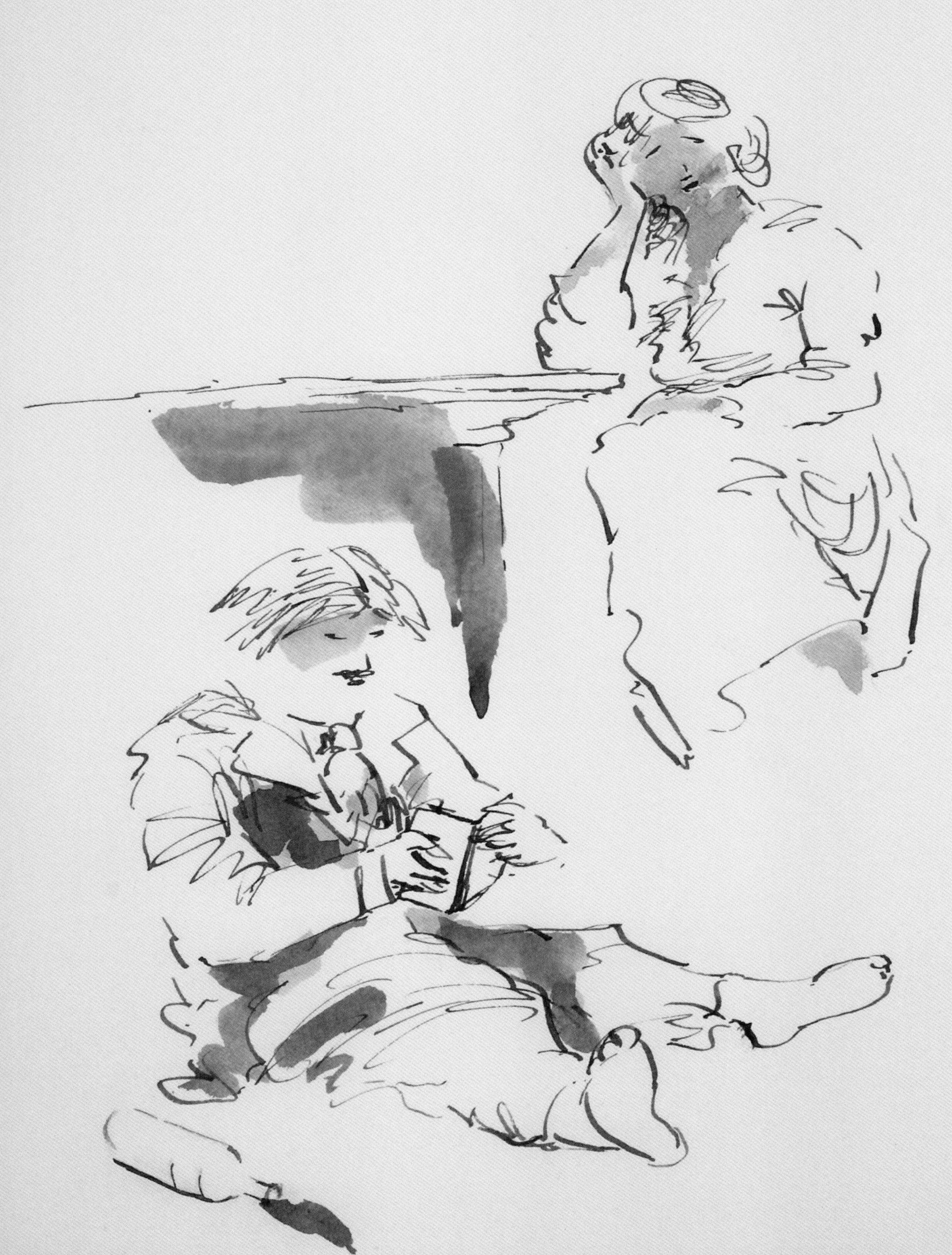

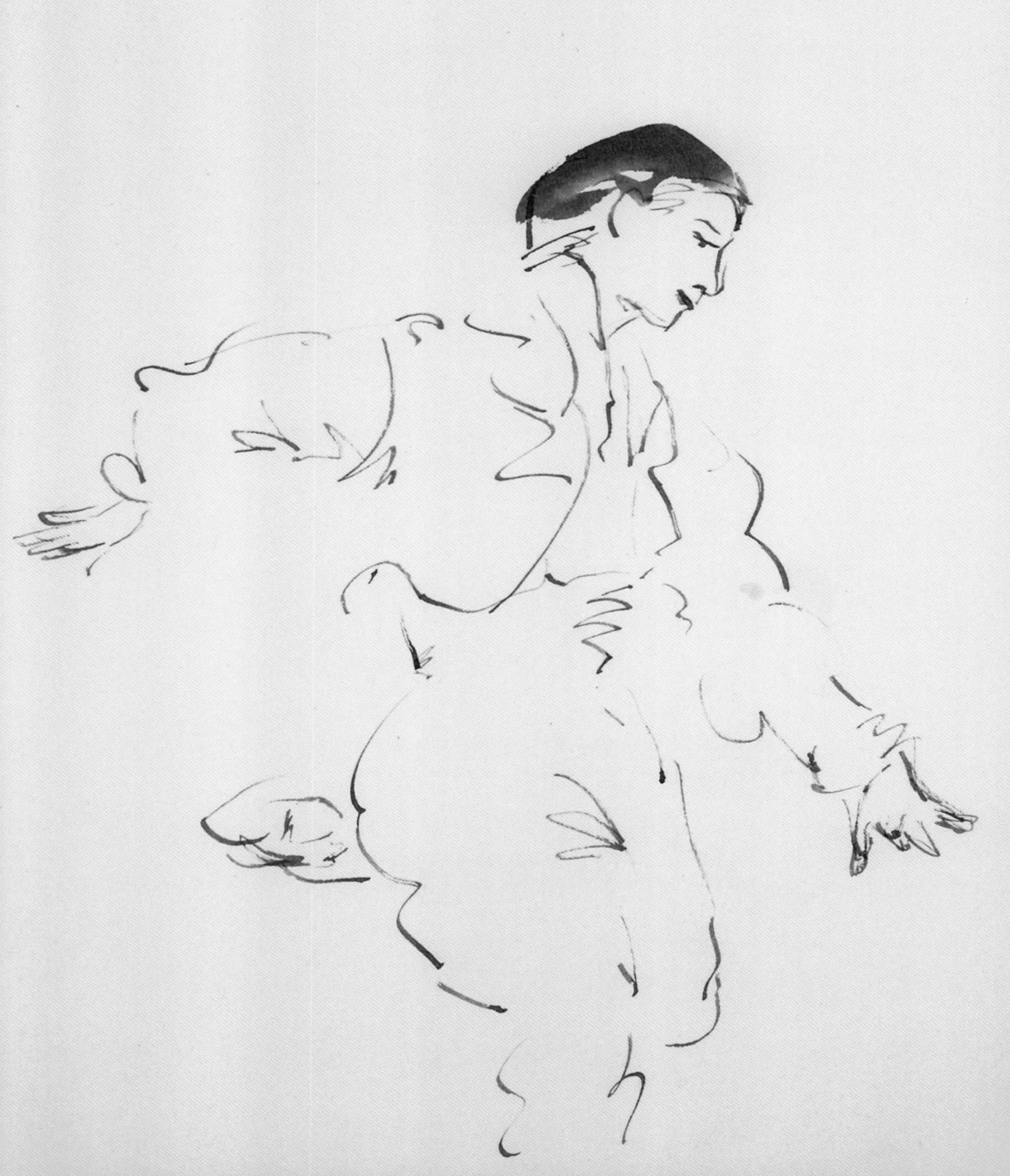

The new wine slid dangerously along the rim of the table.

"A friendly Bordeaux," Fat Jules had confided. "From the town of my brother-in-law. He is a miserable miser and only brought me one barrel." His great red paw stroked my arm. "Take it to your poet, *ma petite chocolate.* It will bring you happiness."

But a broken ankle cost a dancer more than spilled wine. I was afraid to come closer.

"Evil blackamoor. What do you know. I have other fish. A young lady is coming. She will lie down with me in my coffin under the table. We will curl up and you will see nothing, you menacing darkness. You will bend low to spy, to pull our toes, cruel Egyptian Princess, Voodoo Spirit, Abyssinian Witch, but you will see nothing for we will curl into a ball of dust, a mite in your eye, and fly away. Free as the dust. Light as the air. Tonight, I will be in Petrograd."

I shut my eyes as the bottle smashed to the floor, spraying a warm velvet liquid on my legs. "12, 13 hours of dancing that cost," I wailed. "You are devouring my life."

"Swolitch! Take back your life! What are you, a stinking watchmaker? Here, I return your life! I spit upon your life! Ho! A gift! A gift from Dimitri! Fortunate woman!"

He lived under the table singing and crying for 3 days and nights, barricading himself behind a growing number of empty vodka bottles. He shouted that I was trying to kill him, "a poor exile, a wanderer," forcing himself to stay awake nights when I was home by crooning lullabies, rocking the table like a cradle . . .

nothing is the same
my shoes are made of leather . . .
I have walked for seven years

When I left for class in the morning he was snoring peacefully.

When I returned home after the evening performance the pile of papers around his quarters had grown. "He's getting a lot of poems written," I thought grimly. "Doing better than me, for sure."

"You are distracted," the old man scolded. "Have you been gallivanting with that moujhik poet of yours? You must rest nights. You are a ballerina, not a flapper."

"I am sorry, Sergei Pavlovitch. There are so many new steps. It's hard to keep up . . . "

"You prefer old steps?" he muttered. "Soon you will dance in tango contests at the casino." He turned away in disgust. He hated ballroom dancing.

"The price of living with a genius," Tanya whispered consolingly in the wings, *pas de boureeing* past me onto the stage. What did she know? What did any of them know? I wept each night at the injustice of life.

On the 4th night, after a performance that had been plagued by endless delays and accidents, he was waiting at the door, bathed, shaved, a laundered shirt open at his neck.

"You look dashing!"

He kissed my hands.

"I have written a mountain of poems. I am content."

The next few days he couldn't do enough for me. He bathed my feet in soda water, floating herbs along the top and then painstakingly removed the bunions and calluses caused by the additional hours of rehearsing the new roles. He read his poems to me, carefully translating the Russian into French so I could understand the most subtle nuances. When I fell asleep he sat up beside me reading quietly into the night.

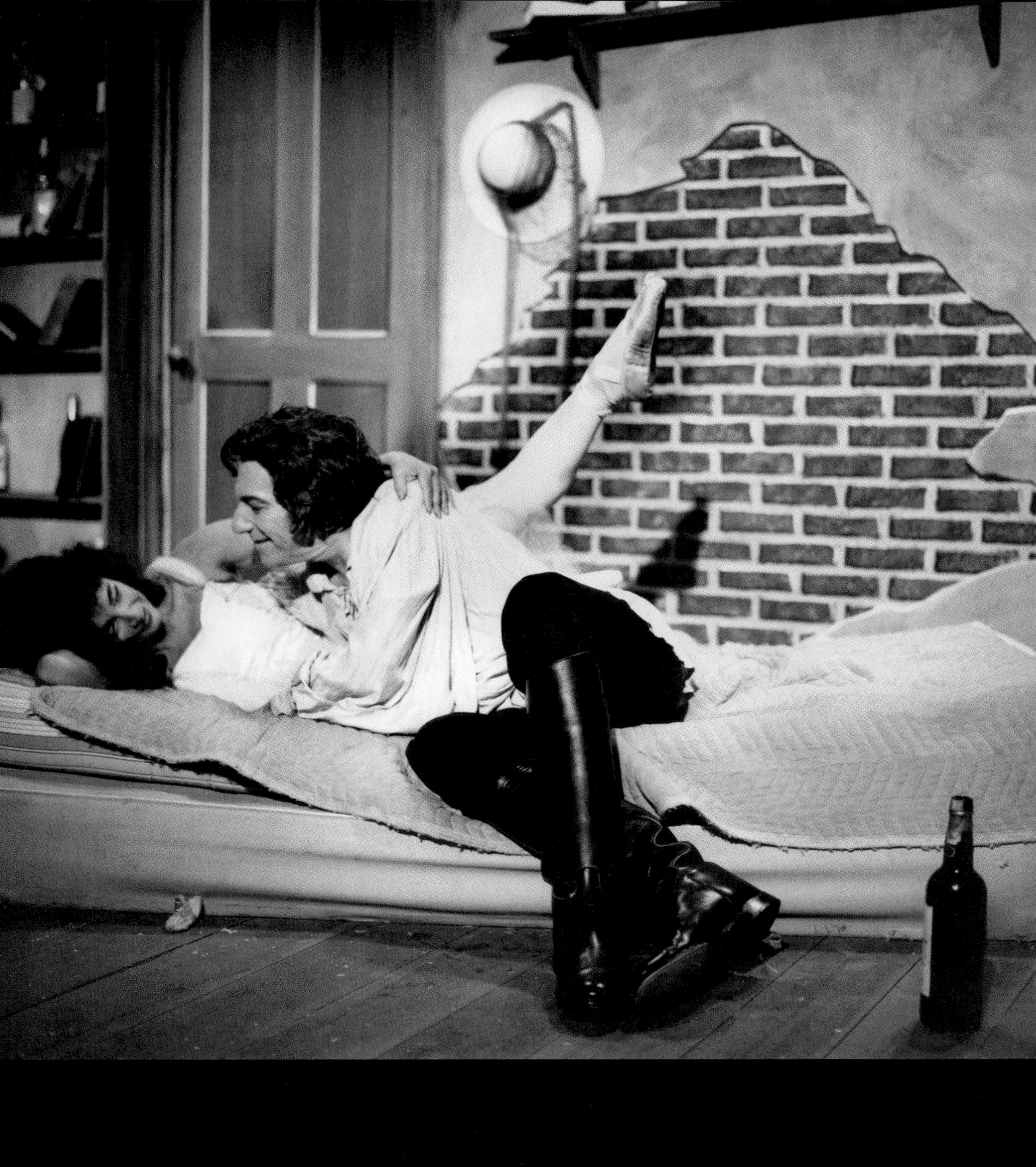

Eleanora Antinova, in *The Ballerina and the Poet*

Chapter 4

Russian Tales

To succeed in life one must become stronger and tougher. You must brook no interference in reaching your goals. If, as is often the case, you don't know your goals, never give yourself away. Enemies wait in the wings for the first sign of indecision. Especially Russians!

I suppose they couldn't help themselves. Half-starved all the time, their meager salaries went for *chocolats* and *crèmes* because sugar cheered them up like horses—gave them the energy they needed to get up again. Always more and more energy, there was no end to it! Never seeing civilians—except for the impoverished dandies, with whom it was a losing battle to get that much needed new pair of shoes or—for the fortunate few—a fur coat to protect their poor thin bodies from the fierce cold of a 30-hour trip in a third class train carriage.

True, it was colder outside than inside, where at least the cigarette smoke and the breath of the others brought some warmth; but when the train slid into a station—even for a short wait—there was always a rush to the door. Inhabitants of sleepy little towns would see groups of threadbare men and women walking up and down the platforms, chattering and shouting in that linguistic hodge-podge that was the Russian of Diaghilev's *Ballets Russes.* No matter that the weather was below zero, that the high heeled pumps offered little protection against the cold. To uncramp one's body—to feel alive again—to move!

They say Trefilova practiced in the train corridors on the two-week trip from Russia to London for her comeback in *Sleeping Beauty.* I don't believe it. After hours of watching the world slip by outside the window, of catching short snatches of sleep before a cramped leg or a distraught companion wakes you up—the only energy you have left is to keep a lookout for the refreshment wagon—to cheer loudly when it finally comes to your compartment—to gratefully submit the francs or marks you have been crushing protectively in your fingers for over an hour.

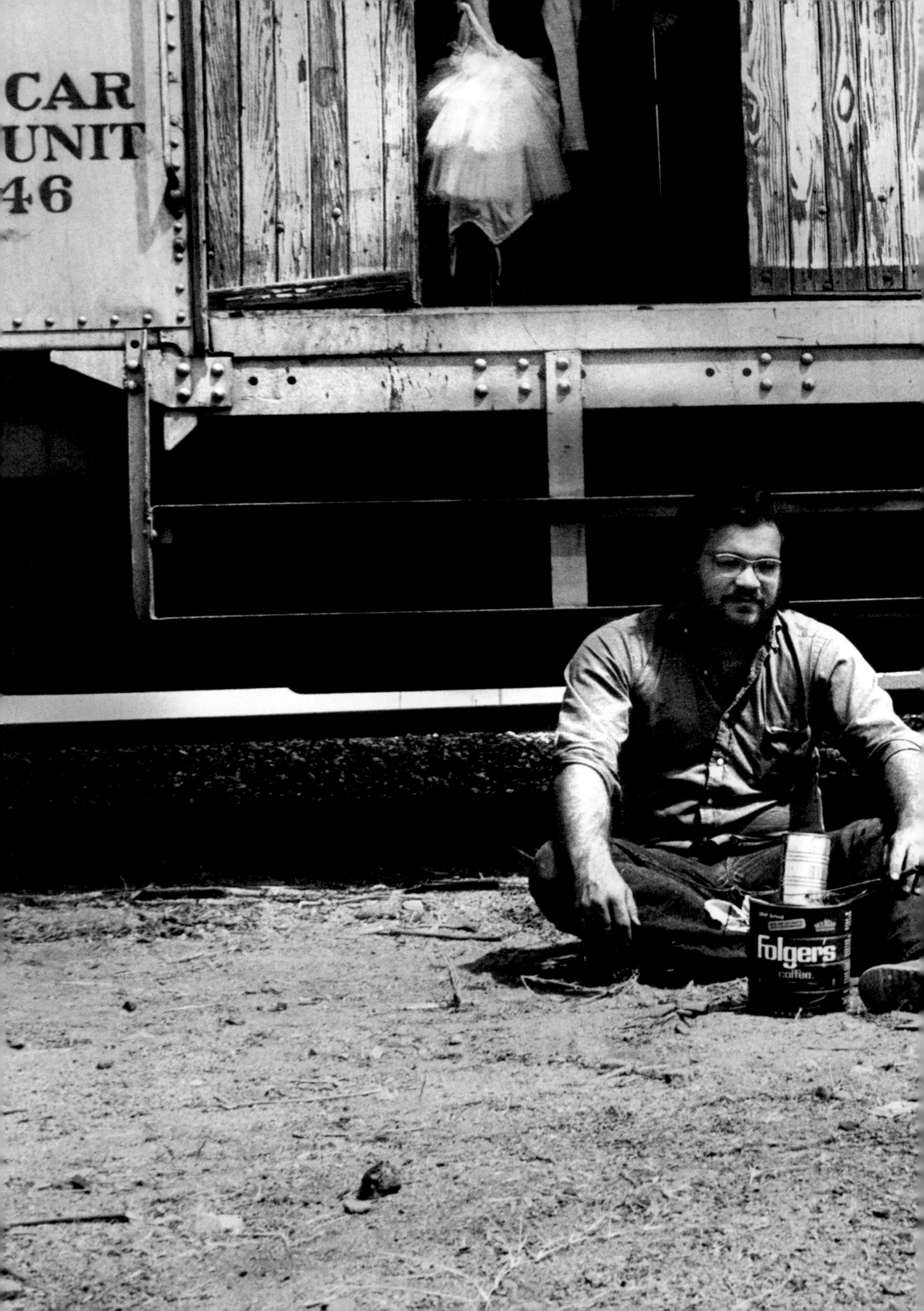
CAR
UNIT
46
Folgers
coffee

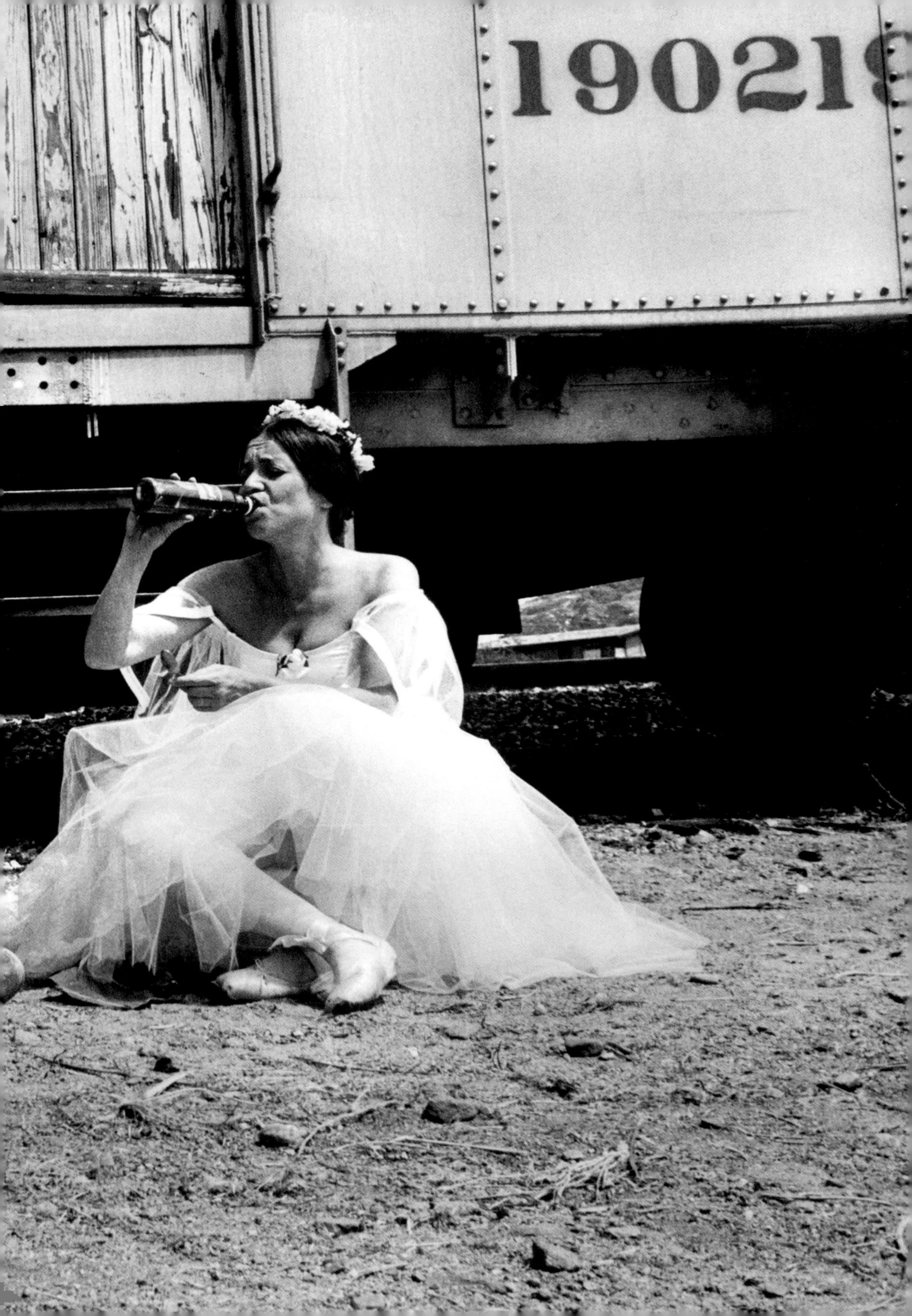
19021

Ah, the warmth of a *café au lait.* Or the lemon-flavored tea that you suck through the sugar you hold in your teeth like a true Russian. You drink down to the last drop and then play with the empty cup, pensive, happy, the familiar hunger momentarily appeased. How confident the men's voices become then, as they call out their bets in the card games that go on for days, while we reach into our crowded bags for the slippers or tights in need of mending.

Somebody begins to strum a mandolin, someone begins to sing a love song—a sad song—a Russian song. Russian songs are always sad, even the happy ones. Someone—maybe Lydia—tells a story—a nasty one but it makes you laugh. You remember you are an artist in the greatest ballet company in the world.

But the train keeps moving and your stomach turns over again.

Small wonder the girls fainted so often in class. But the Maestro was decent about it. A quick slap in the face and you got up again, as though nothing had happened. You returned to your place, and—coolly, just as if you had had 8 hours of continuous sleep and a real dinner the night before—you moved through a magnificent set of *grands jetés* and ended in a whirl of *pirouettes.*

Just as long as you didn't faint in rehearsal, at least not when Sergei Pavlovitch was there. That always meant a fine of a few francs and the loss of 2 or 3 cups of coffee.

In Monte Carlo or Paris, where we spent several months each year rehearsing for the new season, there were always *balletomanes* under our feet. Dounia had a spaniel with a long face. "He is my cross," she used to say and pinch his cheeks. He followed her wherever she went. When a rich Englishman took her to dinner, he spied through the window. She pulled his ears and made a terrible face. "But where will I go?" he whimpered. It comforted him to see her. She saved food in a napkin and he ate it from her fingers.

Once he was a *grande seigneur* with lands and factories. Diamonds. Furs. They spilled from his manicured fingers. He owed thousands to the best tradesmen. It was an honour to do business with such a gentleman. Could we throw him to the wolves? Was it his fault Lenin made the Revolution? He was a kind man. A generous man. Dounia took him in. When she had an assignation with a rich Englishman, he waited patiently in the lobby. He always took the oldest and poorest chair for himself. When you saw him there in the corner you knew Dounia was at an assignation. She was often at assignations. She had a fine wardrobe and liked to be up-to-date. "Tell Dounia we rehearse tonight," we told him. He blushed, he stammered. He was grateful to be noticed.

He was her family, that spaniel. He played the balalaika. He sang the old songs and made her cry. When things went badly at rehearsal she bit his hand and punched his ribs. Without him, she too had nothing. Once I asked why he didn't get a job. He would make a good maître d'. She looked at me scornfully. "He was a rich man," she said. "That was his profession. He did it well. He doesn't know how to do anything else."

But I was a scandalous creature. What did furs or jewels mean to me? I never missed them. The girls could teach me nothing. Lizavetta tried to take me in hand. "You must save for the future," she said. "Soon you will be old and ugly. I will find you a rich Englishman. He will give you many presents." But I laughed at them. What did I care for the future? Even then I had a weakness for poets. "But they beat you," the girls said. "They are peasants." Dounia offered me her spaniel. "He will carry your slippers and play the balalaika when you are sad." But what did I want with spaniels? My poets were fierce and proud. They were on fire.

Not like musicians. Stravinsky talked only of his bowels. Mitya used to call him the rodent because they leave droppings wherever they go. "Are they dropping, Igor?" he would shout in a great voice, smacking him on the back. Igor was terrified of him. "He is not a man, he is a mountain." But even Igor could do nothing. Mitya was a great poet. Poets can do anything. But Igor found a friend. Irina Federova was a genius of herbs. They consulted for hours. She picked fresh grasses for his enemas. He was a modern man. "Experiment," he said. "Experiment." When it didn't work so well, he looked green.

This Irina Federova was a Ukrainian. Big like a horse. When she escaped from Russia, the old man took her in out of pity. None of the men would partner her. It is like pushing a battleship, they groaned. She will break our backs. We will become doormen. But Stravinsky was desperate. He shouted at the old man. "My bowels will be hard as rocks. I will take to my bed. I will never compose again. Who can compose with rocks in his belly?" The old man saw the logic. He gave her small solos—queens and duennas. That horse continued to flourish in the *Ballets Russes.* It was a disgrace.

And if we didn't get away fast enough, she used to lecture us. "For your own good, poor babies, you know nothing." She hated the modern era, blaming it for the loss of her pensions and benefits, though in point of fact, we knew the Bolsheviks refused her pension out of spite: for she had been the mistress of Vassiliev, a high police officer in St. Petersburg. Sometimes she opened the locket around her neck to show us a faded picture of a square-faced, serious man with receding hair.

"Is this the face of a murderer, my little ones? This gentleman of the old school, this patriot of advanced ideas? A man of culture who installed grand pianos in the police stations of the better neighborhoods! But the people were crazed by the Bolsheviks. I myself saw a child of 10 years blow a whistle and people come running out from the neighboring streets waving flags and shouting 'Strike! Strike!' The German spies were everywhere, even in the highest circles. One morning I heard the march from *The Little Hump-Backed Horse* playing in the street—was the revolution over at last? Could I be happy once again? But when I rushed to the window it was the Grand Duke Cyril riding at the head of the Guards, and the cursed red ribbons were fluttering on the points of their bayonets. I met 8 Generals going to the Taurid Palace to take the oath of the new government, and 4 wore the Cross of St. George, but they all wore red armbands. The last was so feeble he was held up by an old peasant woman crossing herself and calling upon God to witness. We wept together. But who wept with me when God struck *me* down? My beloved was burnt to death in a barrel in Mokhovaya Street, and afterwards they hurled the piano through the windows of the Mokhovaya Street Station and they say that when it crashed on the pavement the strings vibrated a dirge. Even the Nihilists crossed themselves. But when I went to the Maryinsky Palace to claim my pension there was no respect. Unshaven students with long mops of hair waved their green caps and laughed at me. The typist looked at me through those little pince-nez glasses they were all wearing—a typical Nihilist—and shoved my petition to the floor.

"'The mistress of Vassiliev, the traitor! You are lucky we do not stand you before the firing squad!'

"'But I was a principal dancer with the Imperial Theatres. The others are receiving their pensions. I am an *artiste.* I am starving.'

"'The people starved for years! And did you care? Ha! You were in the arms of the monster of Garguan Street.'

"They made a circle around me and wagged their dirty fingers.

"'Perhaps the firing squad is also hungry. For you!' they shouted.

"But God took pity and sent the Comte de Rohan, the attaché from the French Ministry, to pass by on official business. He recognized me and they could do nothing—he was a foreigner—a diplomat—they were still allies then—how they gnashed their teeth and looked fierce! I was faint with fear. He escorted me home. 'Join your friends in Paris,' he whispered in my ear. 'All is lost!'

"But even his Excellency could not know how much more I was to lose before God saw fit to rest His servant."

She paused here, her fine brown eyes filled with tears, and as they rolled down her dry wrinkled cheeks, she relaxed with an almost voluptuous relief into her mother tongue. Prayers? Curses? I never knew. She made the sign of the cross and continued in French.

"For in my own beautiful home on Gatchina Street, I myself clothed and fed Judas Iscariot, may he rot in Hell! For the length of two lifetimes, my mother's and my own, he waited—lying low

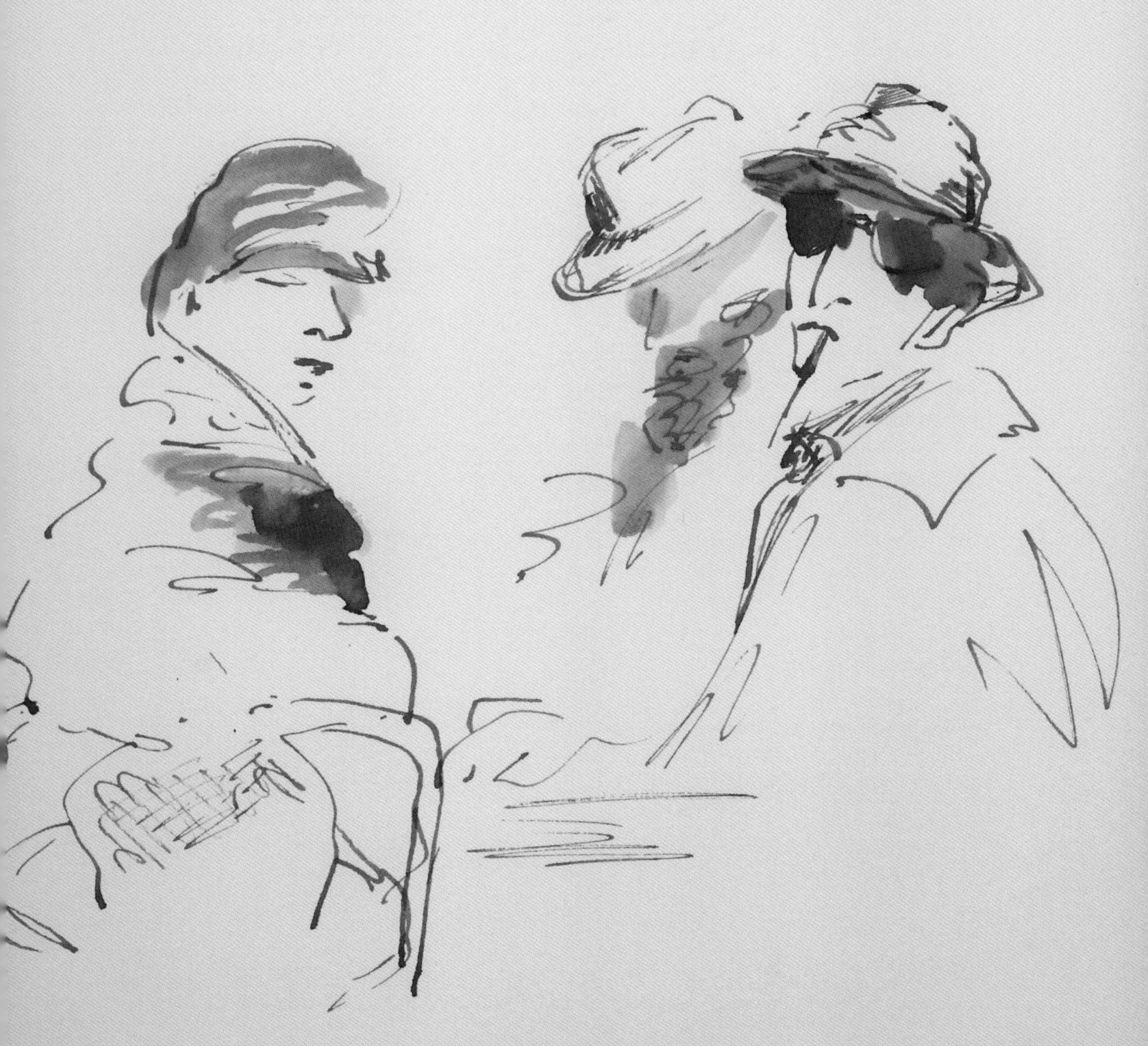

in the body of Dounia, the rat, may she burn with the force of 70 Hells! For 20 years I kept her; she couldn't sew my slippers already, she was so blind and old. Did I send her away and get a quicker servant? She couldn't even get up in the morning to light the stove; her bones creaked; she was disgusting; my beloved used to spit over his left shoulder for fear of the evil eye when he saw her.

"'Ah, beloved,' I tried to explain. 'She is a serf from the old days. A fossil. A gift from my mother who got her from Prince L . . . ' And then a new servant would have been sassy, counting off her workdays. Dounia was of the old school. Christmas and Easter Sunday were her days off, and she always kissed my hands when she went to visit her brother.

"'Come, Dounia,' I say. 'The Reds are coming. I can see them from my window. They have already killed your beloved master, Andrei Lubovitch. They will now search his house. Go to the little fig tree by the wall in the garden and dig up my jewels. They are in a little handkerchief buried in the roots. Thrust the handkerchief in your bosom, and when I rid us of these assassins, we shall flee to Paris. If you do this task well and not in your usual slovenly manner, I promise to take you with me.'

"Fortunately, it was young Tereschenko whom they sent to arrest me. They all said his star was rising, and just think, he had been an ordinary attaché to the Imperial Theatres only a year before. He owned factories in Kiev and was very handsome. Now he was a Red Commander. Such are the ways of God!

"The young man was embarrassed. After all, he was a man of breeding, a well-known *balletomane.* I poured tea from the samovar in the little blue sitting room, and we conversed in French. He took lumps of sugar out of a secret pocket and dropped them into my tea. On that afternoon we forgot the cursed Revolution. How handsome he looked with his rosy face and golden curls. If I looked deeply into his eyes I could not see the red armband . . .

"I know now that it was the last moment of happiness vouchsafed to me in this earthly life. When he left several hours later, I rushed out to the garden. My heart sang. 'All will be well again!'

"But the jewels were gone.

"And so was Dounia, the ungrateful one . . . "

Her voice began rising until her words came out in short dry shrieks. I was afraid she'd have a heart attack.

"... Aiiii, the one-eyed gypsy, may she boil in all Hell's cauldrons at once for betraying her kind mistress!"

Sometimes she got so worked up you could leave and she didn't notice, she was so intent on her grievances. Other times she pulled herself together and, betraying a kind of weary humour, told of her escape from Russia. If I hadn't known her better, I'd almost believe she enjoyed the last adventure. I think she felt like a desperado by then.

"I received word I was to follow a boy with a sack of potatoes. When you trust no one, then you must trust everyone. I followed him to where Petrograd is separated from Finland by but a few versts. Two fishermen crossed me over the frozen ice in a sled with a French woman, her child, and a maid. The trip was treacherous. It was one of Petrograd's white nights and a pale blue light lit everything. We could be discovered by patrols at any moment. The child began to cry out in a high baby voice. '*Maman, Maman. A la maison. A la maison.*' His mother hid him in her arms, but the high little voice carried far over the silent ice. The fishermen mumbled to each other. I supposed they were planning to give us up, strangle us maybe, or break our heads with their poles. They had our money already. I could hardly blame them ... But the child fell asleep ...

"The Finns put me in a third class carriage to Paris. I was by then so stiff and drowsy with cold I would have frozen, but for a fellow passenger, who took off an extra pair of woolen socks he wore and slipped them on my feet; and an old Danish woman next to me rubbed me and held me close. Still, I arrived in Paris more dead than alive."

That was the state in which she made her way to Sergei Pavlovitch. But Massine—he had no heart—he would have none of her. She couldn't deliver the dry, jerky movements his numbers demanded. She was too big and grand, not unlike a battleship. "There are times one longs for marble," Sergei Pavlovitch insisted, and cast her in the secondary roles of dowagers and queens though she was hopeless as a mime and so obviously hated the modern steps.

Chapter 5

Felix

Then one day the war came. I understood nothing. I was a provincial. What did I know of glory? Americans walk on sidewalks. Americans stumble and fall. They put on Dr. Scholl's corn pads and keep walking. The nettles slip into the soles of their shoes and they light a cigarette and keep walking. I will never understand the passionate happiness that the assassination of a measly grand duke, Ferdinand of Serbia, brought to the peoples of Europe. And the artists, they longed to fly over lakes and seas to kill people they didn't know, who were also spiraling like dervishes towards them to the roar of cannons, the glory that was war.

That war, their war, ach, it gave me a headache. I do not like blood. They said it was fire. I said fire burns. They said burning is passion. But I like to eat *pirozhkis* and drink wine with friends. They said better to drink wine with warriors. Our dancers, artists, composers rushed off to make war. Everything came to a standstill.

So Diaghilev said we would go to Spain. Those of us who were left would go to Spain. He said there was a lot to be done there. He said Spain would be a place for making a success. There was a war. Spain was not in the war. The old man always had these ideas. Sometimes they didn't work. But Diaghilev had spirit. So we went to Spain ... What could we do in Spain? Stranded. We were stranded. But we danced. There were audiences. People came. Even the King came. What's Spain? An oriental country. Almonds. Orange trees. Siestas. Bull fighters. It's not a country, it's Asia ... But he said it shouldn't be a total loss, we would do a Spanish ballet. The old man always knew how to go on. We went hunting. In low dives. We were poor. We were dancers. We were brought up on hardships. But those places he took us to, looking for I don't know what. There in a low dive in Cadiz, an old man playing a guitar, drinking brandy ... a miserable out of tune guitar ... the contralto with a cracked voice singing ... and a bunch of drunken gypsies sitting around, dark like they could cut your throat any Tuesday. There was one ... a little man ... Felix. That's who he was. Felix ... Yes, his name was Felix. That's who I want to talk about. I want to tell you about Felix ... Yes, Diaghilev. He discovered Felix.

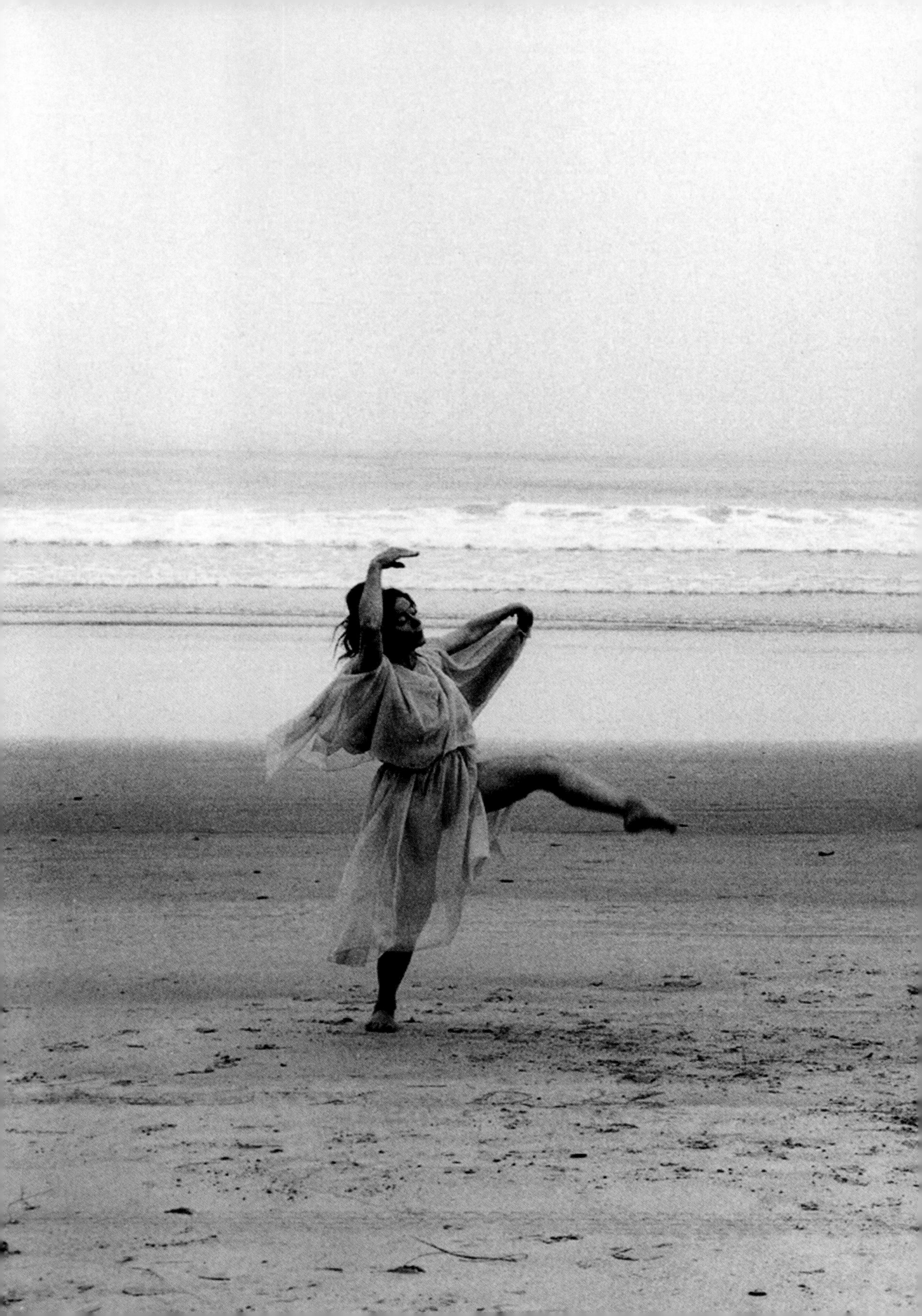

But it wasn't really like that. Felix . . . Felix. I'm sorry. Don't look at me with your reproachful eyes. Your dark hungry face. You wanted so much to be a success.

And Felix starts to dance. It is not dancing as I know it. No. Not like that. It isn't dancing. It's drumming and courting. It's high heels and drumming. It's pounding the heels, beating the floor, the body is upright as if it's hung from a hook. And he moves as if he's dancing around a handkerchief. Drumming on the edge of a handkerchief. It is all fire and blood. The rhythms are uneven. We try to count them. 13. 11. 7. 9. What kind of rhythms? The music is going one way, the dancing is going the other. He has hands. He claps. The dancer moans. Somebody plays castanets. It is wonderful. But it is not art.

Art is what you do every day. You do it once. You do it again. It is the same 365 days of the year. Art is what you do over and over again. It is perfect when it is good. When it is not good it is not perfect. But every day it is the same. That's what makes it art . . . Felix was not art. He was fire. He was bad moods and good moods and bad brandy and rotten food and dark cafés. That's what he was, thunder and lightning and misery and jealousies and fire . . . that's what he was . . . and he was magnificent.

No. It was not that way. It was not quite that way . . . We adopted Felix. The old man adopted him. "Felix, you will be my son," said the old man. "Come with me. You will dance with us." And Felix came. He came out of the dark into the light. It was very light and he was wearing dark. All the time he was wearing dark clothes. What was he doing in the sunlight with us? But the old man was a kingmaker. He made Nijinsky from little Vaslav, the son of a Polish acrobat. He made Fokine. Bakst. Stravinsky. And now he was making Massine. Massine. An actor from Russia. A handsome boy. Dark. Ambitious. Hungry. Careful. Obedient. He created new ballets. Good-bye Fokine. Good-bye Nijinsky. Massine was the star of the moment. We all admired him. Diaghilev, the Silver Fox, a giant. Portly. With holes in his shoes. Always in full dress suits. Leading behind him this dark shadow of a young man who was to take the throne. The new choreographer. The new genius. We were in love with him. He was very pretty in his fur coat and white gloves. A pearl pin in his lapel. He was a sharp little character, that Massine. But the old man would send us packing if we set our caps for him. He used to spy through the keyhole of his dressing room. General Bezobrazov teased him once. "Seryosha, you are mad. The boy is a holy virgin." But once burned . . . after Nijinsky got away the old man took no more chances.

Massine and Felix. Two crown princes, but only one could inherit the kingdom.

Now Felix was of the inner circle. He and Massine were always together. Like brothers. They wore the same clothes. But Massine was a whip, thin, quick. Felix was chunkier. Coarser. It was the gypsy blood, I suppose. We were in love with both of them. We argued who had more burning eyes . . . I always chose Felix. The other one had a black heart. I wouldn't have turned him out of my bed . . . but I don't think I would close my eyes.

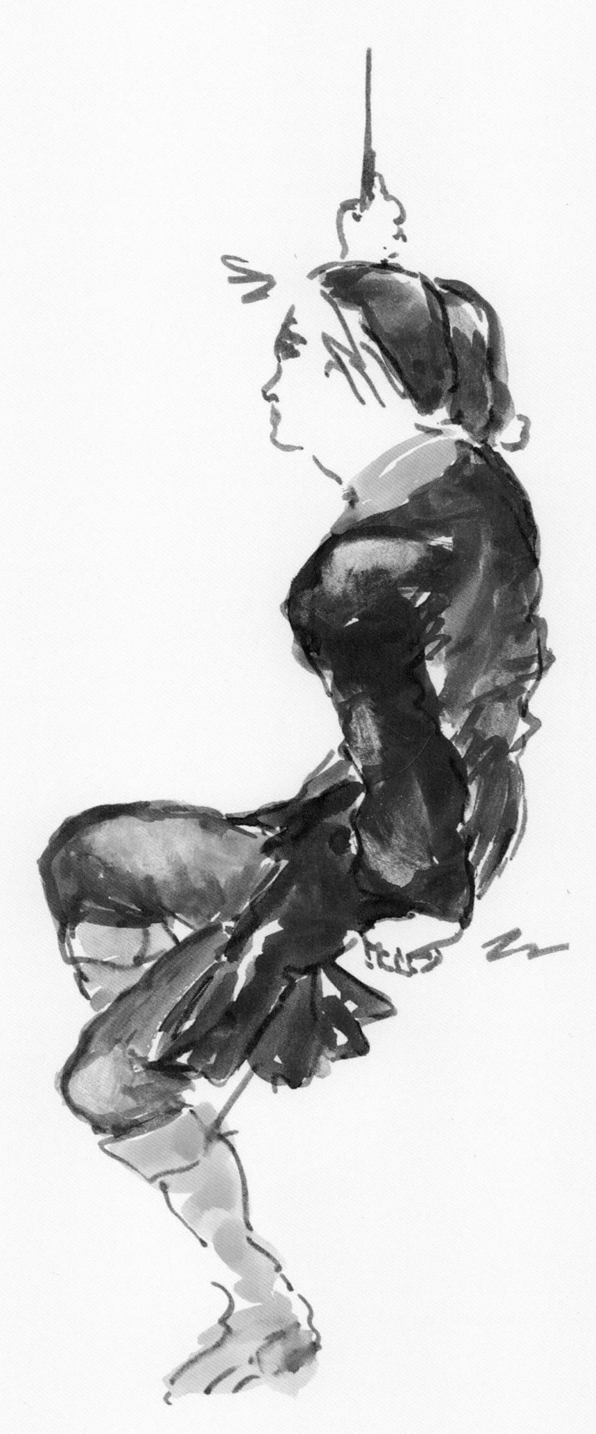

When we got to England, Felix began to teach Massine the Spanish dances. Later, Massine would create a dance for Felix. A dance to bring the house down. A *farucca* to end all *faruccas.* But first Massine must learn the correct steps. The new Spanish ballet must be authentic. But Felix cannot repeat the same steps twice. Do the waves of the sea repeat themselves in a storm? He is a gypsy. He improvises. And like a true gypsy he cannot come in on the same place in the music. De Falla turns red. He is an apoplectic man. "You are a gypsy, not an artist," he screams. "Listen to him," the old man shouts. "He is the composer. He is our father."

But Felix was an orphan. He had no father. He danced with his eyes closed. He was a mystic. He tried to explain. "It is the pulse of the music. I can come in anywhere as long as I feel the pulse." "But what if you do not feel it," they shouted. "Where do you come in then?" He looked at them. They must be mad. Why would he come in if he could not feel it? He would take a walk. He would visit his cousins. He would make love. But talk to the walls. To the air. Ballet is an art. It is not life. It is not authentic. It is frozen. Felix is fire but art is ice.

They gave him a metronome. He would learn to count. So he will know where to come in on the music. He is not a fool. He is merely without education. He cradles his metronome in his arms. He carries it with him wherever he goes. It will save him. I saw him on Shaftsbury Avenue walking so his feet move in time with the ticking. He is mumbling like a crazy man when his feet lose the regular count. Those feet erupt into combinations of complicated off-rhythms. He cannot imprison them. He looks about with wild eyes. They are not the same eyes. The fires rage. They are out of control. He is burning up.

Everybody talks about the new ballet. It is in all the papers. Photographers come to the rehearsals. Diaghilev is followed everywhere by critics, reporters. Picasso comes over from Paris with the new curtain. He paints it himself. He will not trust the scene painters. There are always photographers taking his picture with a brush in his hand. "I am a Spaniard," he tells them. "I will paint the Spanish curtain." He paints bulls and sunlight. It is very modern. Like him. Olga dresses him in English suits. A suede hat. A cane. The girls are impressed. What a rich painter. Lucky Olga! Outside, it is cold. England has not a hospitable climate. The sun only appears when it rains. Every day it rains for half an hour, maybe less. The sun comes out. The air is clean. When we can, we run outside to bathe in the sweet London rain like sparrows . . . Soon it will be Christmas . . .

Felix sits in the wings. His ear is to the metronome. He is counting. Still, he is counting. He is desperate. It is his last chance for success. He is the only one without a part. There is no *farrucca* for Felix. He cannot count. Even the last girl in the line can count. There is always a giant sandwich in his hand. I do not know if it is a different one or the same one. Maybe he remembers when he was hungry in Spain. But even when Massine tells him to show us a step he does not put down that miserable sandwich. There is a lull in the music. It comes to a close. But the metronome knows no close. Its tired heart goes on beating. Massine is tired. He has not slept for days. He is a perfectionist. "Get rid of that *imbecile* toy," he shouts. "It's making me crazy." Even De Falla is shocked. Picasso puts down his brush.

Dounia moans. Felix turns pale. Massine is ashamed. Maybe for us. Maybe for himself. Who can tell? "Listen, *galoupshik*," he calls to Felix. "Come down here. Show me how this part is to be done." Felix demonstrates but it does not matter anymore. The ballet is finished.

On opening night, the Spanish numbers bring down the house. Massine dances like a possessed man. "A demon has possessed me," he cried, coming off the stage. "I was not myself." He had 17 curtain calls. History was made. Felix watched from the wings. Then he was gone. We never saw him again.

A few weeks later we were off to Paris. Paris was our biggest season. Diaghilev cared only for Paris. But nobody thought of buying Felix a ticket. Maybe he was there at the train station when we left but we were busy. There were bags to check. Lovers to say good-bye to. Massine posed for pictures with the old man. He was holding court. We always did a lot of business in train stations. Arrivals and departures were very important to us. Felix did not know how to arrive and depart. He had no money. The old man paid for everything. He was a maker of kings, Diaghilev. He was gracious. Generous. He opened his hands. Gifts fell to the floor. But it was all a figure of speech. When you are always arriving and departing, everything becomes a figure of speech. It is not the lover of the week you mourn for. It is the metaphor for love.

Later we heard Felix was arrested for dancing on the altar of a church somewhere in South London. It is a neighborhood I do not know. I believe it was Christmas Eve and the police were indignant. He stamped and clicked and played the castanets until the priests were beside themselves. They thought he was an anarchist. The English do not like foreigners anyway. They searched him. Maybe he had a bomb. Nobody spoke Spanish. They did not know what to do with him. But there are no cantinas in England, you see. No guitars. It was Christmas. He was lonely. His heart was broken. The only thing that looked like home must have been a church. He had no money. He used to stay at the Hotel Dieppe in Old Compton Street but they put him out. By then he was forbidden to eat in restaurants. He behaved in a crazy manner and upset people, and Diaghilev was afraid he would give the Russian ballet a bad name. I think somebody said he kept food in the hotel room and they put him out. But somebody else said there was nobody to pay rent for him. Grigoriev was in Paris. I don't know what happened. But he had no friends. No money. Such men are dangerous. We heard he was arrested. They put him in a mental hospital and he stayed there for many years. Later, much later, he died, during the war.

We knew nothing. We were busy. Who was Felix? Who remembered? We didn't need him anymore. Art is not kind to her children. Why didn't we send him home? Felix. Felix, how you cried when Diaghilev introduced you to King Alphonso. You kissed the King's hand. It got so wet from your tears you tried to wipe it off with your sleeve. Even the King was embarrassed . . . just a poor gypsy from the mountains . . . and we stole you away . . . like the ears . . . the tail . . . of a prize bull.

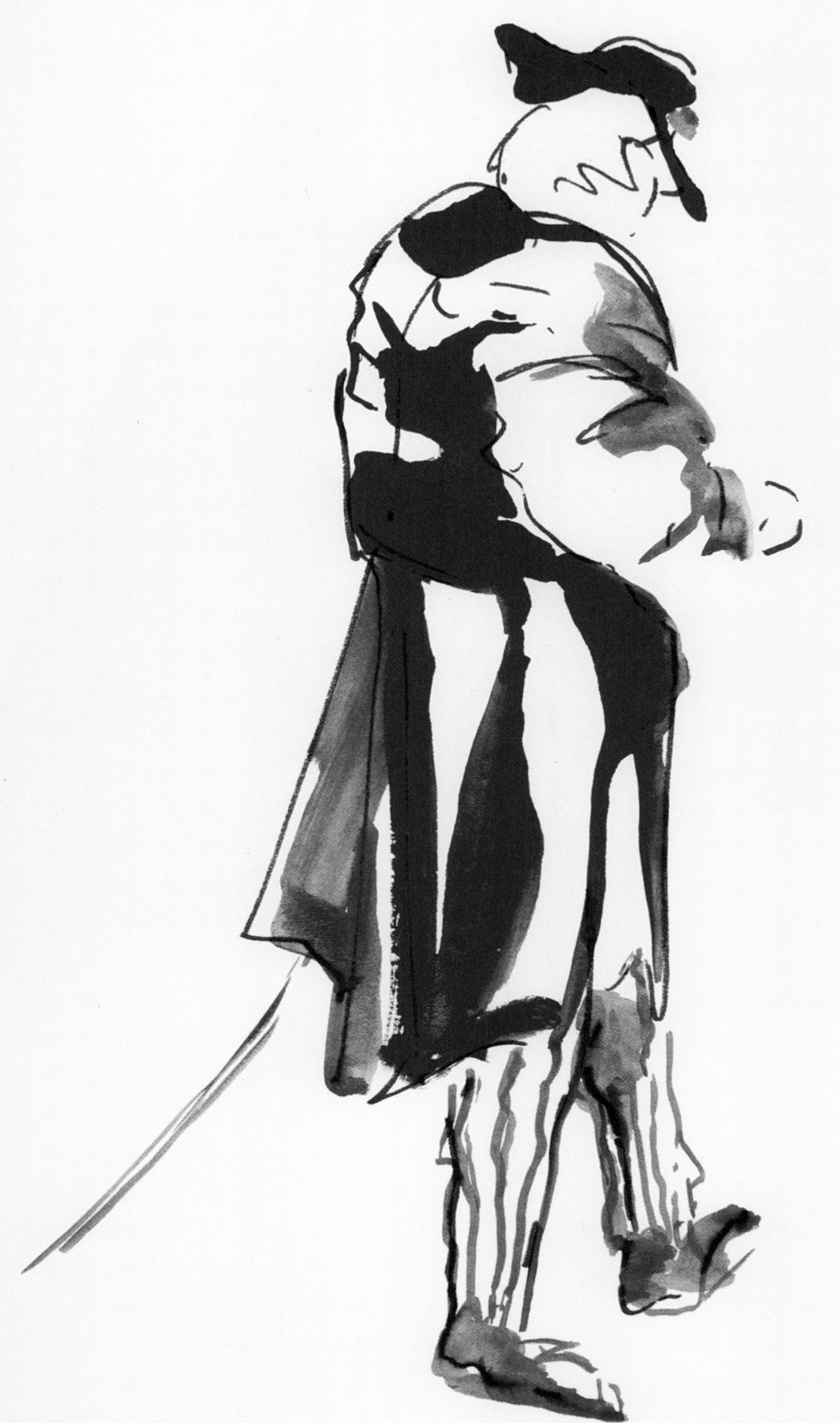

Chapter 6

After the Great War

After the Great War, I went to Russia. So much was happening. The Soviets were making history. Everybody was talking about them. Wherever you went, it was the Reds this, the Reds that. You can't understand today what the Bolsheviks meant to us. Such a robust subject. How could Art compare? Our wars were over. We won. Diaghilev was the 8th wonder of the world. All of Paris rose to salute our modernism. It was so boring . . .

One night I had a dream I was dancing for Lenin. Tears ran down his face. Worn. Tired. It was my father's face. The orchestra struck up the Internationale. "Arise ye pris'ners of starvation." My mind was made up. I was going to Russia, my spiritual home . . . So I was born in New York. So! Nobody asked me. I am a mature person. I can pick and choose. But it wasn't an easy decision, let me tell you. I danced with the *Ballets Russes* . . . White Russians! On the anniversary of the Czar's death, they wore black. They scared themselves with tales of Red Devils. I was in peril for my life. The stage was their battleground. Broken glass under my feet. A partner who moves two steps to the right, I could hear my legs break already. My career was doomed . . .

But it never happened. Diaghilev, himself, took me to supper at the Grand Hotel. He ordered caviar. Wine. I ate for 10. Maybe I didn't know what was what, but I wasn't a fool. Dancers are always hungry. He took my hand. "Eleanora, beloved child. You must make them understand." Who? What? I didn't understand. But he wanted to go home, you see. Once a Russian always a Russian. He wanted to reorganize the entire State Theatre System even if they were Bolsheviks. Make it a model of modernism. The 8th wonder of the world. He pressed a bundle of letters into my hands. "For Lunacharsky," he whispered. "Tell him . . . tell him . . ." He choked on his tears and couldn't go on.

Then Mathilde Kschessinka grabs me in the wings. “Hey, Pushkina.” She always called me Pushkina after Pushkin who was black. Mathilde Kschessinka was a ridiculous person. But she was our Prima and that was that! She wanted me to steal into her palace in St. Petersburg and dig up her old love letters from the Czar. *Vanity Fair* was going to give her a million francs for them. 5% for me if I found them. We bargained.

“10%”

“7%”

“8 ½%”

“What are you, an Armenian?”

“But Madame! Your palace is a Red hangout. Lenin himself lives there.”

She wept and tore her hair. “I have 3 Grand Dukes to support. Dimitri alone, the gambler, what he cost me. Yesterday, the miserable wretch bet my diamond earrings that 17 women would cross the Chausee d’Antin in 60 seconds. The man is a fiend, a viper.”

“Did he win, Madame?”

“One was a dwarf. We split the difference.”

She appraised me with her cashier’s eye. “So now I have one earring left. You can have it for 300 francs.”

“Madame,” I wailed. “Where would I get 300 francs?”

She looked at me in amazement. “Where does any woman get 300 francs?”

Soon everybody came to me with presents for an old mother, lover, sisters, cousins. I left with a bag this big. On my way to the Revolution, I became a mailman. Sweaters, jams, cigarettes. I could sell the lot on the black market and be a rich woman like that. Who would believe I wasn’t a capitalist? I could be jailed. Shot, even. “The walls have ears.” An old Russian saying. The Czar himself supported half of St. Petersburg with his secret police. Everybody was a police spy or in training to be one. Spies had their spies who had their spies. It was said of St. Petersburg that there were more spies than bedbugs. It was a bureaucracy of spies. Do you think that a man changes his character as fast as his politics? So now they spy for Lenin . . .

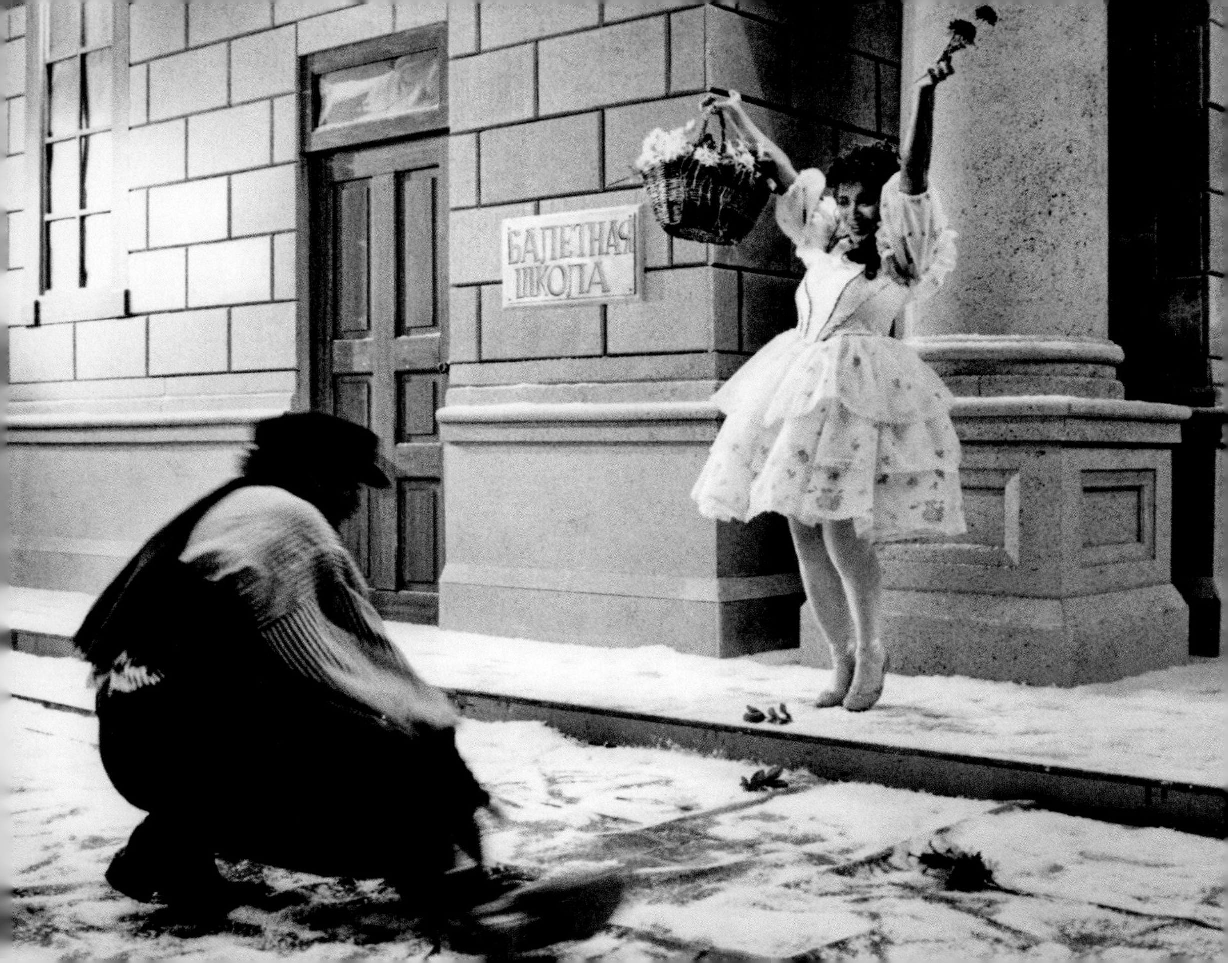
БАЛЕТНАЯ
ШКОЛА

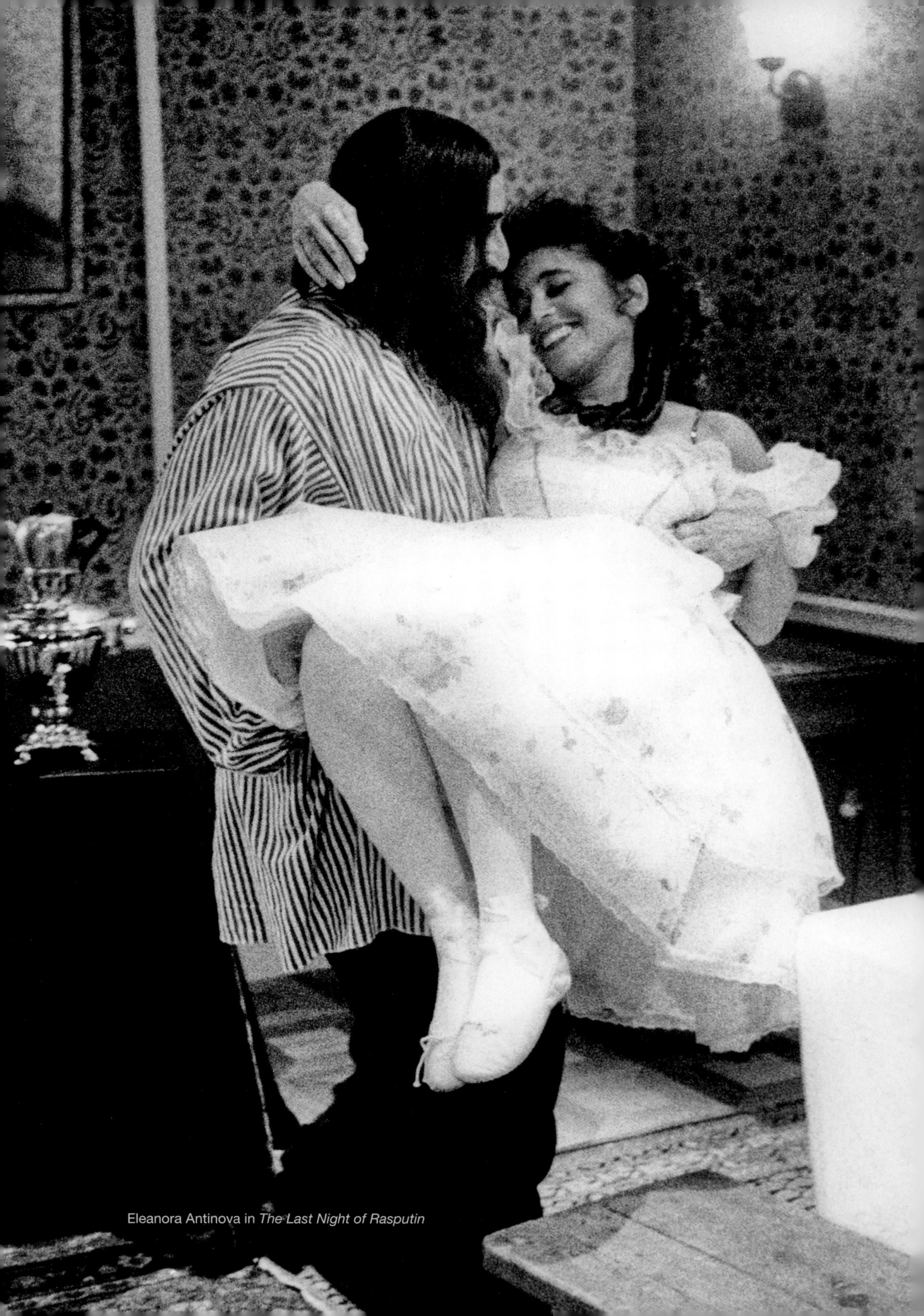

Eleanora Antinova in *The Last Night of Rasputin*

I had a spy. My very own spy. All to myself. I considered myself fortunate. She was a cultured person. A librarian at the Maryinsky School. It was an honour to know her. She attached herself to me and believe me I was grateful. She took me in hand and showed me the ropes. Got me a room next to hers. Helped me deliver my packages. Took me to the best cafés. Pointed out important people. When I complained about the scarcity of food, my friends advised me to tell my spy. "She is a good person," Olga Kokhlova said. "She will help. Foreigners are treated well here." The next day they delivered a herring, butter, some sugar. The artists came and we had a party. I invited my spy. She wept from happiness to be in such company. She was a humble person.

But don't think I spent all my time carousing. I was assigned to the cinema workers. I protested. "I am a dancer." But the artists cheered. Cinema was the future. And to us the future was everything. They introduced me to Pudovkin, he was an actor then, Abram Room, Kozintsev, the actor Morrissov. It was Morrissov who introduced me to Antinov. He was making a film. I must have a part . . . a handsome fellow, Antinov. Small, but handsome. I always had a weakness for men I could look in the eye. He wore a little round pince-nez like Trotsky. Trotsky was his god. "A man of culture," he would say. "He read French novels in the tanks." A dandy, that Antinov. Never without his grandfather's gold watch. Even when he was hungry later in Paris, he refused to sell it. "The food will leave me in an hour," he would say. "But the watch . . . it will never leave me." As for me, I have little attachment to the things of this world. I sold my diamond for food. I am an American. Easy come, easy go. But the Russians never had anything. So what was new? Except poor Antinov. He had a ballerina. He howled. What could he do with a ballerina in a film about Rasputin? But Morrissov took up my cause. He was in love with me. I was very pretty in those days. And he was playing Rasputin. He had pull.

"How can a Russian turn down a ballerina? What are you, a Nihilist?"

They came to blows on the Nevsky Prospekt. And I? I went home with Antinov. Such are the ways of the world. Besides, that Morrissov was a fanatic. Who needs a fanatic to tell you what to do? He was his own man, that Antinov. He fought with the Reds, the Whites, then the Reds again. His mother swore he was born with old eyes . . . What can I tell you? He made a place for me in Rasputin's life. "Our politicians rewrite history every day," he said. "Am I not a better artist?"

But later, Olga Kokhlova told me he stole the idea of the ballerina from her husband Lev Kuleshov. This was the sort of paranoia you had to deal with in those days. I respect Kuleshov. He was a great teacher and they say now he was a great director. I'm just a dancer, what do I know of such things? I'm sorry the government treated him badly. The government treated everybody badly. That's what it means to be a government. They should have given him film. I would have given him film if I were a government. He was a true artist. And very clever to make films without film. That was ingenious.

He had a school of film acting but it was during the war, there really was no film around anywhere. What could he do? He wasn't going to close down his school. So they acted without film. On a stage. In short takes. Da da da, like that. They laid out the sight lines with sticks and strings. They spent a long time sticking an actor's elbow out of the frame. They could cut a profile on its ear. They spent a long time framing. The montage, they acted. They came forward and looked big—close up. They stepped back and looked small—wide shot. They disappeared though everybody knew they were still in the room. They were just off camera. Back for the reaction shot. It was very tiring. But it was a movie. The final cut without the film.

In one of these movies, a dancer is kidnapped. It was an American plot. The gangsters fight over the loot. That loot was Kokhlova. Some ballerina, Kokhlova. Big like a horse. Hands pawing the air. She was not a great beauty. I am a ballerina. I dance on the tips of my toes. I am a feather. She is a horse. And that's that. So where is the same? . . . Holy Mother . . . I am defending a dead man from a dead woman. But I fell into the habit of defending him. He was always a suspicious character to the Bolsheviks. He used to say a certain E was a Judas to him . . . That E was Ermler, the famous film director. But then he was just a diligent spy out to advance himself. He was always writing in his little black book. He sucked on his pencil till his teeth were black. But Antinov always saved a seat for him. "He is not like the other comrades," he would say. "This one works for a living."

And he was at his best when Ermler was around. There was no getting away from it. He looked at Ermler and became a poet. "Art is organic," he said. "It must breathe naturally like the human heart." Then he winked over at Ermler. "Not like you, comrade. You regulate traffic." But Ermler was quick, too. "Irony is counter-revolutionary, comrade."

They gave us a professor of Ideology. This professor was an imbecile. He sat in front of the stove and snored. It was a factory whistle that snore. It killed our inspiration. But Antinov refused to wake him. "He is an old man," he would say. "He fought in the 1905 revolution. When we sat in the cafés, he rotted in jail. He deserves a sinecure. Leave him in peace." Who had peace? We used to nail the set to the floor at night so it would be there in the morning. It was the Moscow Art Theatre. They would come and take your set out from under your nose. Stanislavski was the darling of the Party. He could do no wrong. They adored him. It was Constantin Gavrilovich this, Constantin Gavrilovich that. They were old men. When they were young, he was their avant-garde. Who could fight it? You can't fight a memory.

Would you believe in all of Petersburg we couldn't find a dagger? Weapons were confiscated, you see. They sent us kitchen knives. Three times they sent us the same kitchen knife. "If it's good enough for the peasants, it's good enough for you!" That was the mentality in those days. Poor Antinov. All he wanted was the Prince to trim his nails with a dagger. To sit at a table and trim his nails with the same dagger he would later use to kill Rasputin at the end. It was a good psychology. But they sent a letter opener. We had to kill Rasputin with a letter opener. That's the way it was in those days. The only thing we had plenty of was uniforms. The theatres were packed with Czarist uniforms. We had a joke that the corpses were still inside them. You could see the dried blood stains. So we played historical dramas. Even Stanislavski. Artists are thrifty people. The girls used to fight over the fancy dresses . . . Antinov liked young girls. It was a trouble between us. He would bring in a girl. Where he found her nobody knows. "Give her a part," he would say. "She is such a beauty . . ." That was the way it was in those days.

Then Lenin died. And you should excuse me, the shit hit the fan. We were drowning in Georgians. There was no end to them. One day, Antinov was denounced in the press. The next day he was sent to the provinces. In an old agit train, can you believe it? They found an old agit train. It was falling apart. The wood was rotting away. It wasn't good enough for the termites. It stank. Old posters were peeling off the walls. In summer, it was damp. In winter, I got rheumatism. But how could I leave him? I stayed out of spite. I am a stubborn woman. Poor Yevgeny. He was a fish out of water. It was too quiet in the country, it scared him. He refused to leave the train. He would sink down into the mud and he worried about his boots. Even on the tundra, he was a dandy.

Our train wandered from one village to the next. I think we were lost. The peasants hated us. They would piss on the train. They came to the shows and pissed on the train. "The Muscovny," they called us, and pissed on the train. To them all city people were from Moscow. We were out in the sticks for months playing Antinov's films. They were falling to pieces. They ripped at every showing, sometimes as much as 5 or 6 times. We had to stop the show to piece the film together. Then the peasants would beat each other up. We wrote to everybody we knew. Lunacharsky, Gorky. Even Ermler. Did they get our letters? Only Ermler answered. "You are doing good work, comrade. Long life!" We were forgotten men. Lost on an agit train in Eastern Russia. Poor Yevgeny! Now they say they are showing his films again. In beautiful museums, too. Lucky I'm so slow. I'm still here. Maybe I'll get to see them . . .

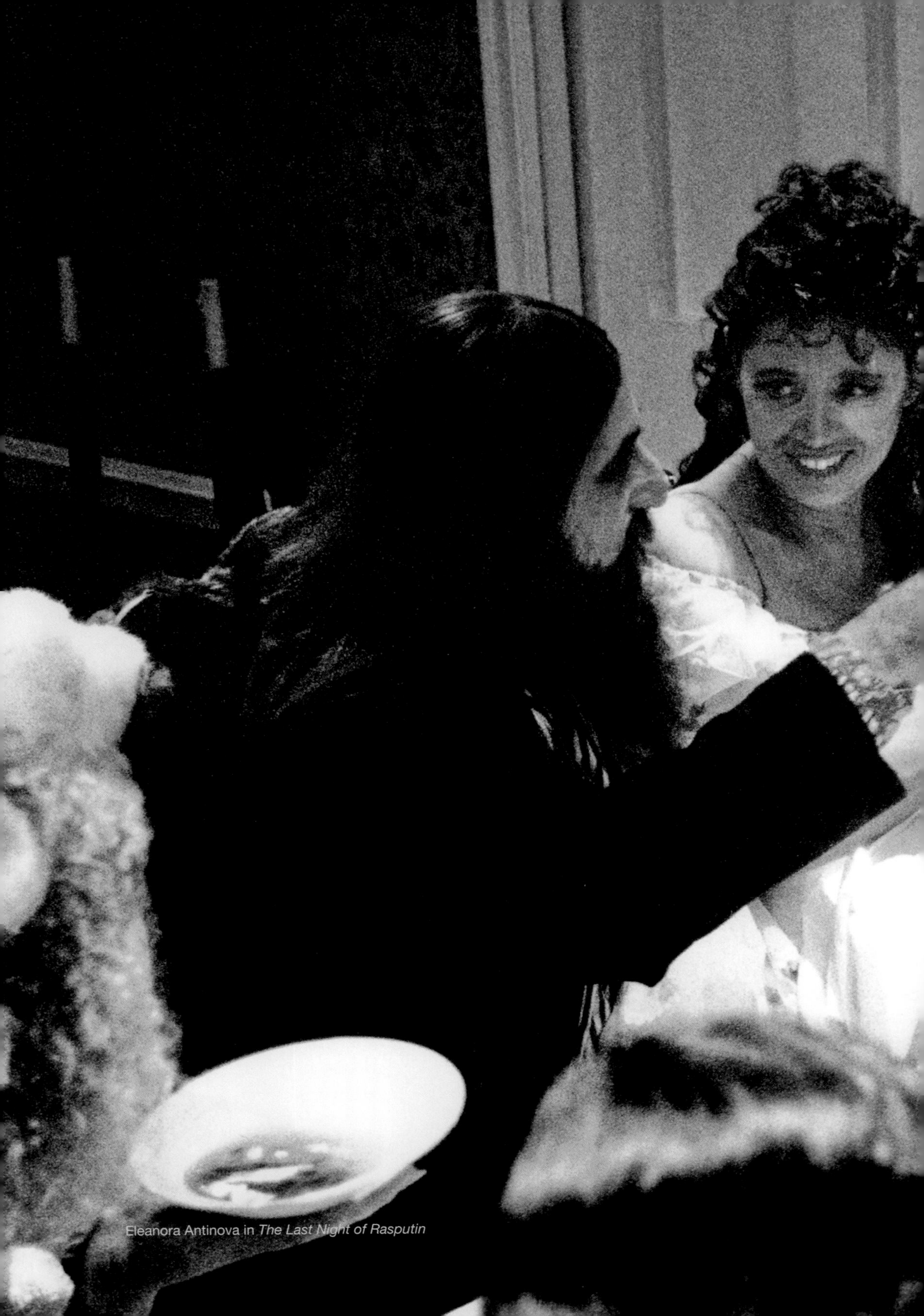

Eleanora Antinova in *The Last Night of Rasputin*

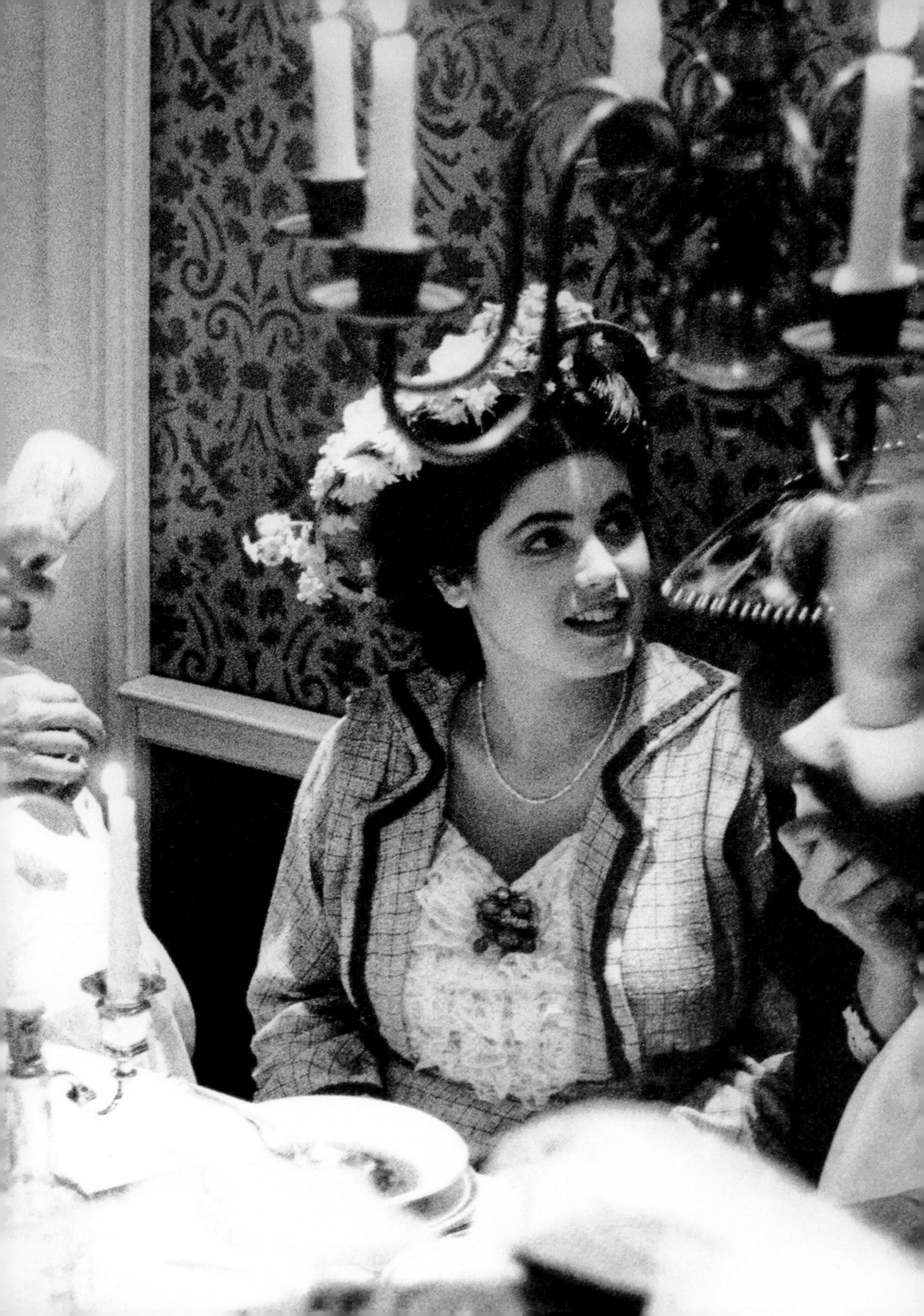

Chapter 7

Boundaries

But it's odd to force one's life into chapters, sentences, stylistic unities. An Eleanora made out of words is such an airy thing. She's even become a natural ballerina and I certainly wasn't. I probably shouldn't have been one at all. I was clearly more suited by body and temperament to be a modern dancer. But I had a vision—a dream—of the beautiful thing, though by nature I was more suited to the expressive thing. Pavlova, Spessivsteva, Karsavina, they had a talent for beauty. You left the theatre feeling warmed, fulfilled, as if you had spent the afternoon with a very generous and talented lover. Perhaps you had!

But I had very little talent for the beautiful. I didn't flow, I exploded. I wasn't ungraceful, it was just that I was so much more apparently percussive. I had so many disjunctive parts it was hard to see the smooth ones. And I didn't know how to be gracious. I had too many opinions, because I cared too much, and I changed them, too. So I wasn't restrained, classical. Though Diaghilev knew the well-oiled machine could do with an occasional juicing. Myself, Mme. Ida Rubenstein, we were there to play the more peculiar, in a manner of speaking, the darker roles.

But I was never sure that I really wanted to do that for them. Typecasting always seemed so vulgar. I preferred the imperfect fit, where you saw the performer intersecting with her ambitions. There, at the edges, they might overlap—the desire and the fact—when two impossibilities come together, a beauty is created, so dense, so rich, so painful almost in its pleasure, the most hardened person must cry.

It was out there at the boundaries where I wanted to stake my claim. Unfortunately, I chose the most academic of art forms. For the entire length of my stay with the *Ballets Russes* I fought them. By and large, I have to admit they won. Not because they were right but because there were more of *them.*

When Massine left to start his own company, Bronislava Nijinska became our choreographer. She was a good choreographer but she argued too much. I think she reminded the old man of her brother. Though why, I don't know since they didn't really look alike and besides Nijinsky never argued. Despair flooded his soul and he just sulked. But I have to admit there was something. A brother and a sister, there is something . . .

Then one day, Michel Montrachet appeared and then he was there every day. It was his time. He was young, he was handsome, his eyes were clear as a river. Diaghilev took him in hand, took him to museums, concerts. He said Michel was a genius only we didn't know what kind yet. "If you are a genius, you do something better than everybody else," Vera said. "He does nothing. So where is his genius?" It will come, the others said. It is waiting to surprise us. "To surprise him," Vera said spitefully.

One day in the studio when we were all standing together, only we weren't together, we were just standing, the old man called out sharply. "Eleanora."

I stood at attention. Why wouldn't that damn Michel stop standing so close.

"Yes?" I asked. "You are calling me, Sergei Pavlovitch?"

"Eleanora," he repeated, "it is your time." He paused and looked steadily at me and then Michel ran his hand through his hair and bumped me with his arm. Diaghilev looked admiringly at him. He did have silky black curly hair.

"Children," he said, "there has never been an American ballet. It is time. You Eleanora will choreograph and dance in this ballet. You will make your debut as a choreographer this spring in London." Then he looked at Michel because he was still standing next to me smoothing his hair. "And you, Michel," he announced, "you will design the ballet."

There was a silence while we all took this in. Or at least I tried to take it in until Bronislava's cold voice demanded our attention. "Sergei Pavlovitch! Are you talking about *Pocahontas*?" He ignored her and continued to smile at me. Or maybe it was at Michel. He was still standing so close to me, the idiot. I stepped back so we would be 2 people, not one, but there was no room. Everybody was there and looking at me. I wanted to hide but Bronislava's voice, it was like ice and it would freeze me to death. "*Pocahontas* is my ballet. I am already working it up for the London season."

"Ach," the old man growled, turning to her. "The little one is black as coal. You are pale and insignificant. What do you know of Indian braves and tomahawks?"

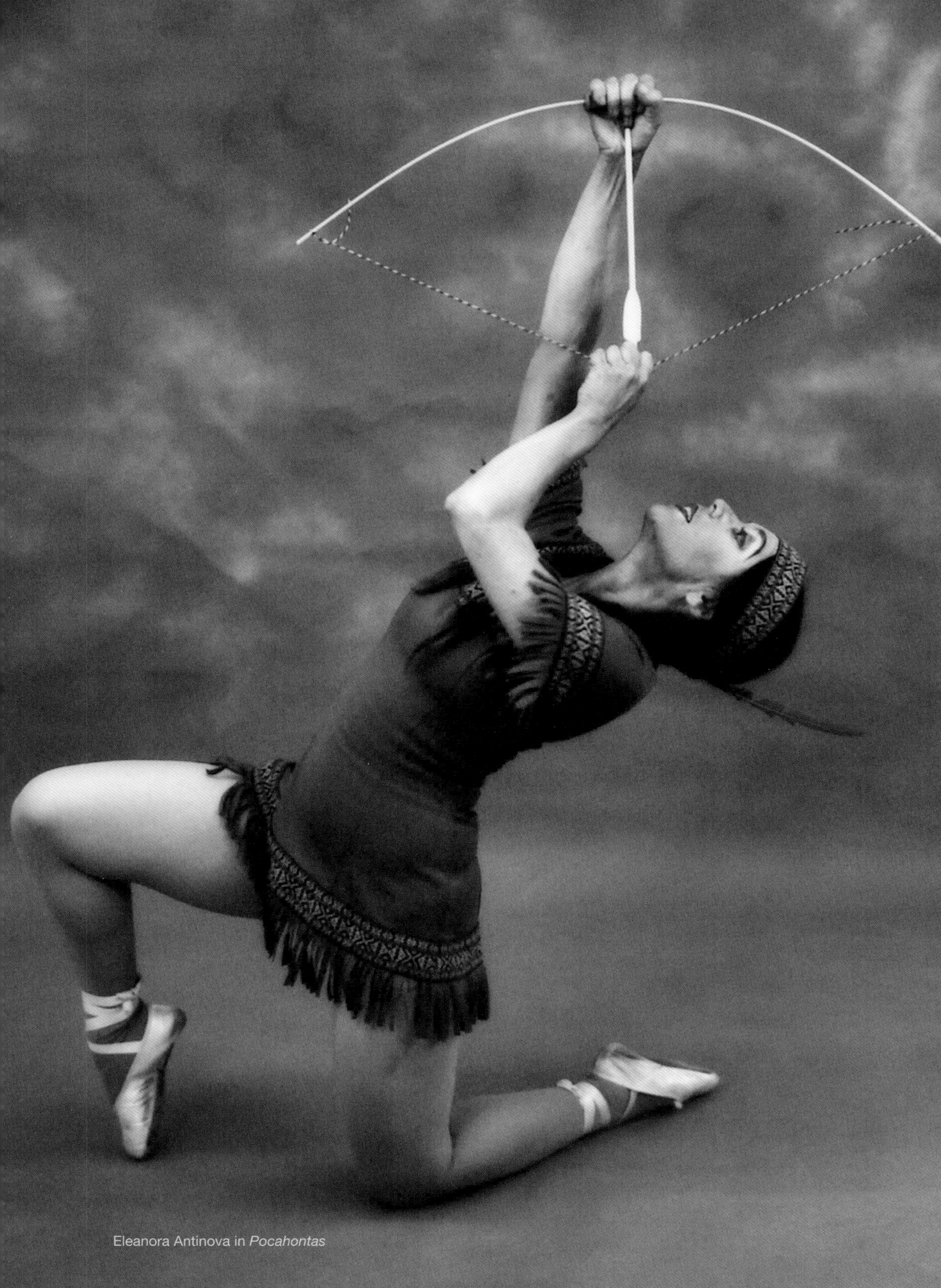

Eleanora Antinova in *Pocahontas*

We all gasped. True, Bronislava was no beauty, but she was not insignificant. She used rouge too, so she was hardly pale. And besides I wasn't black as coal, either. I was considered quite light as a matter of fact. "You are a mulatto," my father used to say. "There is a lot of white blood in our family."

"And you are not even an American." The old man continued glaring at her. "Are you an American? Tell me, what do you know of primeval forests?"

"Don't be ridiculous." Bronislava's voice was rising. Now it was close to a shriek. "Of course I am not an American. I am a person of culture, an *artiste.* I am Russian. You know I am Russian."

"You are mad like your brother," the old man shouted. "He called himself a Russian too . . . Ach, I am a gentleman. But now I am saying, 'How dare you call yourself a Russian. You are a Pole. You come from an insignificant country.'"

Bronislava turned red. It was an insult. It was true but it was an insult. She stormed out of the room.

"*Pocahontas,*" the old man relished the name and turned back to us, a great smile lighting up his face. "*Pocahontas,*" he repeated. "For the British. Later for the Americans. The season is saved."

Maybe the season was saved. But I wasn't. The role of the ill-fated Indian princess and young braves with tomahawks was the old man's fantasy of primeval forests and Elizabethan England —more Petipa than Longfellow. It would begin with the death of Pocahontas in an English tavern.

"Wait! What is she doing in a tavern?" I asked.

The old man looked at me incredulously.

"Have you no education? History!" he scowled. "This is merry old England. Shakespeare!" he shouted when I didn't look convinced. "This is how the English passed their time. Always merry." He raised his arms threatening to dance and be merry.

I thought fast. "Well, then, we have to dance the story backwards. From merry old England back to primitive Virginia." I waved my arms at the dancers who were leaning lackadaisically against the *barre* waiting for the bosses to shout it out. So now I was a boss. I remembered the loudest usually won. "Look at them," I screeched. "They are dancers. Deaf mutes not actors."

Diaghilev's expression was getting darker and darker. I had to save my ballet. "OK, OK," I said. "We'll tell the story on two stage levels. I'll compress the action into an Elizabethan present and a Virginia flashback."

"Magnificent," Michel shouted. It was the first time I heard his voice. It was gruff with a Southern French flavor. Was his genius coming out? Would it help my ballet or destroy it?

"I will turn the upper level into a timbered balcony," he continued. "Beneath will lie the unconscious body of the mysterious Pocahontas. The forest primeval. The moon mourns behind the trees looking for her in vain. Where is the princess? Why does she not return to us?"

The merry Elizabethans caroused around me on the top level, bear baiting, pocket picking, tumbling, doing jigs, hornpipes, Morris dances, while I made delirious gestures from my bed. Michel painted the top stage to represent a timbered balcony. At least he knew how to handle a brush. Later I threw off my diaphanous gown and leapt out of bed in my Indian costume to dance the dream of my youth, after sliding down a pole twined with exotic vines. I ran through the trees of my unconscious, teasing the dashing young braves leaping over rocks to catch me. This flashback included a fancifully constructed dream boat, sailing over waves represented by a rope held by 2 slithering mermaids who flailed it around to cook up a balletic storm while some ethnic types from the upper level performed a dumb show of my nuptials with a stiff-necked British farmer.

The dress rehearsal was a debacle. They forgot the plot was of their invention, not mine. Diaghilev flew into a rage and threw out most everything—the 2 stage levels, the bed, the boat, the forest, the wedding. The final version found me lying on the stage obscured by revelers brawling and twirling to some Russian version of Elizabethan music. At some point—for no reason known to anyone—the crowd parts to reveal me lying flat on my back, waving my arms helplessly above me. I think they thought I was making waves. When I leap up—bow and arrow in hand—to dance the delirium dream of my youth, expressed mainly by spins, leaps, and cartwheels, 2 dancers heavily padded in front, grasp opposite ends of a long rope, and for reasons mysterious to everyone, wave it gracefully in the air until I collapse and die.

The shortened version had some success in London but never made it to America. My parents were disappointed. They were looking forward to getting free tickets but I was secretly pleased. Pokey, as I called it, stayed in the repertoire for a couple of years. It was revived once by the de Basil company and there was some talk of reviving it for the recent Bicentennial but it came to nothing.

Michel disappeared after that. It was generally agreed that he hadn't a modicum of genius and didn't belong in the *Ballets Russes.*

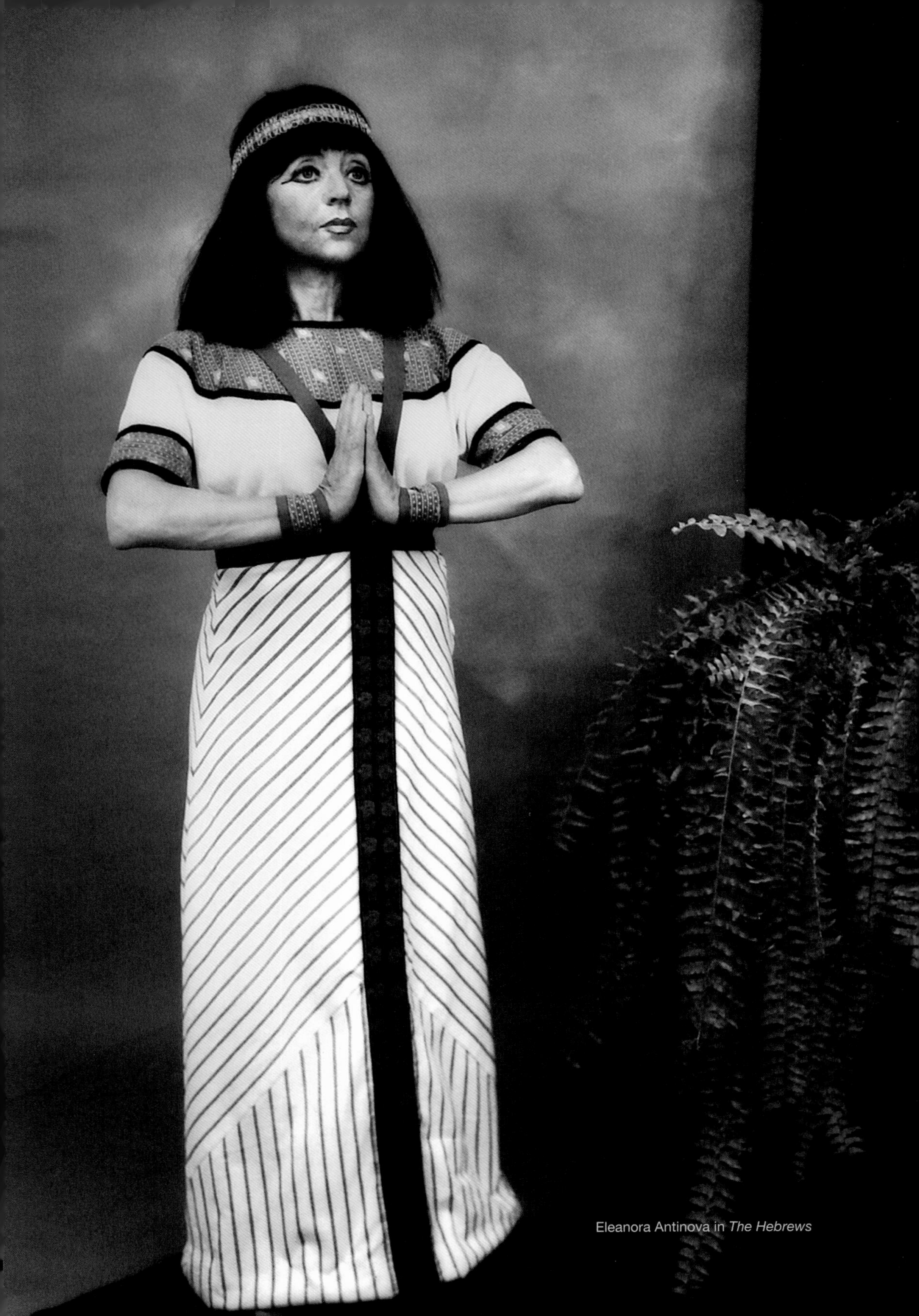

Eleanora Antinova in *The Hebrews*

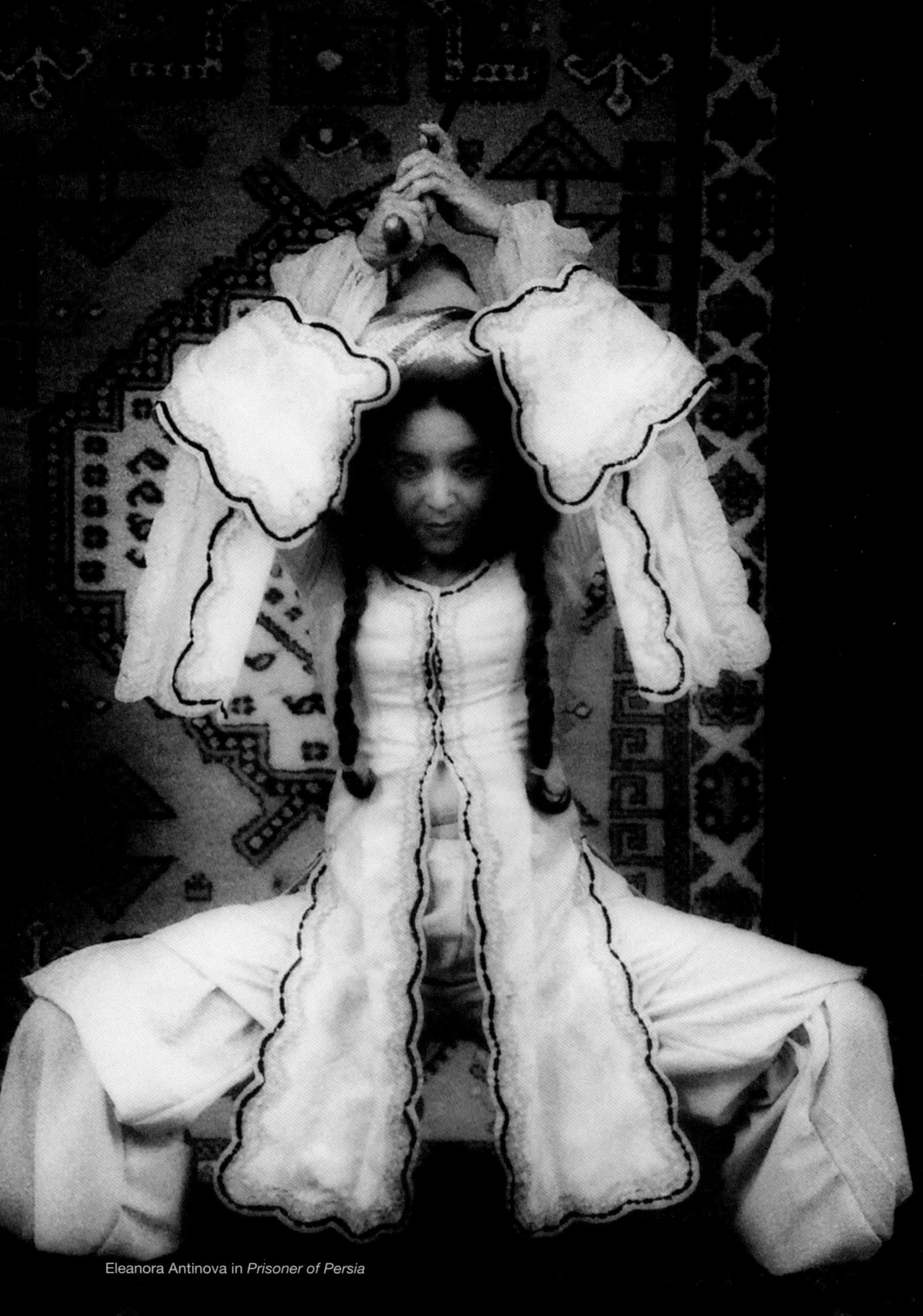

Eleanora Antinova in *Prisoner of Persia*

Chapter 8

The Third Act

I danced with Diagheliv for 10 years. Where did they go, those years? Here. In my head. They are all in my head. And when I'm gone—pshaw . . . They were my family. Sergei Pavlovitch was our father. We were sisters, brothers. We slept 4 to a bed. It was cheaper. Two bargained for the room while the others sneaked up the back stairs. And took the best places. You should remember the friends who share your bed. But the nights blend into one night. Sometimes I can't remember any night . . . I'm ashamed to confess this—I hope you won't misunderstand —I can't help it—to this day—I am partial to Russians. I feel friendly to them. Maybe not friendly, but familiar. A Russian is a Russian, even a bad one. I remember St. Petersberg better than London or Paris and I was never even there. By my time, most of the Russian girls hadn't been there either. Paris rats. The last they saw of Mother Russia was racing through the ice fields of Finland on a sled. But there is no St. Petersberg anymore. What's the new name? A ridiculous name, very likely. I always get it mixed up with Moscow but it isn't. Moscow was always there. Stanislavsky was from Moscow. Chaliapin, too, I think. Leningrad. That's the new name. A stupid name. Tanks, not white nights. Am I a snob? It's hard to live with Russians and not be a snob. Even Lenin *was* part of the family. There's no getting around it. A Russian is a Russian.

I knew the girl he lived with in Paris. She found him in a café. He was starving. She took him in and fed him like a stray cat. They say she was very beautiful, one of the famous artists' models. All the girls in those days were from Martinique, Jamaica, Haiti. She was from Martinique. I was the little girl from America. They felt sorry for me. They looked at me like I was a savage. But that was later. I came later. By the time I knew her, she was over the hill. Absinthe. Syphilis. People didn't know about health then. Later, when Lenin made a name for himself, they wrote to him for help, but he wouldn't answer their letters. They say he had a hard heart. But why should he remember those days? What was there to remember? That he was poor and wretched? Now he was an important person. He lived in Kschessinska's palace and made revolutions. I think Kschessinska was secretly proud that he chose her palace. They made the revolution from that palace. And it was only a little palace, new, not very important. So look at Eiffel. That was only a tower.

Indeed, she was a great ballerina, Mathilde Kschessinska, but narrow in her outlook. A terrible snob. We were all terrible snobs. Not a penny in our pockets but we sailed through the doors of the Ritz as if we owned the place. We did. Kschessinska's Grand Dukes were the doormen. Grand Duke Andrei formally pinched our bottoms. It was an honour. Wasn't he the Czar's brother? "Go little flowers," he would say. "There are two counts from Alsace. They are old and ugly but their pockets burn with gold." Our stomachs rumbled. We lived on *piroschkas* and *café au lait.* Dounia adjusted the veil of her red hat. That afternoon we lunched on oysters and frog's legs and *escargot* and salmon roe and wines from the private cellars. Everything fell before Dounia's delicious red hat. It had a spirit, that hat. And why not? It came from a corpse.

Though she wasn't always a corpse—the tall skinny lady who crept close to the walls of the *pension* and never smiled. "Opium!" Dounia announced. "She is rich but will not last long." Dounia had spies everywhere. She gave the maid some extra francs. When the poor lady died in her sleep, the maid knocked on our door. Later Dounia showed up with a red hat. A Chanel dress. Silk underthings. She gave me a pink chemise. She was furious. "That whore Katya. We fought over every piece. What does a slut like her need with a Paul Poiret dress!" We were shocked. A Paul Poiret dress! What couldn't we conquer with a Paul Poiret dress?

For who knew how the day would end. Fortune came and went. There was no reason. No cause and effect. Things happened. Fortune came or it didn't. By not coming, it didn't. So much of the time, it didn't . . . I never did what I should do. I always did what I wanted to do. In the end that's what I did. What I wanted to do. And the dances I made. I made the ones I wanted to make . . . Did it matter? I don't know. In the end it's all the same, isn't it? Gone every one, except here in my head. Was that what it was all for? For some pictures in my head? A couple of phrases, an embarrassment or two? Yes, I still cringe when I remember some of the things I said and did . . . I'm so ashamed . . . In life things come out wrong . . . as in the theatre—events cross, mix up, mask, pretend—like life . . . But it all works out in the third act. There was a ballet I wanted to do, nobody would produce it. If there is nobody to produce it, there is nobody to dance it. I called this ballet "Act 3." All ensembles. No solos. The *corps de ballet* working in perfect harmony . . . I loved third acts . . . You are happy in the third act . . . I never even got to the third act . . .

When Diaghilev died there was nothing for me in Europe and I came home. To a desert. America was a desert. The roads were empty then. And the nights. The skies were black. The lights weren't on yet all over the country. You saw the stars. How many moons did I see over Kansas? The country was silent. It was waiting for cars. The diners waited. The filling stations. We rode the buses down those empty roads to one nighters in church halls and movie houses. Sometimes we did 3, 4 shows a day. Between Carole Lombard and Ronald Coleman. Ballet was a foreign word. What

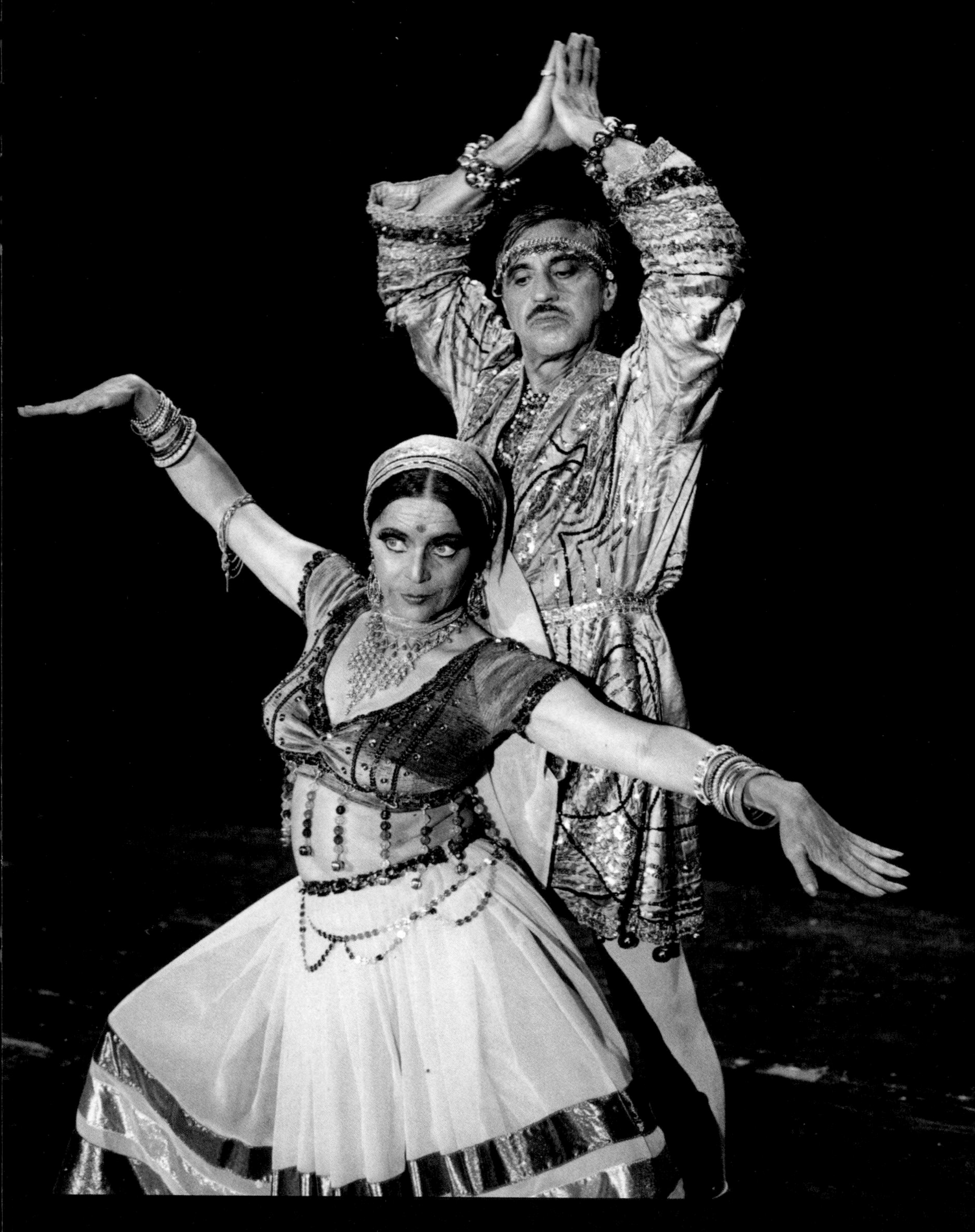

Eleanora Antinova in *In a Bazaar in Bangalore*

was an American dance? The people were harvesting the wheat, rolling steel, making cars to ride the empty roads. America was singing. I heard her. I was a native, after all.

Europe was decadent. I came home to find my roots. The intelligentsia was in a ferment. They were searching for an American idiom. A new culture was at hand. We had high hopes . . . but it was not meant to be. The Great Depression. Those were terrible times.

Theatres were closing left and right. Bookings were very hard to come by. People were on bread-lines. Jumping out of windows. I worked up some lighter numbers. I had to eat. I heard the *Ballets Russes* was starting up again in Paris under the Count de Basil. I had hopes. There was talk. But it was a new generation. The baby ballerinas were in demand. Still things were looking up. I did a number in the Greenwich Village Follies which was well received. The young Martha Graham was on the bill. A couple of shows. A safari number with an elephant. He was dropped in New Haven.

America was a Corsica. What did she know of the dance? So many unemployed dancers. Though I was fortunate. The American girls were all running off to have babies. But after 10, 12 years of training, a Russian girl does not run off to have babies without a good return on her investment. That was how I met Orlando. In Madame Albierti's studio where I taught the beginning classes in exchange for attending the advanced classes. His last girl . . . pfft . . . off to have babies. "I have lost 3 in one year," he wept. "I am a doomed man." I had been living off of a snappy little diamond but the proceeds were running out. "I have no babies," I said. "They all say that," he shouted. "It is a plot to kill me before my time." I looked at him closely. This man was no spring chicken despite his powdered face and darkened hair. "I do not know of what time you are speaking," I said. "But I have no use for midgets." We went on that night. It may not have been *Swan Lake*, but it was an honest job. The theatre had a real dressing room. And the manager did not run off with the money.

We took to the road. Did a lot of touring over the next couple of years. They were very lonely those tours. For years I lived in trains and hotel rooms. I was always cold. I used to wear a coat even in June. And after spending so many years with Russians, Americans said I talked funny. "I am from Azerbaijan, Bessarabia, Kazmestan, Shirvan, Karabagh," I said. "Take your pick." It was safe to say the name of a rug. They were less worried about my dark skin, which wasn't exotic here like it was in Paris.

At first we danced acrobatic ballroom numbers. It was the vaudeville circuit, after all. But maybe we should try something classier. Perhaps dance for a better element. Orlando had ballet training. We worked up some interesting numbers. Audiences seemed to like them. We would try them out on the road, then hit L.A. and New York. We dreamed of the big time again.

For a while, I had a friend who was like a daughter to me. A little soprano with a sweet voice. She sang old mountain songs about her home in Tennessee. Later, I told her about Paris and the

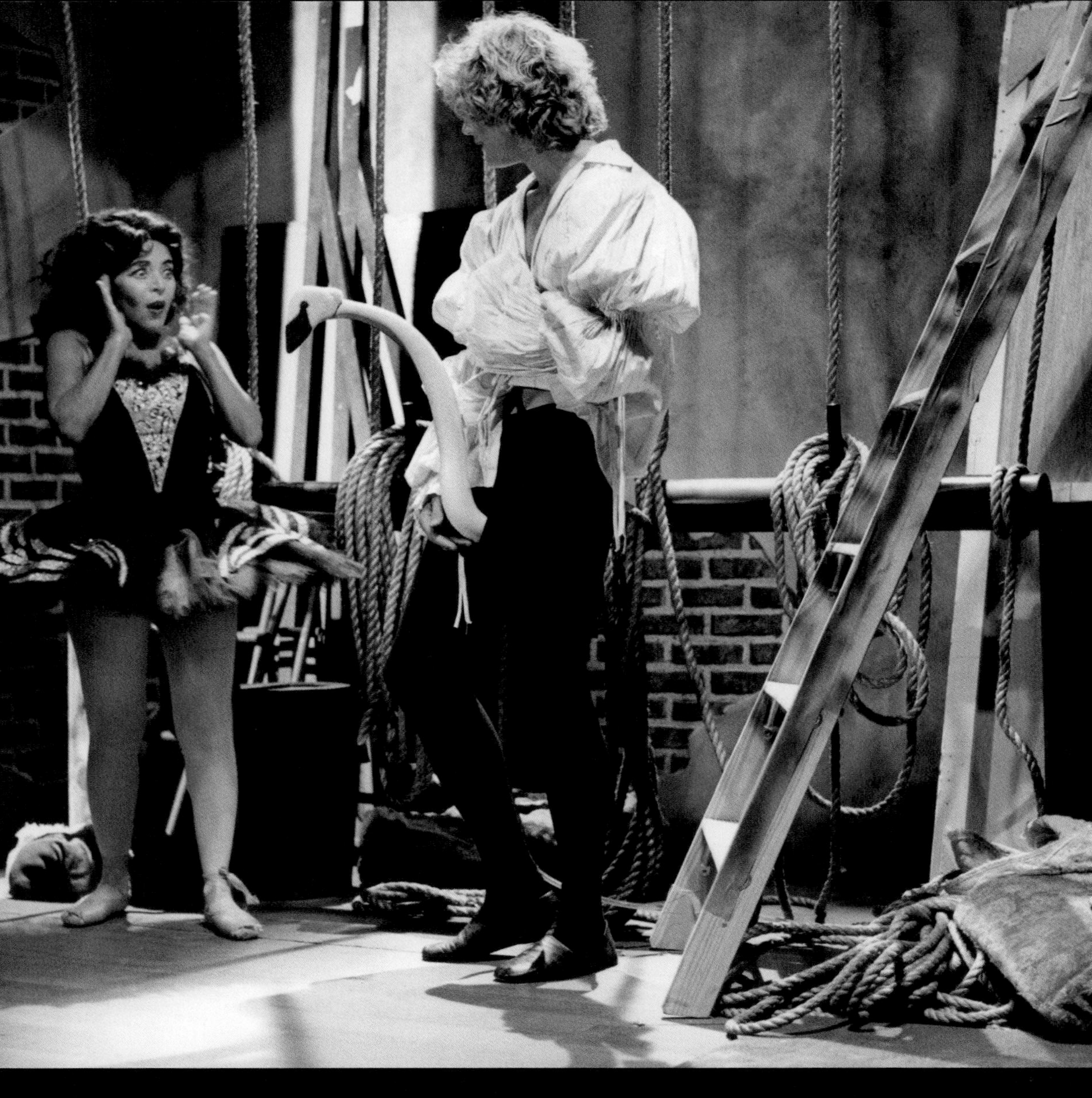

Eleanora Antinova in *Swan Lake*

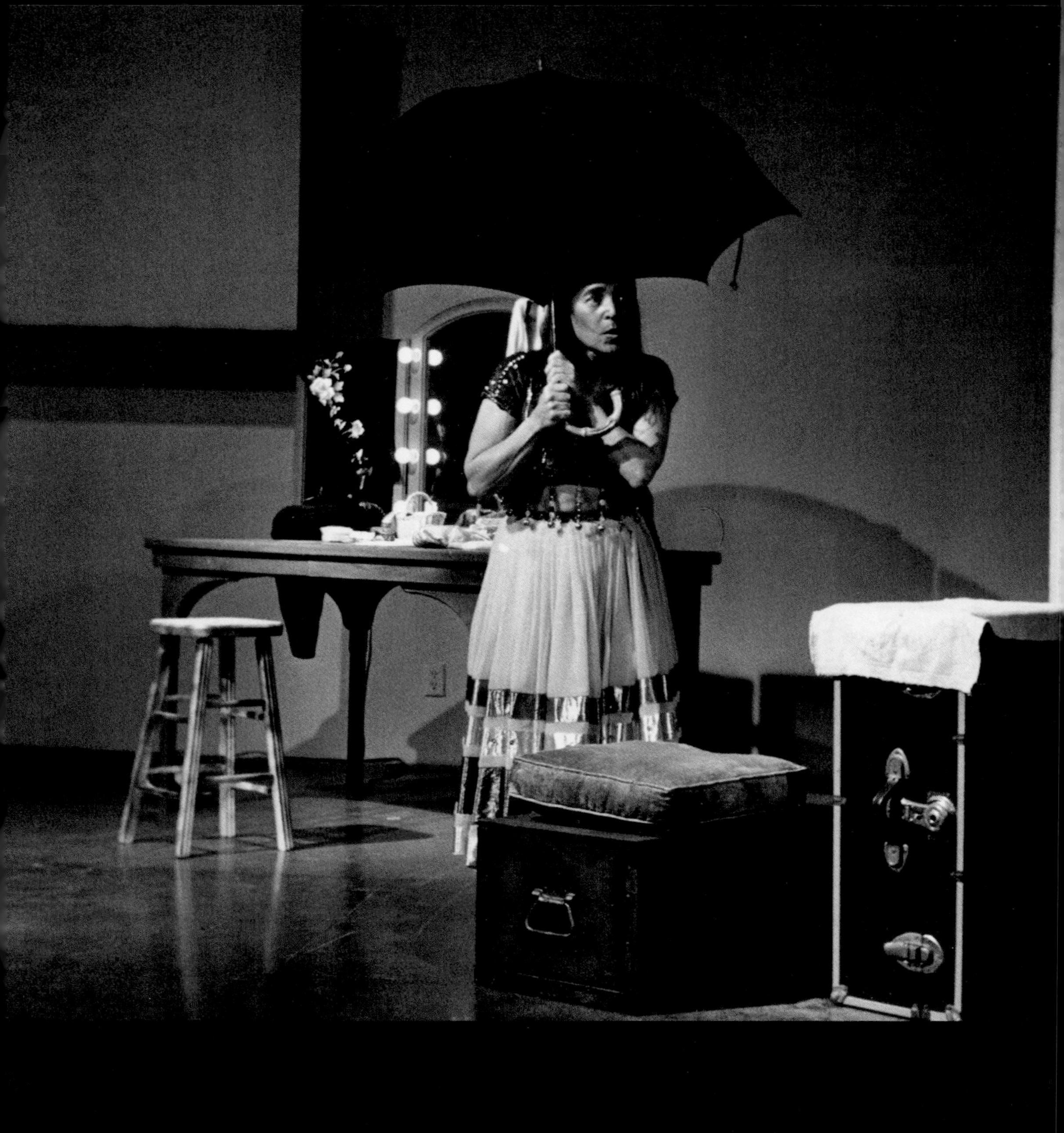

Russian dancers. The dear little soprano hugged me. "How lucky you are, Eleanora." Her nasty husband sneered. He was a pirate, that one. Kept pinching me under my coat. But maybe he was right. Maybe it was a fairy tale. The snow was falling all around us. It fell in my heart, my soul. In the morning it stopped. A white blanket covered the windows. We heard the train whistle. We kissed. Promised to look each other up. We knew we wouldn't. But it warmed the heart to say it. The camaraderie of the road. The family of artists. And who could tell? The next week you could hit it big. We had some good club gigs. A show here and there. A couple of films. We started a school but nobody came. I still dreamed. A letter would come. A phone call. "Eleanora, return to us. We are starting a new ballet company." But everywhere there are spies. Toumanova's mother spies in Los Angeles. Slavenska's sister in Houston. They will say terrible things about me. They are not to be trusted. I have danced with the Russian ballet. I know what's what. There will be no letter.

The hotels are such nasty places. Evil smelling closets. Often there is no window. It is the custom here to give the show people the first floor rooms. They are over the kitchen. We are always awakened before the sun rises. We are lower than the salesman on the second or third floor. He appears for breakfast smiling, rested, hungry. He rubs his hands with vigor. Let the day begin. He will sell many Bibles today. We look at him. Our eyes are red. Our hair is wild. How ugly we look. "The hotel is empty," I protest. "There are only 3 salesmen in the dining room. Give us rooms upstairs. We must sleep." Is there a species lower than the hotel clerk? "This is a fancy establishment," he shouts. "Every room is spoken for." He jumps up and down. He is indignant. "We don't want your kind here." Rita, our strong lady, comes to my aid. "Leave her alone, you two-bit jerk." She makes a fist at him. The muscles ripple up her arms. The clerk is respectful. He drops back. "That is how they treat us," she says. "Stinking cowards!"

At night, after the last show, I come back to the hotel. My trunk waits at the door.

"You are mistaken," I say. "I am not leaving till the end of the week."

He is jumping up and down again. "Your room is rented."

"You are very nervous for one so young," I advise him. "You will get apoplexy. You will die of a stroke."

"You people always cause trouble," he says.

"I do not want to cause trouble," I say. "I am tired. I want to sleep."

He pounds the bell on the counter. Two men come out of the back office. One is chewing on a greasy turkey leg. They are old but there are two of them.

"Call the sheriff. One more colored down there cain't make no difference."

My companions are not robust. Even my friend Rita, the strong lady, turns away. After holding up 500 pounds of chairs and wriggling bodies over her head 4 times a day, her muscles are weary. Her soul droops. She does not want to be noticed. She wants to sleep.

Greasy fingers reach for me. "I am an American citizen. I have done nothing."

"Yeah, well," he sneers. "I thought you was a princess from India. This is a free country. We got no princesses here."

I turn away. I'm bored with the whole business. I'm not even angry anymore. Just tired.

But the bastard won't let up.

"You ain't nothin' but a dirty nigga, ain't ya. Comin' in here tellin' lies. False pretenses, that's what it is. False pretenses."

"Yeah," the senile one grunts, waving his turkey leg in the air. "False pretenses. That's a crime, surely."

"Go to Hell," I say, while Rita hoists my trunk onto her shoulders and walks me back to the theatre. "I'm sorry," she says. Her eyes avoid mine. We kiss and she goes back to the hotel. The old super lets me into my miniscule dressing room. I make a place for myself on the floor and wrap myself in my old fur coat. I am comforted, But first I take some crumbs from my pocket and place them neatly on the floor in the shape of a heart.

A little boy, an acrobat, used to perform here. They say he was tops. His father had big plans. He wouldn't let him eat. "Later you can eat," he would say. "When you are a star in the big time." He wasted away. But he was beautiful. He flew through the air like a glittering bird. He tried to hold on until the big time. He dreamed of chocolates and lollypops. But he grew weaker. The show people slipped food to him when his father wasn't looking. It only made him sadder. "I must become a star first," he would say. "Then I will eat and eat and eat." On Christmas Eve there was a party. The little acrobat sat up on the ropes. The smell of chocolate maddened him. His friend, Dainty June, waved a chocolate angel. "Finish up honey. It's Christmas." With a cry of pain the little acrobat offered her his shaking hands. The old super is a hundred years old. He saw him fall. He just broke, he said. They could hear him crack. And to this day you must leave food for his ghost or he will keep you up crying into the night.

But vaudeville is dying. Old timers work for $10 a day. My friend Rita, the strong lady, tears telephone books in half. It goes over big with the yokels. But this is a 4-a-day house. She must tear up

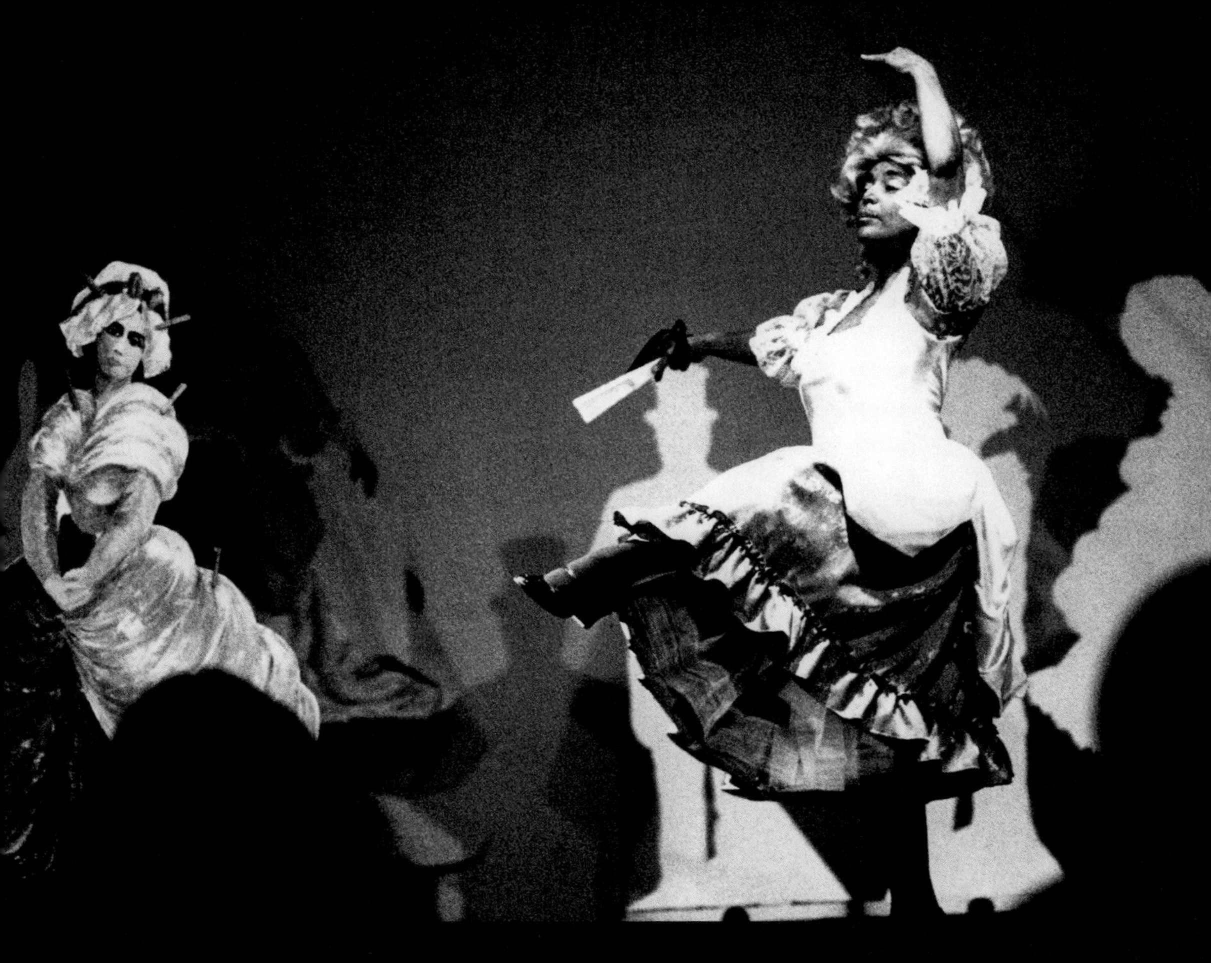

Eleanora Antinova in *Before the Revolution*

4 telephone books a day. A book costs 50 cents. That's $2 a day. $14 a week. "I have to steal them," she confesses. "I am so ashamed." She even saves the nails she bends. She just bends them back before the next show. These are terrible times. I must get out of this business. I am looking into the nightclubs. They are patronized by gangsters. Gangsters can be very generous. I know a singer in Chicago who did very well with a gangster. A handsome fellow with satin lapels and derby hats. They put on the dog together. When the bookies shot him, she wore white fox to the funeral. She looked stunning. Now she has a new gangster. Not so handsome perhaps, but generous. There is no shortage of them, it seems. I am not so snobbish as I was. One gets older. There are setbacks. A girl must look out for herself.

Time is irresistible. In Seattle, I remember a singer, Sylvia Froos. "The Little Princess of Song." When she skipped out on stage shaking her Shirley Temple curls, the band played "My Heart Belongs to Daddy." Once she was a class act in the big time. And she still dresses like one—pink frocks, petticoats—long white gloves with rhinestones. Once I saw her without gloves. When she saw me she hid her hands behind her back. But I saw how wrinkled those hands were. Like an old woman's. She cries in her dressing room. Drinks.

Life is short. Memory is longer. I think sometimes of *Before the Revolution*, my most famous, perhaps my least understood work. It was the only ballet that was mine all the way. It was produced during what turned out to be our final season, since Diaghilev died soon after in Venice. He always knew he would die on the water and he did though I don't believe he ever dreamed it would be Venice. He loved her so much. Maybe that should have been a clue. They say all men kill the thing they love. But maybe it's the other way around.

We were at a real low point that spring and money was scarce. Besides the old man seemed to lose all interest in the company. Perhaps it was his way of saying good-bye. So I had little trouble convincing them to let me dance the role of the white queen.

Marie Antoinette was the first, and as it turned out, the only role I ever danced that fit my own skin. She was my balletic swan song. The White Queen dancing through the empty streets of peasant villages and dairy farms was the spirit of ballet . . . as the flightless white swans gliding swiftly over the little pond in the *Bois de Boulogne* were its soul. She neither touched history nor was touched by it. The revolution erupts in her dream and kills everybody with a fountain pen. Like ballet she had the innocence of childhood . . . and its cunning. Her dance was as lovely and futile as swans on the royal pond . . . I wonder if there are still swans in Paris . . . My friends are gone, of course. They're all dead except for the ones who are still dying. Pascin too died a long time ago though he was still a young man. How generous he had been, how kind. But he painted in an unfashionable manner. Later he killed himself. Art is not generous to her children. A young man asked me recently how one knows that a work of art will last. Nothing lasts! All those years I worked and dreamed. Some mornings I woke up famous. I don't think I ever woke up feeling understood . . . Sometimes I wake up in the dead of night and can't remember where I am . . .

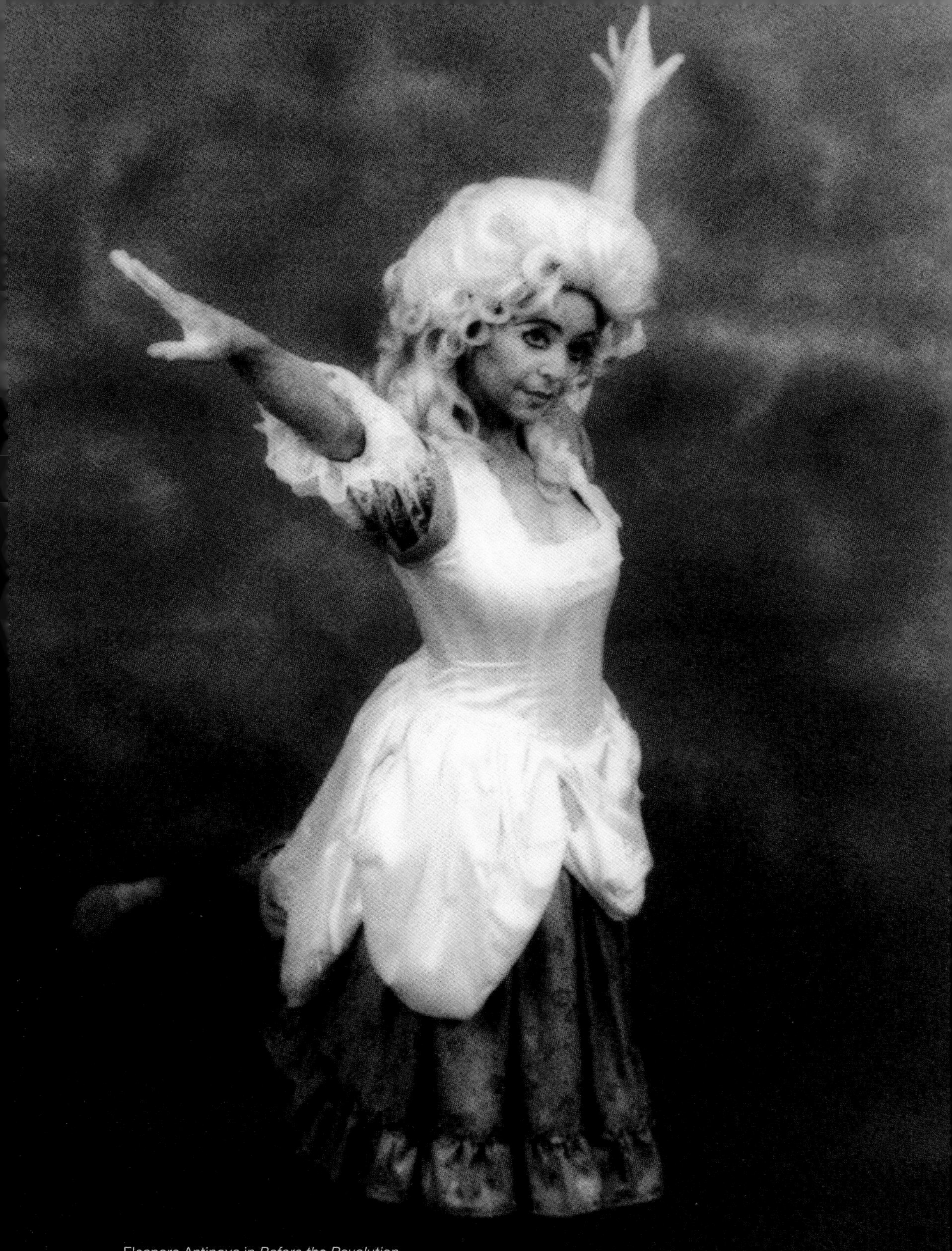

Eleonora Antinova in *Before the Revolution*

Chapter 9

Waiting in the Wings

You have to be careful of a talent. A talent has to be helped to find a certain planet and a certain time. You cannot blame it on money or good looks or connections. The time must be right . . . I was always on my own, you see. There was nobody to take me in hand, to take charge of me . . . my talent . . . to say, Eleanora, on such and such a day, you must do such and such a thing . . . Not even Sergei Pavlovitch . . . How I would wish . . . if I were a boy, then, yes, perhaps. Had I caught his fancy, who knows? Massine was a fortunate man . . . but you can't have it both ways . . . Such eyes he had. How could Sergei Pavlovitch resist? None of the girls could. We were all a little bit in love with him. If he hadn't had such eyes? Who knows? But I had to write my own letters, knock on doors, so many doors, doors and doors and doors. I was always waiting for the elevator to take me upstairs, a big burnished door. I would look back at myself for hours. But the others were restless. "Push the button. Push the button." "They are making deliveries," a young woman explains. "Don't you have any manners?" But the people are angry. Some leave. They have better things to do. These aren't the only doors in the world. That shocks you. You are ashamed for yourself. You have such a limited view. For you, there are no others. Later, you are looking the other way, dozing in the armchair, maybe a drink, maybe you are having a drink with a handsome young man. He has dreamy eyes . . . shhhh, just like that, without a by-your-leave . . . without a warning . . . without a sound, the door slides open . . . just like that . . . you are pushed to the rear of the elevator, you can't breathe, you can't reach the button. "Please push the button," you call out. A tall woman twists around to see you. "You are very rude," she says. "What floor do you want? I wish you would get off." "So do I," you shout. "Just push a floor, any floor. I want to get off, settle in, get down to business, begin already." She gives you a disgusted look. "You people!" Now everybody looks at you. "There," the woman says triumphantly, "I pushed 14." The people laugh. The woman is pleased with herself. She says it over and over. "I pushed 14." They are all saying it now. "She pushed 14. She pushed 14." The door slides open and a number overhead lights up. 23. "This isn't 14," the woman says. "Can't you read?" But it is a high and airy room. The bronze evening light falls through the long windows. The clouds below are flushed with pink, as the sun sets behind the sandstone bluffs across the river. A little

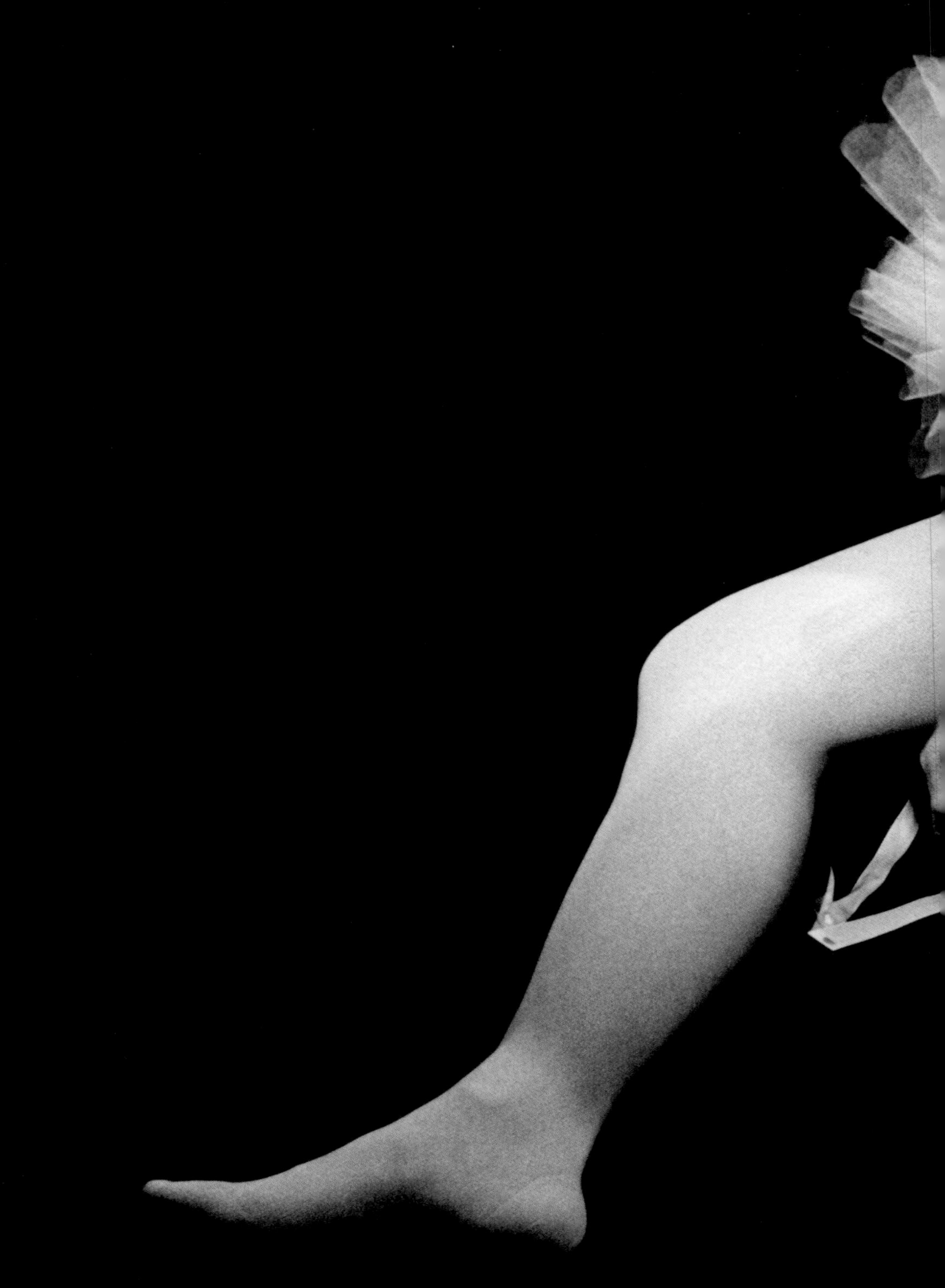

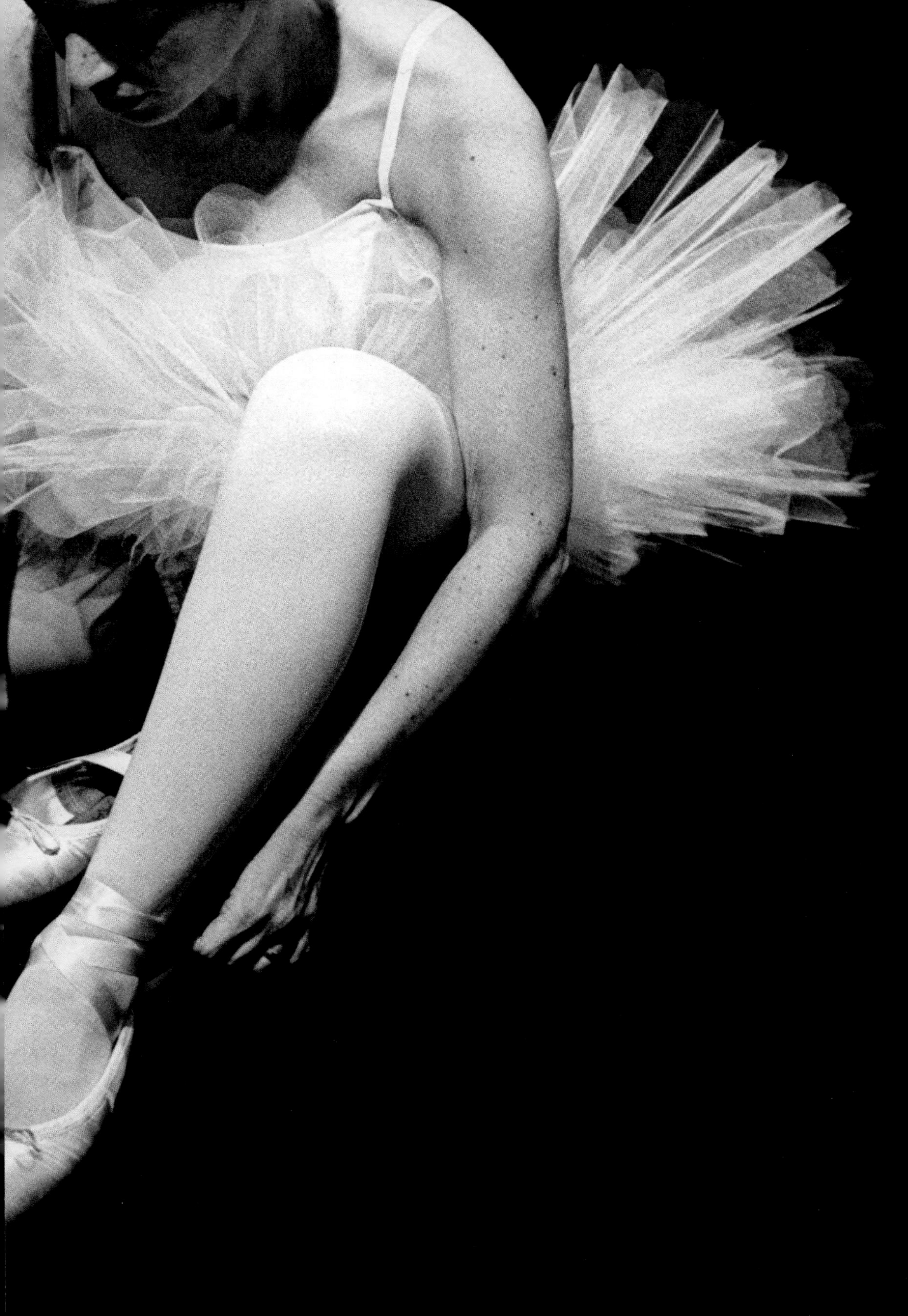

boat chugs through the water followed by screaming gulls and a wake of white, pretty foam. "That's the ferry," somebody says. "No, the tour boat," somebody else says. "Can't you tell?" A purple wash sits on the horizon. "Hawaii," a man says, giving you a tall drink. There is a party going on here. The guests are pleased to see you. They are all talking at once in an amiable manner. They applaud politely, throw flowers, diamonds. You pocket the diamonds when nobody is looking. You're a smart cookie, you've been hungry for so long. Later you go home, eat a steak, one must eat, there's no getting away from it . . . The next morning you are the first to arrive. The room is blazing with sunlight, there isn't a cloud in the sky, the little boats are out dancing on the river, you throw off your shoes and sink into the soft, thick carpet, warm with sun and the rich red color of earth. It is the same on the next day and the next and the next and the next. "Too much play makes Jack a dull boy," you joke to your neighbor. This makes her nervous. She looks quickly around to see who is listening. She laughs in a loud voice. How droll you are. You must be the life of the party. The people seek you out. They want to rub shoulders, hold hands. The men are handsome, they have little moustaches. Sometimes you are bad tempered, you pull their moustaches, bite their ears, their fingers. Some mornings you're too tired to get out of bed. You play hookey, hang around the house, watch television. People are getting prizes, winning academy awards. The next day, you are the first to arrive. You are the life of the party. You cheer on the ferry—or is it the tour boat. Sometimes there are sailboat contests. The little boats lap up the water, they look like toys, proud, smart, snappy little beasts, you make book, take bets, you always win . . .

Then, one day, the elevator breaks down. There's a sign on the door: "Out of Order." You are not worried. You can use the day off. Maybe you'll take a walk around the city. You can play a joke. Take the tour boat and wave to the people at the party. Later you will shop, you can use a new pair of shoes. But the next day and the next day and the next day, it's the same old story. "Out of Order" . . . The weeks go by, the months. You can't read the sign anymore . . . the letters fade . . . the rains come, storms, they turn the heat on in the lobby, but it's big and drafty, people keep coming through the swinging doors bringing wind and snow. Sometimes you see a familiar face from the party. He moves swiftly through the crowded lobby, goes through a side door, it says EXIT. You try to follow but the door is locked. Once you try to squeeze through with one of them but she gives you a terrible look and slams the door in your face. People are such shits . . . Excuse me, ladies and gentlemen, doubtless you are fine and intelligent people. You have liberal opinions, progressive ways, but how do you look at a person when her shoes are run down and her fur is ratty, and she is ashamed to be seen in such a smart lobby, and you are ashamed to see her shame . . . At first, I went home at night, the same as always. I showered, put my hair up in curlers, sewed the hems on my dresses. Later, I lost heart, home was far away, so I spent the nights in the lobby. In an armchair with a nubby texture. That texture got smoother, I sat in it for so long. Soon, I was afraid to get up. I was a mushroom. I stank. The people would hold their noses and make bad faces at me . . . I began to worry . . . What if the repairmen came . . . I would have to get up, stand next to people, disgrace myself. Everybody would know I stank . . . I fell into a deep despair. The door would open and all I could do was sit and watch the others pile in. I was doomed . . .

But then, later, when it happened, when the repairmen came with their tools and blowtorches, I forgot my dirty underwear and smelly feet and rotting teeth and rushed ahead of the others through the gleaming brass door. Would you believe it, after all that! Again the crowd shoves me to the rear. I feel young and gay again. I know this scenario from way back. "Careful honey, that's my corn you're standing on." I just hope their sinuses aren't too good . . . I spray myself with a perfume atomizer. That should take care of indignant noses. Where there's a will there's a way . . . The people are singing and calling to each other. "It's always like this after the deliveries are made," an old gentleman says, tipping his hat. I don't introduce myself. I can't trust my breath in such close quarters. "23," I call out. "Please push 23." How nasty! Who has such a cracked voice? Whose voice is that? A voice in the desert! I hope I don't arrive at the party with some wrinkled old woman and get typecast at the door. First impressions are so important. But when the elevator stops at 23, I'm the only one to get off. Damn, it's dark. The party must be over. I'd better come back tomorrow. It's so tacky to be early. But I find the switch. A bulb hanging from the ceiling flares up. The dull glow bounces off the green walls, the worn kitchen linoleum on the floors. There are a lot of crates around, they seem to be jammed with pots and pans and dishes, and salad oils and boxes of barley, and millet and dried milk. A broken television set lies shipwrecked in the corner, just spilling out its wires and fuses for all the world to see. Shameful! Like a corpse lying in its own shit. "What floor is this? I've been tricked." But the elevator door is closing. "It's 23," they call out. "Have a nice day." "You're lying, you bastards. It's 14. I know it's 14." The voices fade out. I'm alone. And this is one hell of a miserable place. I get the shakes. Better sit down. I'm scared. I've never been so scared in my life. A cockroach jumps into my lap, but I'm shaking so much he falls off. The couch smells of bug spray. At least there's a telephone. Operator! Busy signal. 911. It's busy, too. Here's an ancient phone book. Once I had a friend, she used to tear up telephone books for a living. What people won't do to make a buck. But you would disdain this one, dear. A telephone book has to be snappy and new, otherwise, what's the point? Elliot Smith. Jean Forsythe. Beverly Willis. I dial a lot of phone numbers. Nathan Cohen. Gene Lockhart. I dial any number I can read. Somebody must be home somewhere, drinking a cup of tea or doing the laundry. But the line is always busy. I'm going to panic in a minute. I'll never get off this floor . . . it's the last stop . . . I'd better put a lid on myself . . . lean back, take a load off my feet. A couch is better than a floor, be thankful for small mercies. I have furniture . . . close your eyes, my dear . . . just a little time, is all . . . you've hung around for so long already . . . what's a little more in the scheme of things? The music will still play . . . the lights . . . we wore *pointe* shoes . . . artists painted our sets . . . stole kisses in the wings . . . famous men gave us music . . . candy . . . there are no surprises . . . nothing is new . . . a curtain will rise . . . flowers will fall . . .

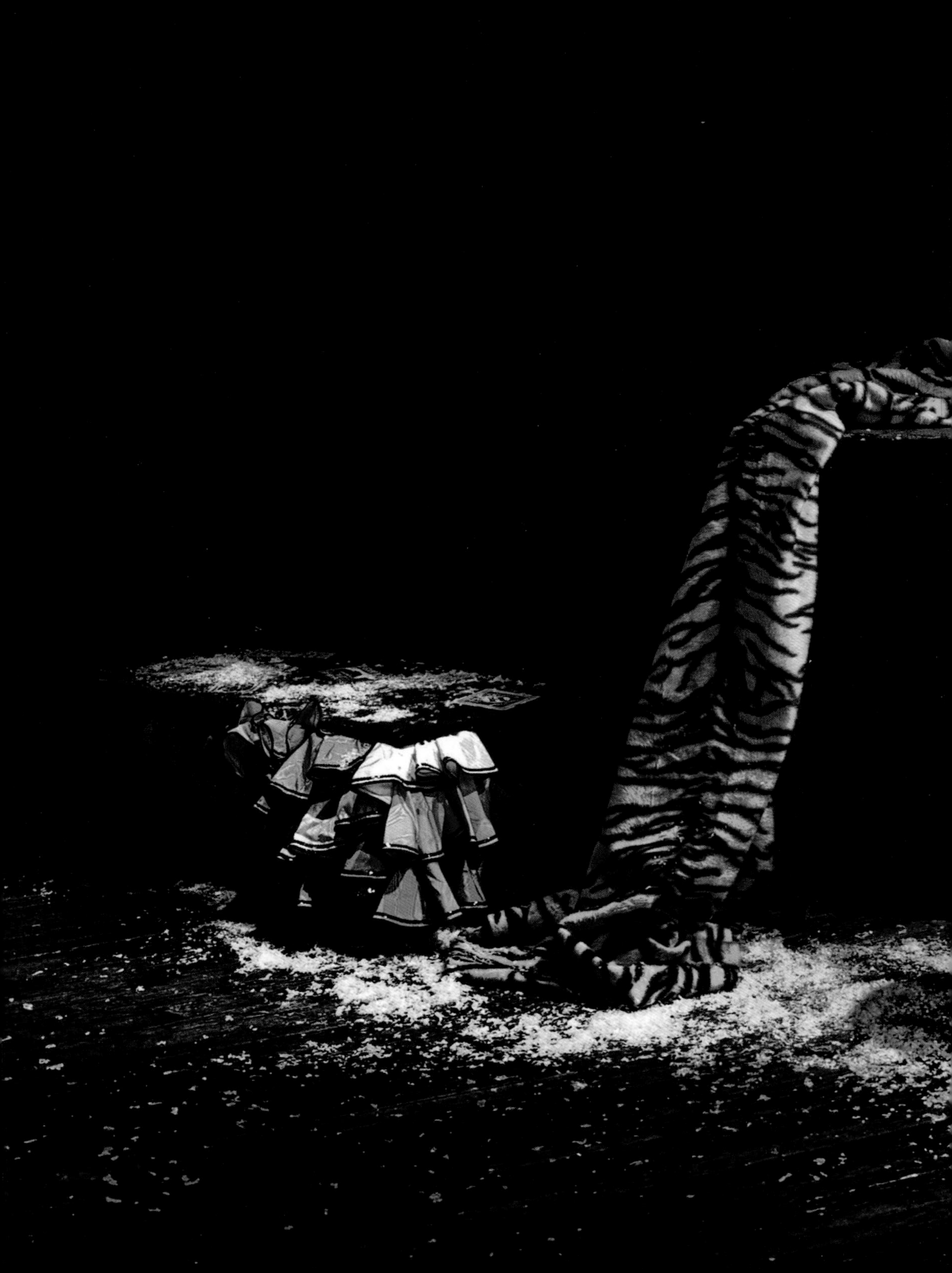

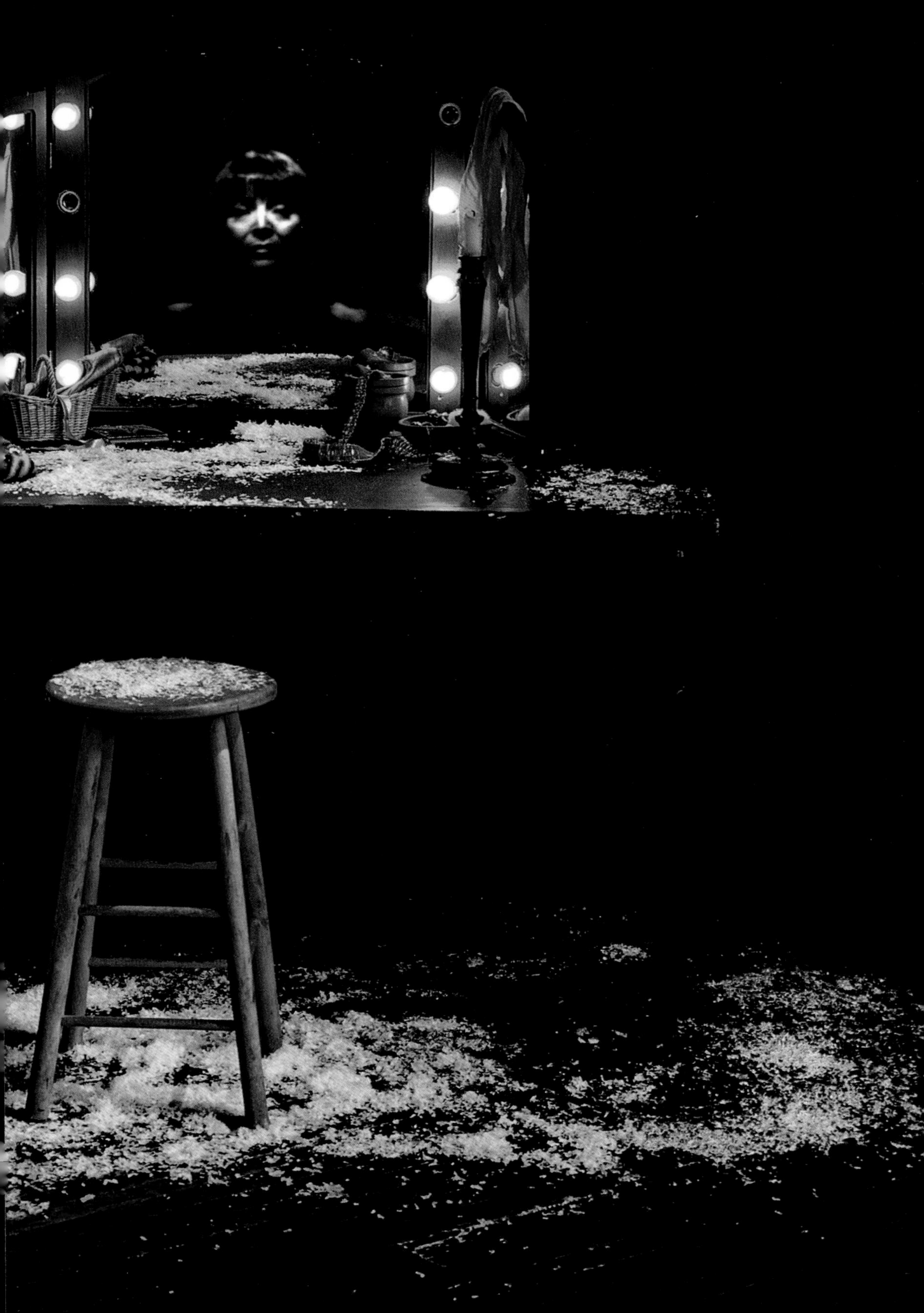

FOR MARCIA GOODMAN AND IDA APPLEBROOG

BEING ANTINOVA

BY ELEANOR ANTIN

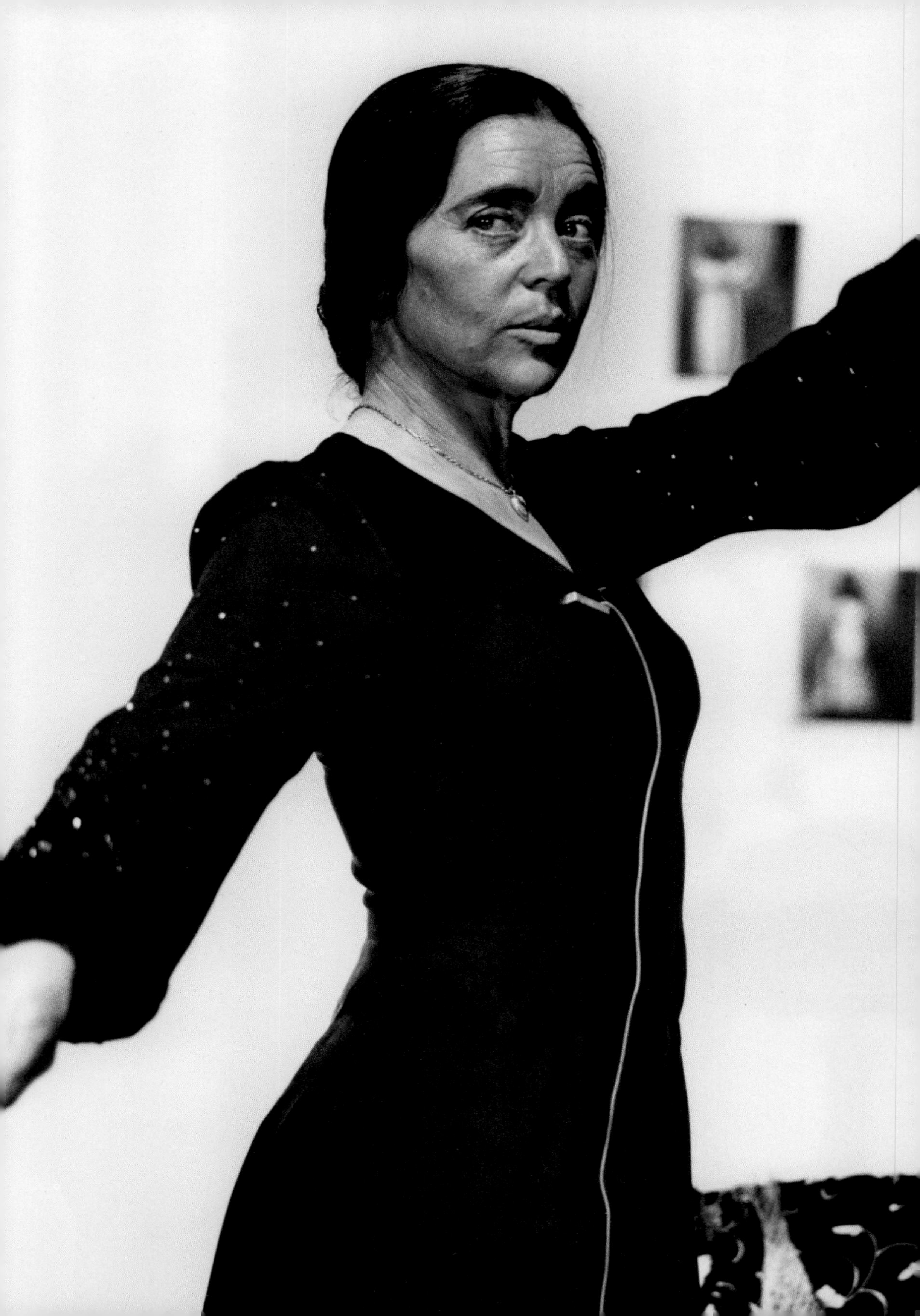

SATURDAY ***October 11, DEL MAR, CALIFORNIA***

Spent four hours at *Madame Joli* preparing for my New York trip by having long porcelain nails attached to my stubby fingers. Now the tips of my fingers aren't the furthest extension of my hands anymore, and they can't reach for the world the way they used to—the new nails get in the way. My hands are confused and spatially disoriented. Objects feel weightless, even when I know they're not—like the drink Gina gave me. I couldn't hold onto the glass, and the wine spilled out all over the carpet.

"Good thing it's the white," she said with disgust.

I was embarrassed by my clumsiness and went to the john for some privacy. When I tried to open the door, I couldn't get a grip on the knob and my nails scraped hard against the wood. They didn't break, but it was a shock. I had forgotten they were there; and that was turning out to be a dangerous thing—difficult too, it seemed, when I couldn't hitch my pants down with my fingers anymore to go to the toilet. Not only could I impale myself with my nails if I moved too fast, but there wasn't the old instinctive rapport between myself and my fingers that I used to have. The new nails have no feeling in them and they can't anticipate what I want them to do. I managed to roll my pants down with my knuckles, helped some by pressure from the palms of my hands, but it took a hell of a long time. Everything I do has to be renegotiated, like using the toilet paper without cutting myself. I began to worry. I had to install an exhibition, do several performances, and live for three weeks in New York with these nails. I hadn't counted on being a cripple.

"You'll get used to them." Gina patted my hand for encouragement. "You'll learn to do everything differently and you'll see, you won't even notice them anymore."

That really depressed me. I had no time to go back to kindergarten. I think if it didn't seem so absolutely necessary for a ballerina to have long fingernails I would have called the whole thing off then and there and asked her to remove them. But long nails are part of a ballerina's stock in trade. They add to her graceful line both on and off stage. I would destroy the illusion of glamour if I didn't camouflage my stubby fingers with their dog-eared, bitten-down nails.

She holds my hands in her cool perfumed ones and begins to apply the deep violet nail color I want. Her movements are neat and efficient, yet her nails are even longer than mine. They extend a full inch past her fingertips. Mine are shorter, somewhere around half an inch out. I'm impressed by the deft way she twists the cap off the lacquer bottle and brushes the color on evenly and accurately. It is close work with little margin for error.

I study her as she works. I don't normally get to observe glamourous women at such close range. Of course there will be the stewardesses on tomorrow's plane. I expect to pick up some tips from them.

She must have felt me watching her because she patted her wet hair wrapped in a towel and fluttered heavily blackened lashes in mock self-deprecation.

"I always look like this on Saturdays," she apologizes.

"Do you always make up?" I ask.

"Of course." (huffy voice) "I'm working."

A man comes in—the accountant from next door. He has just bumped into her ex-boyfriend who's selling his office and moving to Aspen next month.

"That Jack! What a life!" He whistles with admiration.

"What does he mean 'going to Aspen'?" Her voice is shaking but the accountant has begun to talk of something else. He encourages her to buy the red Corvette from the guy who's got the dealership in Encinitas.

"I'd buy it myself, if I was in the market," he says and leaves.

Gina has become very pale under her bright pink makeup. She stops working because her hands are shaking. It turns out that she and Jack are together again, which the accountant doesn't seem to know yet. In fact, they plan to be married when her divorce comes through.

"Oh, my heart is fluttering," she whispers and pours a glass of wine to calm herself.

(me) "Are you sure Jack wants to get married?"

(her) "Damn right he does." (bitter voice) "I was the one who didn't even want to start up with him again after we broke off a couple of months ago."

A young man in shorts comes in followed by a teenage girl. We go out to see the yellow Corvette Gina is thinking of buying from him. When they leave she admits she doesn't trust kid drivers. They soup up the engine and fall behind in repairs because they don't have the money. Unfortunately, the better car, the red one belonging to the guy with the dealership in Encinitas, costs several thousand more. With the divorce under way, she isn't sure whether she can meet the payments.

"I have a 16-year-old son," she explains.

I ask if she needs a new car.

"I've got a Datsun," she answers. "It's just not my style."

She gives my nails a second coat of polish and we start talking about Jack again.

I suggest she might not mind living in Aspen. After all, it's a famous resort community. Didn't she like to ski?

She gives me an irritated look.

"I have a business in Del Mar," she says.

I looked dubiously down at my nails.

"Is it successful?"

I surprised myself. I would never suggest to an artist friend that she pull up her roots and follow a man. Luckily she wasn't sensitive to my snobbery.

"I'll call his wife. She'll know if he's going."

"His what?"

Why should his wife tell her anything?

But the wife wasn't home, so she called her hypnotist.

She began filing my nails again with what felt like unnecessary vigor.

"I'll hang him," she said.

"Who, the hypnotist?"

I thought she should confront Jack in person. It was absurd to fall out with him because of the accountant next door.

"You have to talk with him before you make up your mind about anything."

Maybe it wasn't true.

She was certain it was.

Rather slyly, I suggested she would have the advantage of looking great that night, with her hair washed and all; so why not throw the information out at dinner and watch his face closely for tell-tale signs of the truth.

She shook her head.

"Can't. I have a date tonight."

I left feeling I had had an adventure. We embraced with the camaraderie of women who have touched in a woman's place. I promised to call the following evening to find out what was happening, though now I was beginning to doubt Jack's sincerity.

It's night now and because of my nails it's taken me almost an hour to write these few pages.

But I learned to dial the phone with my knuckles and was as excited as a kid when the person who answered turned out to be Moira. This day I got the first taste of the strenuous life of the glamourous woman, whose simplest activity is some kind of achievement.

MONDAY ***October 13, NEW YORK***

On the plane to New York I'm haunted by Lucy Lippard.

As she gets older, Lucy's fierce New England relatives have taken over her face. She reminds me lately of a Quaker printer whose dark little shop on 18th Street used to turn out abolitionist memoirs, or family anecdotes of Mother Bloor down in Harlan County.

In my daydream she pursues me, one finger in the air. "You are a fake," she announces indignantly. "If you washed the paint off your face you'd be white." In my dream I take a long time to raise one eyebrow a long distance. "If you cut off your hair, you'd be bald. So what!" While she tries to figure that one out, I sail by her with a straight back.

I've got the new autobiography of Sono Osato. But the first Japanese-American ballerina is hopelessly American. Her memoirs are leaden, there isn't a romantic or outrageous personality to hold them together. So when the action slows up, Lucy's disapproving face repeats her accusation and each time I dwell longer on my part. It's not much of a blockbuster, that line—pretty dismal really—it will need a good delivery to pull it off. Maybe I should just change it—I *am* the playwright, for God's sake. But it's too late. That scene is engraved on my mind with all the finality of the printed page. It's up to Lucy to change *her* line before I can change mine.

"Are you a ballet girl?"

The stewardess interrupts my reverie. Flipping through the pages of Osato's book, she slips into the empty seat beside me. I'm flattered to be chosen. Stewardesses never talk to me. By and large they prefer men or young mothers with babies. It must be my nails, and I notice with some satisfaction that mine are longer than hers.

It turns out she likes dancing, or used to, until she was shocked deeply by the language and nudity of *All That Jazz.* The drug-taking too. She wouldn't let her 10-year-old daughter see it, even though the little girl wants to be a dancer and is very talented.

"If that's an exposé of the dancing profession, I won't let her take dancing lessons anymore," she says in a tight angry voice. "Is it?"

I'm ashamed to admit I didn't see the movie since she takes me for some sort of an expert. But the truth is I don't go to the theatre anymore. Why would I go? For Balanchine, a Pop Art character with a dream of America born of Western movies and Fourth of July weekends? Back at the Maryinsky we had a nobler view of our audience and its aspirations. We didn't patronize them, we respected our audience—aristocrats, *balletomanes*, we dined together, drank together . . .

With a clear conscience, I agree that dance today has become rather common. But she's protesting in the name of the moral majority.

So what? No way will I defend middlebrow culture.

"Nothing but cheap exhibitionism," she is saying.

"Formalism and vulgarity go hand in hand," I acknowledge.

"Who do they think we are," she says.

"A contemptible beast called 'The Public,'" I answer.

"Well we aren't going to take it anymore," she repeats stubbornly.

I thought of those long sleek legs sawing the air, the high energy of professional Show Biz.

"You shouldn't," I agree.

Since we are polite people and don't look too closely into each other's meanings we can agree on the dismal state of cultural taste. Before she leaves I have a twinge of guilt and put in a good word for her daughter's sake.

"Remember, dancing is good for her health."

Left to myself, I map out a playing script for Antinova.

1 - Focus my attention outward. Look at people closely. This will give me a romantic appearance. It will also force people to notice me—who can resist the persistent stare of a stranger?

2 - Kidnap them. Grab them off the street and chuck them back into the Old World. So the broad-shouldered young man I see on 6th Avenue will become a yachtsman from the British Regatta, sporting white flannel trousers and a malacca cane on the boardwalk at Monte Carlo.

I like this script. The Invasion of the Body Snatcher.

Marcia meets me at the airport with a dozen yellow roses. We drive off in her white Jaguar, which in my ignorance I call a Mercedes, to my new home—25 Central Park West. *The Century.* Emily moved out several months ago but Marcia's been holding the apartment for me.

"Maybe it's not the thing for my daughter," she said over the phone, "but it's the stage set for Antinova."

The Century is one of those genteel West Side buildings with a sculpted Art Deco facade that I used to envy as a kid. It seemed to me then that the most terrific place in the world to live would be behind a solemn, protective front like this. Unfortunately, the closest I ever got was the doctor's office on the ground floor. But this building that I was moving into now was more impressive than the ones I remembered. It took up the whole of the park side of the block and made it halfway down to Broadway along the side streets.

The main entrance faced the park. Marcia introduced me to the doormen and had some trouble with my name.

"I felt like a criminal calling you Antinova," she explained in a whisper. She pushed me through the door ahead of her. "It's their job to detect disguises."

"Wait till they see me tomorrow."

The floor of the lobby is inlaid with cinnamon and black tiles in the hard edge decorative style of the thirties. The geometries erupt into ornate leafy tailed birds or an occasional flying horse, icons who crouch underfoot, grip the walls or take in the scene from a high perch up between chandeliers. The walls are lined with mirrors reflecting the soft glow bounced off the bronze mouldings by the hanging crystal lights. My elevator was at the end of a long corridor to the right. Getting there was a theatrical act.

But the apartment is startling. It opens on the rear. Only a small courtyard separates us from the building across the way. On closer inspection this turns out to be just another part of our house. *The Century* is so large it appears to close in on itself. The sky is blocked by the apartments across the way and the rooms are hopelessly dark. I'll have to keep the lights on all the time when I'm home. The apartment was probably split off from a larger sunnier one so that the landlord could extract two rents instead of one. These back rooms must have been the servant's quarters. The discrepancy between the outside and the inside reminds me of the contemptuous description given by the servant of Miss Julie's mother. That she always rode out in a dashing carriage with a team of horses but the linen at her sleeves was yellow and frayed and there were holes in her underwear. This was supposed to illustrate something important about the difference between the aristocracy and the bourgeoisie, but I never knew what until now!

Emily must have used the place only for sleeping. There's a large mattress on the floor of the bedroom with a tiny TV set near the pillow. It would fit in my purse. The screen can't be more than four inches. There are a few pots in the kitchen, a small frying pan, a few cups and saucers, silver for two. She must have prepared a minimal breakfast and eaten it on the bridge table in the alcove. There are two folding chairs. Perhaps she had a friend camp out with her for a while. Marcia has hinted at an unhappy romance. The floors are polished wood. I can do a *barre* in the living room. There's only a tattered sofa and rug in one corner. I'll probably have to work out in bare feet though the wood feels slippery.

Emily hung sheets over the windows to keep the neighbors out. This makes the rooms even darker; and they were probably unnecessary, since the windows across the courtyard are curtained and shuttered, and the people across the court wouldn't have noticed if she danced around the place naked. But I left the sheets—on principle.

There's a dress in the closet, late twenties, perhaps early thirties. The black silk falls straight from my shoulders over my hips and rustles at my knees when I move. Jet and silver beads emit a rich and somber glow over the bodice and flowing sleeves. There is a distant perfume. What short haired beauty wore my dress to illicit clubs so many years ago? What Charlestons, tangos, what whispered words through long lost nights? My dress is beautiful. I stroke the fragile silk and thank my sister.

It turns out to be the first dress I ever wore that I didn't have to shorten. It's an omen. I decide to make it my performance dress.

Later when I try to sleep I am afraid of the dark. The floors of my empty house creak. The sheets over the windows sigh like ghosts. I keep the foyer light on all night long. Morning is D-day. Who will go forth from *The Century* in the morning? Who will Antinova turn out to be out there in the world? I hope I like her—or the next three weeks will be living Hell.

TUESDAY ***October 14***

D-day.

Let me try and pull it all together. It's nighttime and I want to remember as much of it as I can.

Antinova's first day out and, no getting away from it, this morning I wished I was any place but here. My stomach kept turning over and I needed a good strong cup of coffee to settle down. Really bugged at myself for having to make do with herb tea. My hatred of cooking is beginning to get me down.

It turns out to take a little under two hours to darken and glamourize myself. That's in line with the time traditionally taken by glamourous women to represent themselves to the world. Osato writes of the peaceful morning hours she was sometimes invited to share with Danilova in her old-fashioned Monte Carlo suite, watching the fashionable ballerina prepare for her day. This morning I understood for the first time what deep pleasure a glamourous woman gets from these preparations. And I used to patronize these women, feeling sorry for them having to waste long hours on themselves!

For me too, it was an unhurried private time to stroke myself and listen to my body. It's a lot like caring for plants. People don't speak precisely about plants either. It isn't that you have to talk to them—you have to listen. I stroked the brown cake makeup into my face with a gentle, rotating motion. Even my wrinkles don't bother me this morning. After all, they're mine, and I'm certainly a distinguished woman, not an ignorant spring chicken. In the mirror, my light eyes blazed intensely from out of my darkening face. I took lots of time over whether to shadow them with green or silver. I was confident and ended up doing both, blending the green into the corners and the silver, where the light would be expected to hit. It was like drawing with a soft chalk. Those parts of the face that come forward have to be lighter than the parts that recede into the shadow. I was feeling very cheerful to be painting again. I always liked doing portraits—chalk, pastel, wash. I'm good at likenesses. I become bolder, touching up my brown forehead and chin with a rose shine, my nose too, though you're not supposed to on your nose, but it's gayer somehow. I want my skin to gleam with rich color like the models in *Vogue.* I sucked in my lips like crazy but still couldn't precisely locate the hollow place under my left cheekbone. I rouged either too close to the ear or too far downwards towards the jaw. Then I had to wash off my mistake and start over again with the brown undercoat. Only I couldn't get the botched part off completely without washing my whole face to do it. After a while there was a dark rim around the troublesome area, a scraggly halo where the water had stained the brown paint at the edges. Now the left side of my face was looking smudged and coarse, and my cheek hurt from all that rubbing. It was becoming like a bad luck spot in a painting that you work on over and over, until finally all you're doing is fighting a losing battle with that vindictive patch of paint and you just want to chuck the whole thing. By then I couldn't get a clean color in that area if my life depended on it. If it was a painting, I'd have no choice but to put it away for a better day. To hell with it. Like Anna Karenina I have two different profiles. On the left side my nose is less significant. Whenever I forget and let them photograph me from that side I look gloomy and uninteresting. I was so nervous by then I started coloring my throat with the cake makeup, which I had planned to use only on my face, because it covers such a relatively small area at a time. So then I had to wash off my throat and start over again with the brown liquid color. It did cover more ground but came off in streaks on my skin. It had to be blended, but it's a nice color and the texture is silkier than the cake, which has the powdery look of face makeup. Whatever color differences there might be, they would, I knew, disappear during the day as my skin transformed the manufactured colors into its own natural tones. My confidence in paint and my ability to handle it is amazing. If it wasn't such a measly profession, I might really have taken up painting.

The morning was moving along pretty quickly and I began to suspect I was deliberately putting off the time of my departure. But that careful, sensitive attention to my body seemed to give me confidence. Not enough, unfortunately, because I had to interrupt the work several times to run to the toilet.

But by the time I twirled around the kitchen in my new Andrew Geller pumps and prepared a second cup of tea, I was feeling a whole lot better.

I had some difficulty fastening the clasp on the gold locket Peter's sister in Hungary sent to Mother when she and Peter got married. No mistaking the heavy European workmanship and design, more German than French. It was originally given to Peter's sister by her husband when they married over seventy years ago, as it had been given in turn to *his* mother by *his* father when *they* married. That gold heart is serious and not to be trifled with! Too bad I don't have any diamonds, but if Marcia had some to lend me I'd be afraid to wear them. She says even in broad daylight they rip necklaces off you in the street. Sounds paranoid to me, but this is the first time I'm wearing a necklace at all, so my opinion can't be worth much. Besides family heirlooms will do fine. Sentiment is higher class than money.

I had a bad feeling that those hours of practicing hair swirls and twists back in California would be a waste of time. I was right. My chignon tumbled down when I turned my head and strands of hair tangled in the pins and flopped over my ears. I got so bugged I pulled the hair tightly into a bun, but this only made me look drawn and old. What's the good of having soft silky hair when you can't do anything with it?

There are two things you can never be in this life, Eleanor, a singer and a hairdresser. That may be unfortunate but it gives me an excuse to phone Marcia and get her to roll up my hair in some way that won't fall down before I get to the gallery. Then, since she's here already, we can go down together. I dread the lonely walk through the lobby. It's those doormen. I don't even know yet what my friends will think of me. I'm not up to being put down by the servants.

Down to the gallery to get to work.

Ron stares at me without recognition, then jumps up to kiss me. I'm sure he recognizes me only because he's been expecting me. It's good to see him and the old gang again. Two new people this time around—Julia at the reception desk and Sean, who is preparing to take over when Tere quits next week to look for acting jobs.

Spent the rest of the day laying out *Recollections* on the floor. I like the early stages of an installation. Still plenty of time before next Saturday's opening to lay out the works in different ways and get the feel of how they fit in the space. Fortunately, it's a space I know well. I've done two shows here before. But each show is its own thing. I can't be too confident.

I exchange the pumps for soft ballet slippers, not really because the high heels are uncomfortable—surprising how light on my feet they turn out to be—but I'm just not used to installing exhibitions on two-and-a-half inch heels and they interfere with my concentration. For one thing my eye level is too high. I'm used to being lower than other people, and through the years I must have adjusted to it without realizing it. I'm also thrown off by my unbalanced forward stance and short jerky steps. It's like wearing stilts. The slippers are fun anyway. I am very much the Ballerina, prancing around in my practice shoes, making full turns and taking dramatic poses. When I bend over to pick up a drawing from the floor I hold my legs and back straight. If someone speaks to me I incline my head in the grand manner, one eyebrow raised.

I'm sprawled on the floor studying some drawings when a black kid comes in with sandwiches from the luncheonette on Madison Avenue. A surprised intake of breath. Curious eyes. He's gobbling me up. The staff comes to attention. Everybody waits. He's waiting for me to turn around but I'm afraid to look at him. My first black person. Eleanor, this is ridiculous, he's only a kid. Cool it! I look up and smile determinedly into the place in the room where his eyes should be. There they are—in a nice friendly face. Unabashedly interested. I like him and smile for real with relief. And gratitude. It's easy. But within seconds—even as we're looking at each other—his eyes go blank. They don't move or look away, rather they withdraw. They seem to be turning inward. He doesn't see me anymore at all. It's pretty clear—I'm dismissed from his mind. He turns to the office staff. Am I imagining his movements are more purposeful, less lighthearted than when he bounced through the door announcing himself?

Well, everybody in the room has got to know I've been snubbed. I'm embarrassed. My face gets hot. I don't for a minute believe Barbara's nonchalance as she divides up the order and collects the money. Good thing Ron pays for my lunch so I don't have to join them. I pretend to study the drawings again but I'm stealing covert looks at the kid. He's very dark, African-looking, the kind of black that appears blue. My hand holding the drawing is much lighter, a warm brown with a sienna undertone. The veins stand out heavily as do the wrinkles on my knuckles. The dark color has settled into the creases, making my hands look gnarled like an old woman's. Ashamed, I hide my hands under the drawing. Hell, he's too young for me anyway. He's not even good looking, looks like a field hand. So why is everybody afraid to look at me? Ballerinas have no relation to delivery boys. This is becoming too personal. We haven't exchanged a single word and I've got a whole scene going.

Later a Swedish feminist comes in followed by a discreet husband hovering in the background. She sets up a future interview when she plans to visit California in the winter. From her questions I can tell she doesn't know anything about me. Another woman artist told her I was in town and she had to meet me. I wonder what she makes of what she sees. Certainly the artist who sent her couldn't have known what she was going to find! What does she make of my long nails? Perfume? Sexy bosom sticking out of tight leotards? Hardly your typical American artist. She's too straight not to be put off.

Her husband looks down his nose at me in the background. She's really watching him while looking at me, and I'm watching her watching him. My eyes are as innocent as hers. We're both liars.

I talk about the show, say something about the problems of being a black ballerina with the Russian dancers. Does she realize her luck? You can never tell with foreigners. She's come up with a winner by accident. A successful woman artist installing a show in a major New York gallery, and she's *black!* She doesn't mention this of course. Too polite! Liberals like to pretend blackness doesn't exist. They turn their eyes away as if someone's slip was showing. I know that if I were in her shoes, I'd blurt out, "You're black! Well! Well! I didn't know that."

Or doesn't she believe me?

But what is there not to believe?

That I am a small lady with light eyes, long fingernails, a big bosom, and a dark face.

I am!

I wonder though if there is still something strange about me anyway. Maybe that's why the delivery boy dismissed me so decisively. Can my darkness create uncertainty—not that I'm not dark—obviously I am—but perhaps I send out strange signals. Maybe they conflict. Or maybe I fail to send out some signals people with dark skin regularly transmit. Maybe people can't read me or maybe they can only read me partially. They become wary and look furtively for clues—like the black delivery boy. Uncertainty may be unpleasant. Suggest danger. Suppose he reacts intuitively, out of long experience, to mixed or imperfect signals, the same way he reacts to white people's signals—and eliminates the problem by rejecting them as he does me. It's an old trick of the weak, getting out of trouble by pretending it isn't there. As a woman, I've used it myself.

My Swedish interviewer is cool. She is ruffled by nothing and acknowledges nothing. Later she will think of me on her own ground and remove anything problematic by forgetting it. This will make her work easier and suits me fine.

At five o'clock, Ron and I go up to Columbia to be guest speakers for a class in Arts Management and Administration. Actually, Ron was the only one invited but he asked me to come along as living proof of the difficulties facing today's art dealers.

There was no parking place so late in the day. We drove up Broadway and swung around 116th down Columbus and back onto Broadway again several times without finding an empty meter. We stopped at a crossing for a crowd of students pouring through the main gates onto the street when I saw Jonathan Crary. I expected him to smile and wave, but his self-absorbed look didn't change. I suppose he didn't recognize me, but I must have been staring so intently that he got curious about the exotic dark lady flirting through the car window. Our eyes locked and I swung my gold hoop earrings like Marlene Dietrich. His handsome face got more interested. I could hardly keep from laughing. My God, here I was in broad daylight on Broadway PICKING UP MY OLD FRIEND JONATHAN CRARY. I was playing a part in a glamourous movie and watching it through the window at the same time.

Jonathan was really intrigued now and cautiously looked to see who was driving the car. A careful man, that Jonathan.

Ron was bouncing up and down on the seat beside me.

"Look, look at him, the idiot. Can you believe it, he doesn't recognize us . . ."

But he did recognize Ron, of course—when he finally noticed him. Holding out his hand, he came over to greet us with obvious pleasure. When he got up close he peered hard at me through the window and an incredulous look came over his face.

The movie was over.

I opened the car door and graciously offered my hand.

"Hello, Jonathan."

"Eleanor, I'm sorry . . . "

"Eleanora," I corrected him gently and he kissed my hand.

The lecture hall was shaped like a sea shell and you had to make 180-degree turns to address everybody in the audience. The class took lots of notes. I couldn't imagine what they found to write about. About ten percent of them were black, but they were not about to give me any special attention. Only one young black man in the last row seemed interested. For some reason he didn't like what he saw, and for half the class he glowered in his seat with a fierce face. Anyway, by the middle of the session my cranky style won him over and he laughed louder than anybody else every time I said something outrageous. His laughter was so pointed he might have been egging me on, but I didn't need encouragement. Before the class I planned to restrain my usual public style and try to come off as gracious, perhaps even with some of that sleepy Southern charm. I'm sure Danilova, who had a fierce temper along with a raucous sense of humour, would have tried to make a good impression on a class of college students. But put me in front of an audience and it's a full-fledged performance. I'm up against the wall, doing battle with my devils—formalists, minimalists, systematists, conceptualists, sexists, racists, government bureaucrats, pollsters, oil companies, corporate sponsors, nuclear power, television, ballet and opera companies, symphony orchestras, painters, collectors, museum trustees, certain museums, doctors, Marxists, Freudians, heavy metal sculptors, genius theory, George Balanchine . . .

I was worried too by my professional New York accent, an accent I never had when I lived in New York, but which appeared one day on a panel in California. Most black people still retain vestiges of southernisms in their voice or speech, and it's unlikely that a black ballerina would sound like a Jewish taxi driver from the Bronx.

I gave up the ghost, figuring the public debut of the black ballerina would be a failure because I couldn't get into her character, or, more precisely, I couldn't throw off my own. But it turned out that though ballerinas wouldn't be likely to come on like that, black artists would. Things haven't changed much since the '60s. My Stokely Carmichael number was a success, not only for the young man in the back row. My New York accent gave the students the illusion of energy, just as the low-down black hipster talk must have given it to the liberal lawyers and politicians of the civil rights movement—the polite young professionals with all the personal style of a loaf of white bread.

Linda Shearer, the new director of Artists Space, sat next to me. Later she complimented me on my tan. I suppose my high color confused her. There are so few of us in the art world, she would certainly have heard.

The young woman teaching the class agreed that it was a wonderful tan. They confessed they were jealous. I smiled mysteriously. I didn't know what to say.

Later, they came back to it again.

"What a great tan!"

When we were leaving Linda shook my hand and praised it again.

The instructor started to agree but I stopped her.

"I know," I said. "I was born that way."

Two black students walked us back to the car—a beautiful young woman and a short young man with a bad complexion. They shook my hand and thanked me. I didn't know what for, but smiled knowingly and hugged and thanked them too. We all laughed with pleasure and they stood there waving cheerfully as Ron and I drove away.

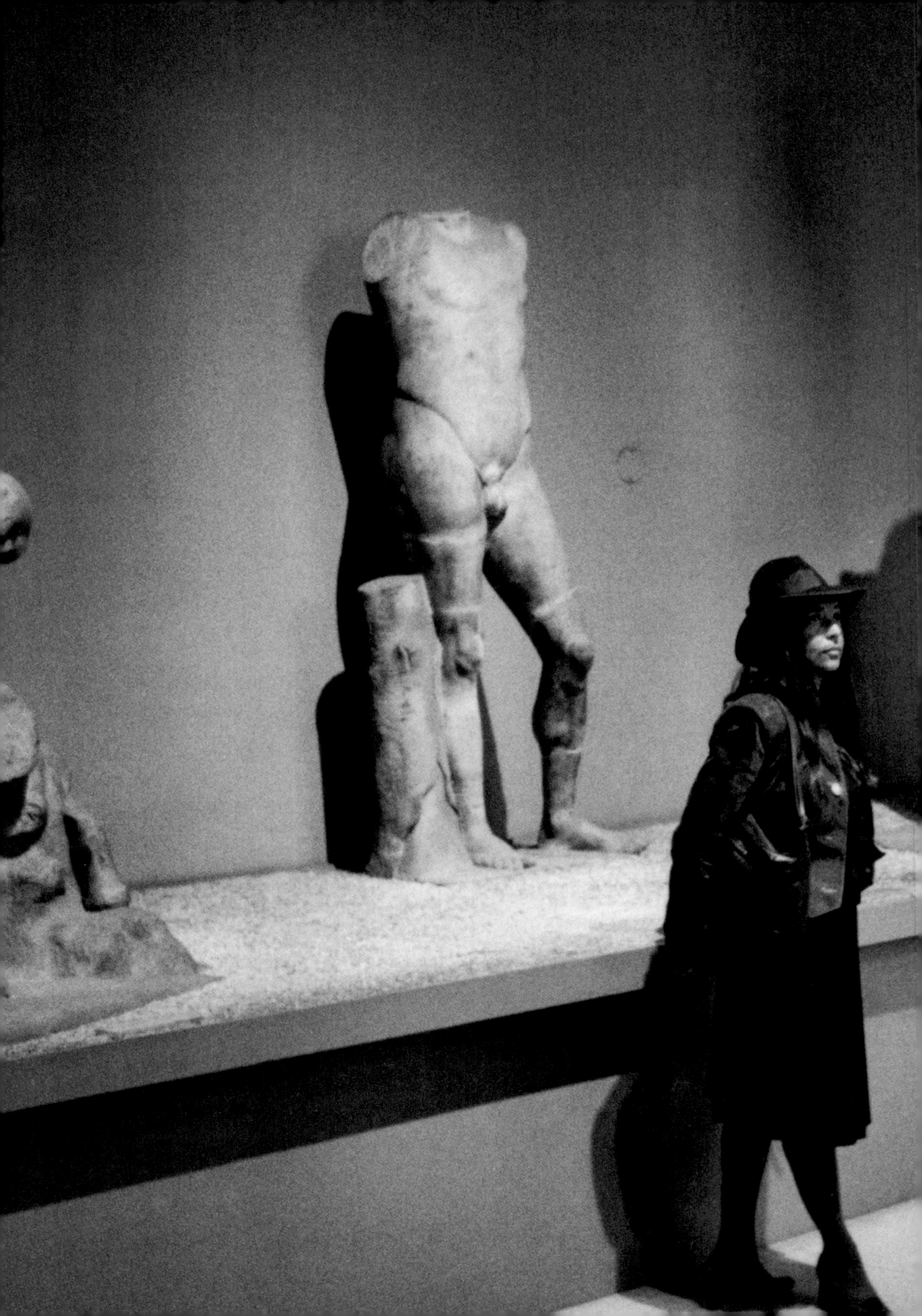

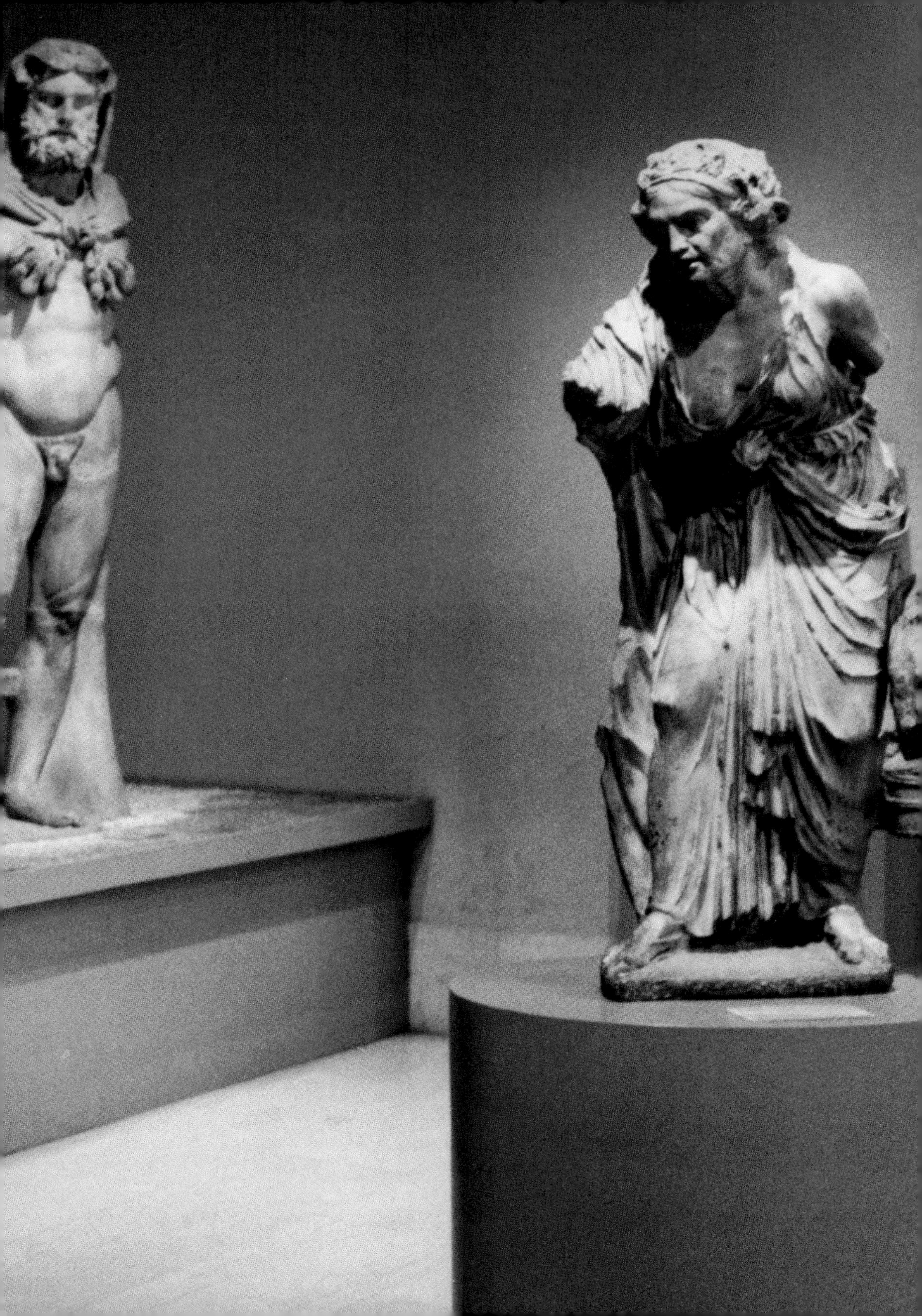

WEDNESDAY ***October 15***

Installed all day. Julia began phoning people from my list to invite them to the gallery performances. We decided to accept between 50 and 60 people each night. That way the seating would remain comfortable and it wouldn't get too hot. Even with that small number I didn't want to do more than the three performances we had planned for the Thursday, Friday, and Saturday of the week following the opening. Unfortunately Barbara Barracks can only make the show a *Soho News* Best Bet for the week after, so we add a fourth performance on the Wednesday of that week. That will be rough on me. I won't be able to put aside the performance after the third one on Saturday night. I'll have to keep the damn thing in my memory another four days. Nothing to be done about it though. We keep to our original reservation plan and sign people up for the first week only, leaving the extra Wednesday night performance open for the readers of the *Soho News.*

Julia is having a difficult time reaching people. Nobody is home during the day and the people in offices have secretaries or receptionists we have to get around. After all, what does the name Eleanora Antinova mean to them?

Julia gets flustered. She's very young. She nearly screwed up with Bob Hughes. He wasn't home, so she called *Time* and managed to get through to him, but he was confused—though friendly—about this ballerina, Antinova. I happened to be passing her desk at that point and heard her begin something about my being a special sort of ballerina, but I shook my head and gestured fiercely so she stopped.

"It's just that he was so nice," she explained afterward. "And I don't think he'll come. He doesn't know an Antinova. He thought I should call the dance critic instead."

Too bad. He's a romantic and would have enjoyed this performance. But there's nothing to be done. In life you can't claim to be somebody else because it's convenient. This is a real life performance, not a masquerade.

Met Carrie for dinner. She took me to an Italian restaurant on Sullivan Street. It was good to be in Little Italy again, in a restaurant with marble statues and murals on the walls and white tablecloths with rolled napkins stuffed into hefty goblets. Most of the other diners were couples or small families, but there were the usual groups of heavyset, middle-aged Italian gentlemen with gold pinkie rings and diamond tie clips.

"The food's great." Carrie took in the scene contentedly.

"And not expensive either."

She winked.

"Mafia!"

Funny how reassured downtown people are by the Mafia.

I remember how smug the people living on Cornelia Street felt because the Bleecker Street Social Club was down at the south end of the block. Nothing could happen to us because the Mafia took care of its family neighborhoods. People used to say with pride that you couldn't find drugs on the block and you could sit on the stoop till all hours of the night and be off-limits to muggers, pushers, pimps, and other dangerous characters. The Mafia became a powerful yet benign father, the best sort too, who protected you without extracting anything in return. Except now and then, short husky men with luxurious white hair and black suits would pass in the street on their way to the Club. In time you got to know some of them and if you looked good that afternoon, or were carrying a friend's baby or a bag of groceries, a polite swarthy gentleman might even tip his hat. You were always a little nervous about looking through the open doorway of the Bleecker Street Social Club, though as a rule all you could make out in the shadows were a couple of ragged plants and some folding chairs. In fact, you made a great show of thinking of something else when you passed because sometimes you would catch sight of pale faces in the gloom staring blankly out at the street. You might accidentally see something you weren't meant to see and perhaps have to suffer for it. In the world of gangsters, who could know where neighborliness and spying might converge. But the feeling of being protected was pleasant. There was something seductive about it, there always is in paternalistic relationships. You were pampered, protected, an aristocrat. I think it was the same sort of feeling a rich kid must have when he's arrested for drunk driving. No way would he be confused with those others who don't have rich daddies and lawyers and who have to stay behind in smelly cells while he is whisked away. And Carrie has hardly been a New Yorker for more than a couple of years. It doesn't take long to become white and privileged in New York. But tonight I was surely not white, and I was too overdressed to be middle class.

Carrie sat there in a loose belted trench coat. The collar of her blouse was white and ironed. Her shoulder-length brown hair gleamed in the light of the electric chandelier. Like the girls in the Breck ads she brushed it 100 times a night. The tall Italian waiter appreciated this. She was a nice girl from an expensive school. She read books and looked at pictures in museums and was a high-class person who did honor to him and the restaurant. It was an honor to wait on such a person.

In this scenario he had to take me for an unsuitable companion. My makeup was streaky after the heavy day in the gallery. Sure, I put on a second coat before coming downtown, but it's not the same as washing the old face off first. I'm a touch-up job at best, the brown paint has settled deeply into my wrinkles and I probably look as old as I feel. I'm wearing too many clothes. I'm fussy. Obviously a low-class person in a Scott Fitzgerald novel. The dark one with a foreign name who sleeps with men and comes from the slums. The Golden Girl is entertaining me. She's slumming.

I know this movie. I played in it a long time ago without understanding it. I was much younger then and cast as the *ingenue.* My cousin's Sweet Sixteen party on Tremont Avenue back in my sophomore year at Music and Art High School. I'm with Morty, the *BTO* who later became a dentist, along with Lenny Sirowitz and a 4'10" music student in spike heels. Her black ringlets curled around her face the way Miss Fury's did in the old *Post* comic strip and she had the whitest skin I ever saw. I remember thinking she was the color of typing paper. She was gorgeous and sophisticated, and I admired her enormously when she slithered through the halls dressed in these clinging silk dresses. Only music students could dress like that. It would never have been tolerated in an art student.

Was her name Fredericka? I'm going to call her Fredericka. She was a perfect Fredericka but I can't really remember if that was her name or not.

The boys picked me up first because Lenny also lived in the West Bronx and he had his brother's car. Then we spent a lot of time looking for Fredericka's house somewhere in the East Bronx. We drove for miles through flat, empty streets with rundown, one-story clapboard houses. Lenny went into the house to get her while we waited in the car a little weirded out by the strange neighborhood.

Morty and I were serious dancers and there was no point in mixing with my cousin's friends, who sat around telling dirty jokes, the boys on the couch at one end of the room and the girls huddled around the piano. They were just dumb Jewish kids from Taft High while we were smart kids from a special school and they weren't worth bothering with. Morty was one of the tallest of the *BTO*s, about 6'4", and since my mother didn't let me wear heels higher than an inch, I only reached to his navel. But we swayed dreamily to the Andy Russell records and the metal clasp on his belt only hurt when we dipped.

But Lenny and Fredericka were wild. They turned off the lights in Sally's kid brother Butch's room and lay on the bed and carried on to the delight of Sally's unbelievable friends, who tiptoed past the open door trying to see inside. They were giggling like idiots and I was furious because I knew that fink, Sally would tell Aunt Betty and Uncle Julius and they would all smirk about Eleanor and her trampy friends and what right did I have to think so much of myself.

"What's going on here?" I whispered to Morty's stomach.

"Lenny says when he went into her house he could tell she was colored."

I was shocked.

"But she's as white as kleenex."

"Only colored people live there."

My mother was a Marxist and a fighter against intolerance so I didn't see how this news, startling as it was, had any relevance to the stupid way the two of them were carrying on. Morty was a senior and experienced. I was just a sophomore and a virgin, so I shut up and kept dipping. But I was in a rage. If the scandal got back to my parents I might have trouble going out with the *BTO*s. If my mother was on a bourgeois kick when she heard about it she wouldn't care that Morty and I were innocent victims.

We managed to get Lenny and Freddy out of there, and this time Morty drove so those two morons could carry on in the backseat.

When he came back to the car after dropping her off at her house, Lenny ostentatiously wiped his mouth with his sleeve.

"Ugh," he said. "I never soul kissed so much in my life."

I never did understand what happened that night. I can understand Lenny, he was always an idiot. I went out with him sometimes because he was so handsome—a dead ringer for John Derek—but a hopeless dope.

But I didn't understand Fredericka.

Now I haven't thought of this story for many years. All that night I felt there was some ritual going on that I didn't understand. I suppose this was what the culture imagined black women and white men did with each other. She was flinging this image back into our teeth. It was something of a performance. Only unfortunately, it wasn't our image. It certainly wasn't mine. Later, when I saw her in the hall at school, she ignored me. When I stood in front of her demanding a greeting, she merely looked at me with contempt and walked around me as though I was a turd. She was probably furious at the failure of her performance and was perfectly content never to say hello to me again and she didn't.

Fuck the whole lot of them. I hate them all.

I glared at the waiter. He'd been pointedly ignoring me whenever I asked for anything.

"That waiter is a racist," I said to Carrie.

She put down the fork she was wrapping spaghetti around and looked hard at me.

"You do not look black," she said.

"No, I'm white as the driven snow." I was angry. With such friends, who needs enemies.

"You have a lot of makeup on, but you're not black. Nobody would take you for black." She sounded upset.

"Everybody thinks I'm black," I insisted.

"No, they don't. You're imagining that they do."

"Well, why doesn't the waiter respond. I've been flirting with him for the last ten minutes and his eyes are like ice."

"Maybe you're not his type."

Carrie sounded distressed. I didn't understand it.

"Why don't you want me to be black?" I asked curiously.

"I don't care one way or the other." She sounded like she was going to cry. "You just aren't."

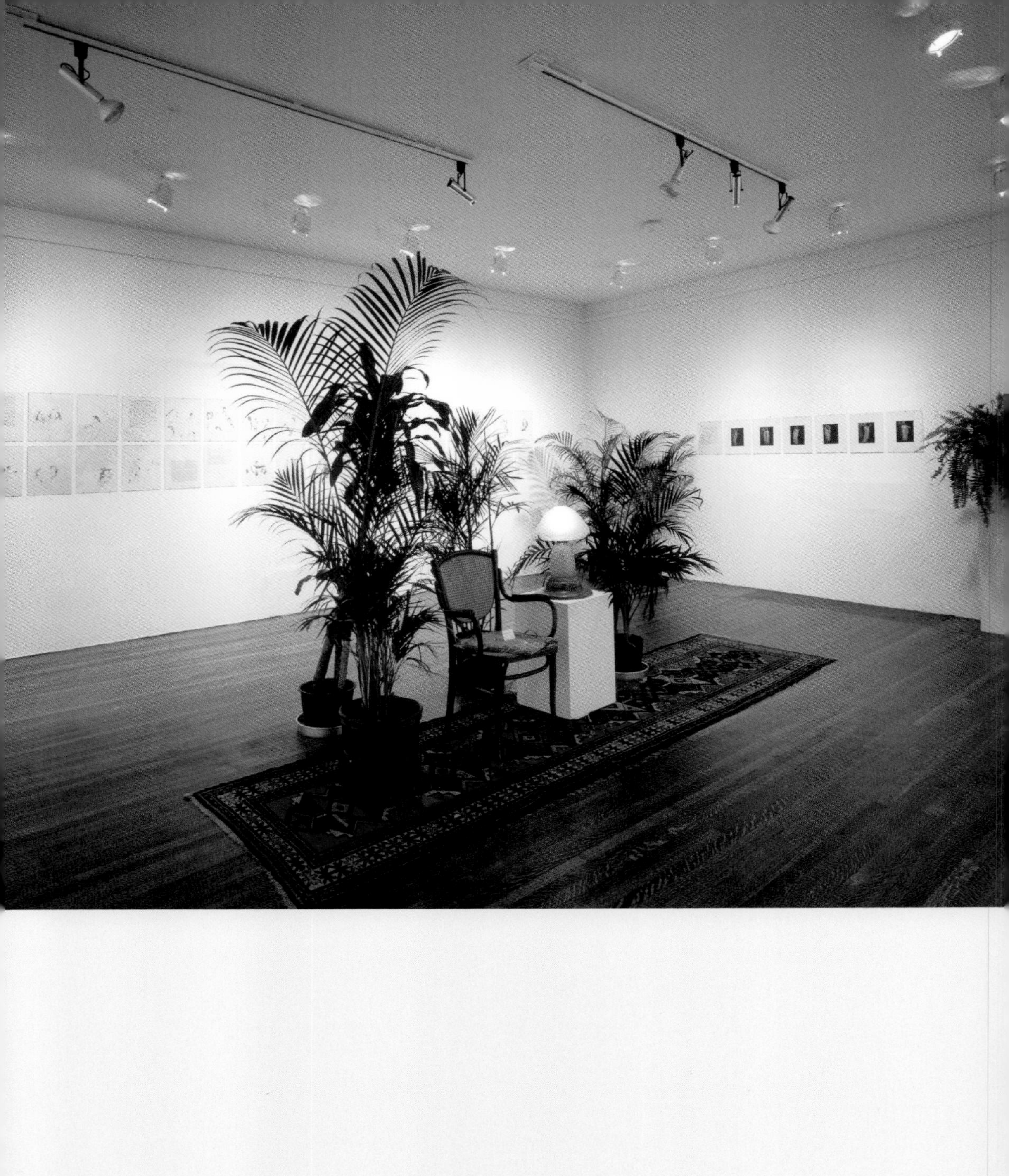

THURSDAY ***October 16***

Installation completed. Except for the lighting. We'll see to that on Saturday before we open at noon. Ron will help out. He has a good eye for lighting. The performance set sits in the middle of the gallery. The first thing people will see when they come in. Marcia lent us a long narrow Persian rug. It acts as a stage for the furniture. Ron borrowed a cane-back chair from a neighbor's dining room in White Plains, and I placed one of the Art Deco portfolios of the *Memoirs* on it, as if I had been unexpectedly called away and would return any minute. The Tiffany lamp Marcia picked up years ago at an upstate auction sits on an ordinary white sculpture stand. A generous number of potted palms and ferns frame the props. Potted plants always add a touch of the Yalta steamer. Dr. Chekhov might be returning to look through the book. Perhaps it was his sudden arrival that interrupted my reading. The '20s easily accommodated a mixture of styles and the set suggests an Art Deco salon.

The plants came from a wholesale greenhouse over by the East River, with large and comfortable showrooms. I could believe I was wandering through a *fin de siècle* greenhouse in some 19th-century exposition. The air hung suspended overhead, warm with the dank smell of plants that are too crowded together and too often watered. Marcia and Sean walked through the aisles studying the plants while I stood listening to the ghosts of gentlemen in frock coats and ladies in plump bustles with narrow trailing skirts. A memory of a parasol brushed smartly past my ear, a mocking laugh, a whispered exclamation. If I turned my head quickly enough I might catch sight of a teasing young lady before she slips behind a tree. The plant creatures tower exotically over our heads. How easy it is to slip behind a great frond and peer out at me without being seen. But I can feel their eyes. Their whispers are always around the corner.

"I can't believe these prices," Marcia said. "They're cheaper than wholesale."

The place was obviously some kind of bootleg operation. Everyone working there, down to the girl at the cash register, looked bugged and aggressive. You had the feeling they were shoving plants out of there before anyone was ready to take them in. That at six o'clock they would fold up their tents and flee into the night. No, it was hardly a scene out of Henry James. The opulent plants clung together for whatever comfort they could take until a man with strong arms swung them up and sent them out into the hands of strangers. Dark, polished leaves glistened with large water drops. When the leaves shook the water slid along the edges but the coat of polish sealed off their thirsty skins. It was a slave market. The smell of fear and helplessness sickened me. The possibility for cruelty was overwhelming. Only avarice kept the workers from pulling off the leaves of these helpless creatures one by one to see them bleed a milky white substance. Or wrenching them out of their life supporting planters leaving them to suffocate slowly. They were squeezed too tightly into their boxes anyway. The roots must be cramped and pained. Is that what they did to the sickly ones? The ones who stayed around too long? What happened to the unsold creatures when night fell? How desperate they must be to find kindly masters. I had the hopeless feeling I get when people crowd around the windows of a pet store to admire the pretty puppies. “Look at that one,” someone cries. “Isn’t he cute?” That one is putting on a dazzling show so one of the faces flattened against the glass will take him away and feed him warm milk and put him to bed in a cozy place. But pet stores are sleepy places. These plants are luckier. The turnover is terrific. There are lots of customers. The cash register never stops ringing.

“It’s a plant theft ring,” I whispered to Marcia and Sean.

Trucks carrying plants and even flowers are being hijacked all over the west. So the merchandise has made its way as far as New York.

Marcia’s eyebrows went up. The collector’s gleam was in her eye.

“So what’s wrong with that? We don’t have to pay outlandish prices.”

But the thieves often dig plants out of people’s gardens and farms and much of their stuff dies because they don’t know how to care for them or they throw them away when they can’t make a quick sale.

“Come on,” Marcia gestured around the room. “These trees didn’t come from a backyard.”

Sure, most of the thieving is done from the professionals. But the big outfits can protect their merchandise with watchmen and armored trucks. It’s the small family businesses like the Japanese ones back home in Encinitas and Leucadia that can’t pay for protection, and many of them are going bankrupt because it’s a marginal business at best.

In the evening we went to Judy Chicago’s opening at the Brooklyn Museum. Suzanne Lacy, Faith Wilding, Jill Soderholm, and Ida Applebroog piled into the Jaguar with us. It only seated four but I was too nervous to let anyone sit on my lap and mess up my paint job. This was my first big social event. I was sure to meet lots of people I knew and I expected trouble.

To get to the liquor I pushed my way past Bella Abzug in a red hat. It was that kind of crowd. Arlene Raven talked of leaving California to settle in New York and become rich. Lucy chattered in her customary manner, too quickly for anyone else to get a word in, as if she was afraid someone would ask her for something. Except for the pain radiating through my toes with the intensity of a dentist’s drill every time I took a step in my three-inch Evan-Picone pumps, things were progressing well. Nobody struck me or challenged me to a duel. Indeed, my friends agreed I had become something of an improvement over myself.

Judy was glamourous talking into microphones. She must have looked exotic on the late-night news with her bouffant Afro and green taffeta dress slit down the front all the way to her middle. Tony Ramos hovered around the edge of the crowd, ready to whisk her off when it got too much. How handsome he looks in a white tuxedo. Like a black movie star.

Here goes nothing!

“Hello Tony.”

I think I glared at him, anticipating a punch in the nose. I’ve always suspected Tony of having a terrible temper. I wanted to bolt.

He looked curiously at me, then a slow grin spread over his face. With a flourish like Toscanini he bent towards me and opened his arms. I fell into them barely suppressing a groan of relief, though I remembered not to press my face too deeply into his white silk jacket.

The bastard—the wonderful bastard—was playing to the crowd all the way. He gave me a long sexy kiss.

I pulled away first. No sense overdoing this. I mean, Judy is my friend.

"You're beautiful," he said.

The people around us were cool and liberal and knew better than to stare but we knew they were watching every move.

"Such a gorgeous black couple," they were thinking.

We basked in their approval.

"We the only ones in the joint, so make it good," he beamed, looking like a kid who's just stolen his brother's birthday cake.

I couldn't stop giggling. It was incredible. Here we were doing a song and dance act in Brooklyn, when just a few weeks before he had been sitting in Bully's Bar back in Del Mar minding his own business, nursing a *Dos Equis* and watching the football game, when two white women turned on him out of the blue and called him a nigger.

"You coming back to my turf?" I teased him.

He kissed the tip of my nose.

"Not on your life. It's friendlier here."

A young white woman smiled shyly at me but dropped her eyes when I looked back at her as if she was afraid I'd bite. I'll be damned if he wasn't right.

FRIDAY ***October 17***

Another pretty day, more like spring than fall. Instead of the usual hour-and-a-half to get dressed and do my makeup, I give myself two hours. By the time I put the finishing touches on myself by spraying on *Opium* perfume I'm kind of dancing around the house. I figure I don't need a jacket on such a day, my wrap-around dance sweater should do fine. Besides, I like looking down at my full bosom snuggled tightly into the sweater. I give myself a couple of feels, taking big breaths while I stick my chest out a couple of inches. God, all those years of wearing blue jeans and loose shirts. I forgot how cuddly and round my body really is. I'm lucky it still is. I lost ten years, at that.

There is the usual pleasure in walking through the Art Deco lobby and hearing my heels tap smartly on the tiles.

"Good morning," I smile at the doormen, wanting to share my pleasure in the day.

They cluster together and don't pay me any attention. Something must be up, I think. Maybe someone is getting fired. I'll certainly sign a petition if they draw one up.

An old lady hobbles through the door behind me, leaning heavily on a cane. She is followed by a middle-aged black nurse with a cranky face, who gives me a disapproving look. Within seconds the two women are settled in a cab by the young Puerto Rican.

Maybe they didn't see me yet.

"Heavy traffic today," I quip. "Do you think I'll get a taxi?"

"I don't know, Miss." The short one's eyes look somewhere over my head.

Just yesterday we had joked about the unseasonable weather.

I could feel my confidence drain away. Bad vibes lay heavy all around me.

The handsome young one is watching us curiously.

My voice when it comes out is tight, rough.

"Get me a cab," I say to him.

He hesitates; but my anger intimidates him, and he moves toward the curb and looks listlessly out to the street.

"You whistle better than I do," I laugh, willing him to admire me, to bring back the comfortable master-servant relationship we have been enjoying for almost a week.

"I don't whistle, Miss."

He makes no move to call any of the taxis that are passing and I am humiliated to acknowledge defeat by hailing one myself.

Fortunately, my honor is saved! A cab arrives. A harassed woman gets out while trying to prevent three laughing children from tumbling out of the car and hurting themselves. In the commotion, I slip in behind her.

"Hey," the cabbie shouts at me. "What a great tan."

I glare at him so fiercely he stops laughing. As we drive off I see him looking at me uncertainly in the mirror.

"Yes, I'm colored," I snap at him. "Now keep your eyes on the road."

He's afraid of me and drives fast. Probably thinks I'm going to rob him. The sunny morning is ruined. What a disaster! The doormen are in revolt and this bastard of a cabbie takes me for Hawaiian. I wanted to turn the cab around and go back home. What, and face those bastards again? But how could I go to the gallery in this state? I can't meet anyone today, anymore. I've been seeing myself in the eyes of my servants and they've rejected me. My confidence is zero.

When I get to the gallery I phone Marcia.

"The doormen are racists."

"Since when?"

"Since this morning. They won't serve me."

I wanted to cry. Until this moment I hadn't realized just how much I enjoyed the little services they performed for me. Their gentle ministrations told me I was lovely, glamourous, important. Passersby in the street used to stare at me, the center of my uniformed support system. In their faces I saw curiosity, admiration, jealousy sometimes—the portion of a glamourous woman. It was what I had spent the last two hours in front of a mirror preparing for. I wasn't going to lose it, damn them.

"I think you're supposed to tip them," Marcia said wearily.

"Tip them? I pay rent!" I shouted.

This wasn't exactly true since Marcia paid the rent, but she knew what I meant.

"You're a visitor and they know it," she said.

I remembered Agatha Christie ladies complaining about the deteriorating servant situation. For me too life wasn't what it used to be.

"You mean I have to have money in my hand every time I leave the house?" I was appalled.

"I guess so," Marcia said. "I'm not good at these things myself. I wasn't born rich."

"But if I've been low-class all week how can I turn around and upgrade myself now?"

"No," she sighed. "People are never complicated about accepting money."

"So how much should I give them?"

"50 cents?"

"I'll make it a dollar."

She thought it might be a little ostentatious.

"Better too much than too little," I said glumly. "I don't want half of their attention. I need the whole thing."

"How much do *you* give?" I asked.

"I don't. I live in places. I give Christmas presents."

I realized then that the rich pay heavily for their pampered nests. The servants exact a price for the warm golden world they wrap their masters in. They had me in their power and they knew it. They had the upper hand. I needed them more than they needed me. Without them I stopped being glamourous. I might be beautiful, I might even be chic, but I wasn't glamourous. I imagined the terrible tall men in red uniforms and gold epaulettes who guarded the doors of the grand hotels in Monte Carlo. With a look—or the refusal of one—they could prick the glamourous bubble of Diaghilev's dancers, decked out in the height of fashion for all the world to see, while their stomachs growled for a full meal. So that's why the hotel clerks at the *Gritti* in Venice and, come to think of it, even at the more lowly *Roma* in Bologna, and the flight attendants in first class *Al Italia,* were so tall for Italians. And the head waiter at *Florian's* in Venice? Him too. Those canny Romanoffs! Exiled to Paris, they took jobs as doormen. After the Revolution, the last position of power is that of a doorman in front of an important door.

SATURDAY ***October 18***

In his zeal to realize my intentions, Ron has turned the lights down so low a pall of gloom hangs over the gallery. Only the stage set is lit, with an expressive light that is invaded by shadows from the surrounding space, creating the effect of a Caravaggio painting. The leaves of the potted plants droop with a waxy despair. In the dim light they look like plastic. Nothing moves. There isn't a breath of air. Instinctively I enter on tiptoe, finger to my lips.

"Where's the organ?"

Poor Ron. Now I've hurt his feelings. He wanted to give me a salon but what I've got is a funeral parlor. A corpse is always the present, the past has got to be alive and snapping. Luckily I have a suspicious nature and was never going to leave the lighting to anyone.

"Take your time," Sean had said. "This is your day. Relax. We'll take care of everything."

(Sigh) It's hard to be an artist. You've just got to keep on top of everything when all you want to do is go home and watch the play-offs on television and gorge yourself on caviar and French bread.

Sean helps me turn up the lights and brighten the place.

Traffic is slow. The usual uptown funeral. There are so few interesting galleries above Soho it's hard to get people to an opening. Especially when they know they'll be coming back again later for a performance.

It's beginning to get me down.

I take a turn around the block.

When I get back, Ida arrives to keep me company.

"Let's split."

We hop into a cab downtown for some Saturday afternoon action. 420 West Broadway first, to catch John's opening at Sonnabend. Here it's already crowded, mostly with kids. Kids usually like John. They understand him. They feel intellectually successful. But the show's tired. What's the matter with him? Is he sick? Conceptual artists often suffer from chronic depression.

I ask for him at the desk. The girl can barely drag the words out. He'll be in some time between five and seven, she drawls.

The bastard! He's watching the play-offs while I'm pestering the menial.

"Tell him Eleanora Antinova was asking for him," I drawl back.

Like a shot the young woman comes awake. Curious eyes size me up. Her expression is speculative. She's seen me before but it wasn't like this.

"Would you like to leave a note?"

She is eager to serve and offers a pen.

"It is so difficult to write," I sigh in a whimsical manner. "My nails . . ."

Just in time I notice that her silver nails are almost as long as mine. The long strong fingers hold the pen with confidence. Yes, sweetheart, but yours didn't sprout overnight like beanstalks.

I disdain the pen and wave my fingers in the air.

She studies my hands with a worried look. Do I have gout? They look gnarled. Why am I shoving them into people's faces? I bring them down behind my back expressively.

"Tell him . . ."

I haven't a thing to tell him. I have no interest in him whatever. Ida looks at me queerly. I'm having so much trouble finding words she may think I'm having a stroke. That's an idea. It would get me out of here.

"Come, my dear," I offer Ida my gnarled hand and sail through the door of the elevator into the oncoming crowd.

"I got lost," I explain to her when the door slides shut and we are alone. "Sometimes you take a wrong turn and you can't get out."

Years ago, when my *100 BOOTS* show opened at the Museum of Modern Art nobody came and I fled downtown to the galleries because that's where the conceptual artists were. I went up to Ileana's, and Michael, the tiny dancing master, looked through my drawings with critical sympathy. They lacked, he explained, expressiveness, and he generously showed me some Jasper Johns and Wegmans, then rushed downstairs to see Joan Jonas' new videotape.

"Are you coming?" he called impatiently from the staircase.

On the day of my opening at the Museum of Modern Art?

"I have an appointment at Castelli's," I lied.

"Leo will be playing the tape."

I wonder what he thought when I never showed.

I looked at Ida gloomily.

"Time marches on," I announced.

Jonathan Borofsky at Paula Cooper. Lively, energetic. I wonder if he enjoys being Paula's *bete noir.* He must; it's too tiring an act otherwise. Ida chats with Irving Sandler and Helene Winer while I stand apart—a shady outsider with too many clothes—ignored by all—until I can't take it anymore.

"Irving," I reproach him, "you don't recognize me."

He is uncertain. My voice is familiar.

"Eleanora Antinova." I am impatient now.

He embraces me.

"My God, I didn't recognize you."

Helene Winer is shocked.

"You look so different."

Later, Ida says that was better.

"Stay cool," she warns, referring to the incident at Sonnabend.

But I don't like being invisible. All my life I dreaded not being noticed. I played the clown, the fool, anything to catch people's attention.

I don't have so many friends that I can afford to spare any.

Back at the gallery traffic hasn't improved much. I'm suffering from the "Hostess Syndrome" and count the house. When someone leaves I groan, but when someone new comes in to take his place I groan again—I'm ashamed for him to see such a small crowd. It doesn't matter that the reservation lists for the performances are filling up, that Thursday evening is already S.R.O. I have a sick feeling when I'm unpopular.

Faith Ringgold comes in. The L.A. feminist contingent, in for Judy's opening, has been visiting her Harlem studio. Suzanne introduces us; and the sudden look of suspicion, with that "what the hell is going on here" look, cheers me up. Especially when within seconds her shoulders relax, the chip falls off, and she is shaking my hand with gusto. She's as comfortable and easy as her miniature bag lady sculptures. It's nice to hug her, she's so solid.

Later that afternoon we notice an elegant old gentleman with a cane in a softly tailored blue suit and a yellow flower in his lapel. He peers closely at the photographs of my great roles and spends a long time over the texts describing my ballets. He looks at the drawings, but keeps returning to the photographs. He takes a pair of gold-rimmed spectacles out of his breast pocket and studies them closely. He seems to come to a decision and, vigorously pulling himself up, asks for me at the desk.

"Antinova," Ron introduces me with a flourish.

The man visibly shrinks. His expression is uncertain.

"But you are too young."

Now his voice is forlorn. I am not what he was expecting. He had seen the advertisement in the *Times.* As a matter of fact, several of his old friends from the *Ballets Russes* had seen it. They have been exchanging phone calls all morning.

"I am just come from the Tolstoy Farm," he says in a softly modulated British voice. "Spessivtseva lives there."

He breaks off, unsure of me.

"Do you know Spessivtseva?"

I don't dare say a word. What could I say that would not break the spell of that name? The years wash away. There is a ringing in my ears.

"An apple came into the world," Cecchetti once marveled. "And Pavlova was one side and Spessivtseva was the other."

"We have been trying to remember you. Later Pat Dolin joined us."

An ironic smile flits across his mouth.

"It was Spessivtseva who remembered first."

"In Spain, she thought. You joined the company in Spain. In Massine's time, Patrick thought it was. In *Las Meninas.* The role of the dwarf. By then he remembered too. Very well. You know Patrick . . ."

We share a conspiratorial smile at his friend's expense.

"It was not a successful ballet, you see. The Spaniards are not an easy people. We thought you might have been of their group when they joined the company. It was a little before my time but I too remembered something . . . Alas, we were wrong."

I go into my song and dance about living my dream. He listens politely and tries to hide his disappointment but it is clear he is suffering.

He was a Surrealist painter but talks like an upper-class Englishman though his name is French. I couldn't catch it because he didn't anglicize it; it rolled off his tongue too suavely for me to understand—that *Ballets Russes* crowd were a multilingual lot. Perhaps he had designed sets, costumes. He could have been one of the smart young men of Diaghilev's circle, perhaps a lover of Pat Dolin, or maybe even of the old man himself. Unfortunately he was out of visiting cards. But he was gracious. After all, as an old Surrealist, who was he to quarrel with dreams, but the effort was difficult. Dejection stood out all over him. He was too old for masks.

I held his fragile, old man's hand to my heart and begged him to come to the performance next week.

"You will understand then," I promised.

"Oh my dear, you are not difficult to understand," he objected gently. But he was already turning away. He had lost interest. He wasn't angry, he just didn't care. He was too old for art. At his age all he wanted was what he could recover from life—some talk of the old days, an exchange of memories of half a century ago.

I watched him leave, moving slowly away from the recognition scene I couldn't give him. I was so sad I wanted to cry.

"Please come back," I called after him. "If you can."

He managed a kindly wave of his hand and was gone.

At night I go to a dinner party for Judy Chicago at Honor Moore's downtown loft. I take a grim satisfaction in honoring another artist on the day of my own opening.

The loft is warm and friendly. The women are relaxed and happy to be there. Diane Gelon though is very depressed. She's holding herself together only by an act of will. Several times during our conversation I thought she would burst into tears but she fought it off. As Judy's second-in-command, she stage-managed the entire *Dinner Party* community. She may have lost the most now that the community is dissolved and the work sent out into the world. In an earlier time she would have made a great convent administrator for an adored Mother Superior. She would have moved the sisters around with a shrewd fairness they would take for granted, without noticing its athletic grace. She speaks now of visiting some alternative space in the Midwest. There's a chance of a job at the Endowment. Her voice breaks as she counts off the possibilities. She is really waiting to be swept off her feet again.

Catherine Stimson talks of her recent book, which I stumbled on among the Gothics and romances back home in a Del Mar supermarket. The mass distribution delights her. She dreams of hitting the jackpot and making it big. Her voice takes on a hearty pop tone, and I can see her puffing a Havana cigar and signing contracts. I half think the unexpectedness of my black silk dress, sewn with thousands of tiny pieces of jet sparkling in the discreet lamplight, brings this out in her. There is a high class lesbian feel to the room. The only men are the servants, one of whom is the French cook. There is a comfortable murmur of women's voices, the rustle of a skirt, a friendly laugh. The wine goes to my head. I expect a golden-haired Renée Vivian to glide weightlessly through the door, clutching the pearls piled on top of her dishevelled little head.

"Honor dear, forgive me. I am desperate. Life is a fuck."

With her own hands, Honor will prepare a green cocktail in an enormous round glass, which her guest will hold precariously in those never still bony fingers capped with nails so long and deeply red they're nearly black. The glass will fall from her hands. Everything does. She is deciduous.

A portly woman in a tuxedo with a stiff jabot rises from a deep armchair in the shadows where I didn't see her until now.

"I am gravely offended," she will say to Renée.

The sound of the slap is clear and shocking like a bullet in a salon, and poor Renée will open her childlike eyes in wonder.

As usual I rush to defend the oppressed but before I can reach her, Renée gives a little cry like a fox caught in a trap, and runs out of the house.

La Chevaliere gazes sadly around the silent room.

"Oh my sisters," she sighs. "Must we too . . ."

"Come see my grandmother's paintings." Honor interrupts my reverie.

They are dashing 30's-type portraits of elegant ladies in toque hats and brightly colored skirts. She had studied in Paris and for a time shown in a New York gallery, when she fell in love and left art for marriage and family. Honor loved the wonderful old lady she had become and has her paintings now that she's dead.

"I'm trying to arrange an exhibition," she says.

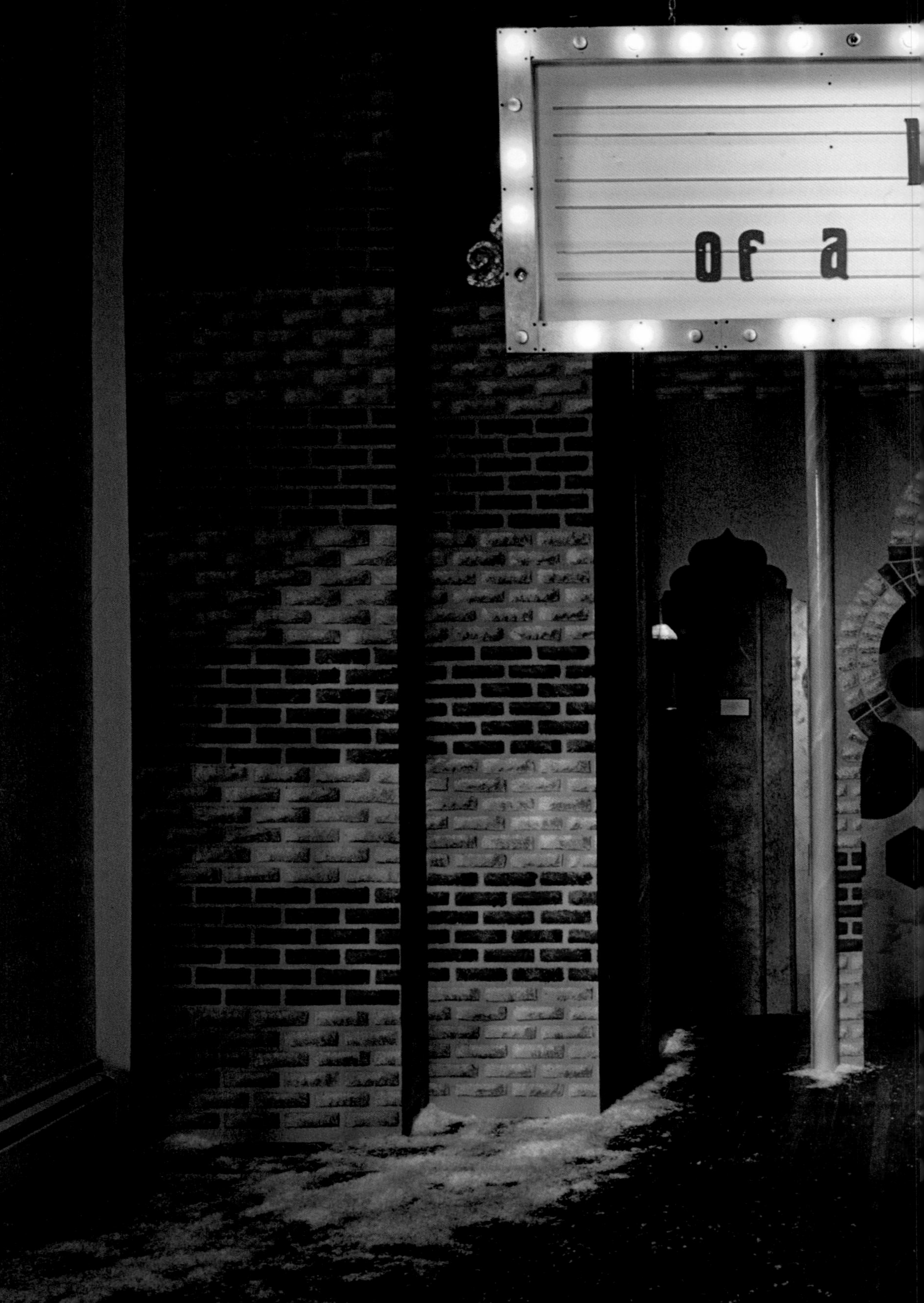
of a

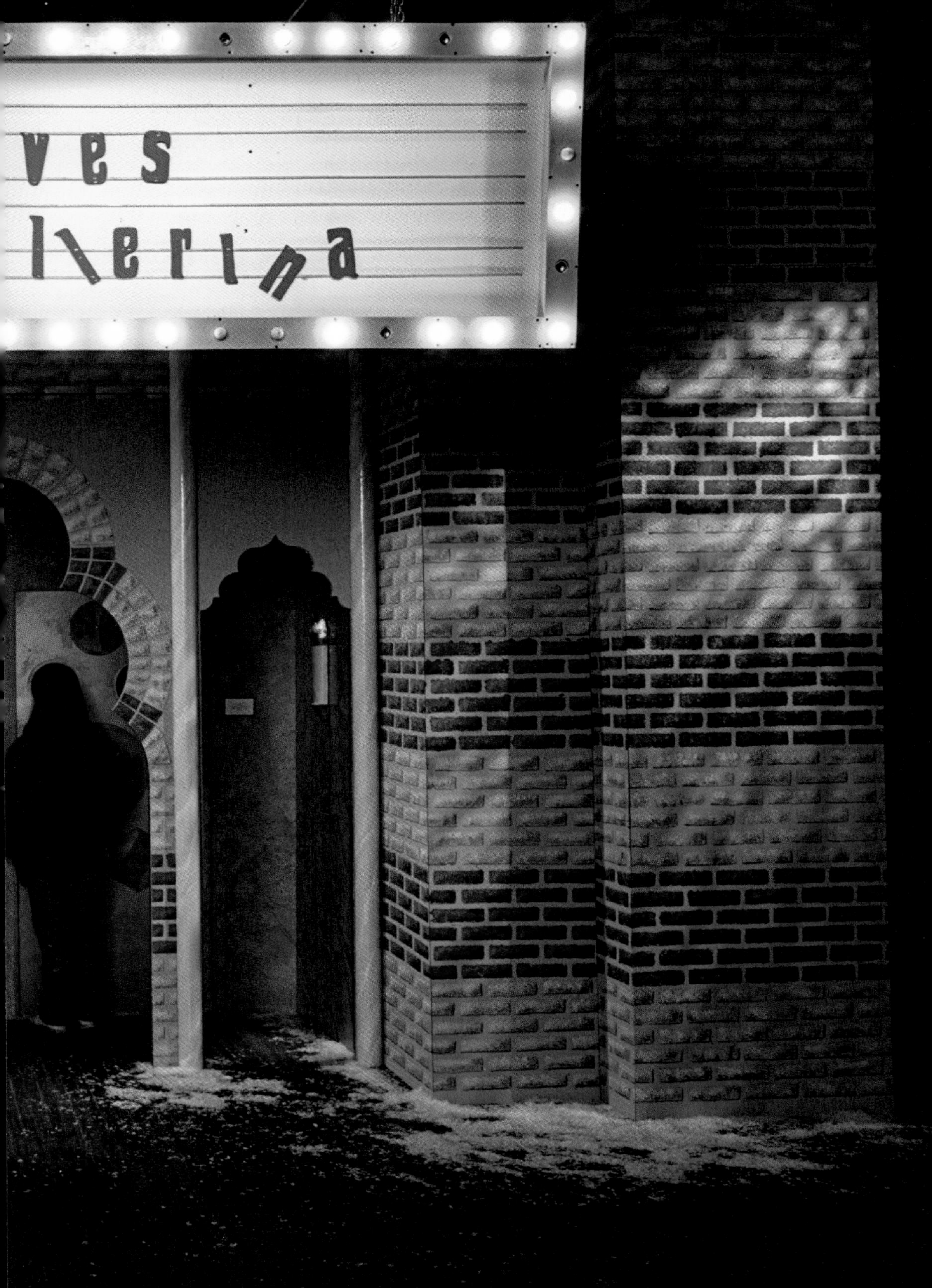
ves
llerina

SUNDAY ***October 19***

Sunday morning in New York. The clock reads 8:45. Somewhere behind the still curtains of one of those windows in the house across the way there will be a young woman drifting up from the quilt puffed around her bed like a jubilant cloud. Warm body smells pull her back down to the rumpled sheets, but an adventurous hand is already making its way to the floor. Fingers tap blindly along the boards, cautiously feeling for the mound of papers. The Book section. Entertainment. News of the Week in Review. Magazine section. Sports. With a snort of pleasure she chooses . . . what . . . I hold my breath . . . what shall I choose for her this Sunday . . . today it will be . . . the Entertainment section. She digs in with voluptuous greed. The pleasure of those thin columns like rows of grey flannel suits. The discreet pallid print suggesting a faint problem in the adenoids, a crick in the neck. How I miss the tired *Times Roman,* so weary and distinguished. Brooks Atkinson on yet another courtroom drama while Crowsley Bother frets about the Method. John Canaday is in Europe again but Ada Louise Huxtable will fill in as the icy breath of Eero Saarinen blows in from the eighth page. In the free-wheeling democracy of the Fourth Estate, Harold Schonberg has moved from the daily sports page at the back to the culture section at the center. He considers the distinguishing features of yet another pianist—or is it peeanist—a perhaps overly fierce interpretor of Bartok and Chopin. The opera is in difficulties again, not so the ballet this week. Mr. B. and Stravinsky have done it again, says John Martin, while little Allegra Kent obeys faithfully as a well brought up young lady should. The Book section has the tweedy look of an independent venture, a pair of tailors gone out on their own. There is Leon Edel on Henry James, the middle years this time around, how far they stretch in both directions as the novel falters and the drama is at hand. The generous Mr. E. B. White shares his summer vacation with us. It appears there are many flies. Somewhere there is a canoe. An 80-year-old unsolved murder. A dish balances precariously on the young woman's stomach. Nova Scotia from Zabar's, thick Canadian bacon, fresh tomatoes and purple onions with shmaltz herring, toasted bagels and cream cheese, deviled eggs, Lithuanian rye with several slices of Ukranian black, good hot New York coffee, not the tepid brown water of Southern California . . .

But the fridge is empty. Only some crusts of dry French bread and a droopy carrot turned black. Why didn't I pick up that jar of herring last night when I thought of it? Gristede's was still open. I fall back onto the bed, depressed, miserable. The Sunday morning debauch is over. How nasty this bed is! I can't untangle the sheets. All night I struggled in them like an octopus in a trap. My face will be a mass of wrinkles today. Dark moons under my eyes. The brown paint will have so many creases to fill I'll look like a road map. Is it really only one week since I left home?

The tiny TV set sits on the chair with a forlorn face. The only channel it plays well enough to see is 13. Late last night I saw Pavarotti talk to adoring students and elderly ladies at

Juilliard. One young girl with bangs and long straight hair wept into the camera. "He's great," she sobbed. "We are so lucky, so lucky . . ." What I wouldn't give to watch the last game of the play-offs this afternoon. But all week I've fiddled with the little beast and the best I can make out is two dark areas on a noisy white screen. One is to the right of the other and slightly above it. There's about two inches between them. I think they are the pitcher and the batter. They are playing in a snowstorm. Kansas City too is going down before the Easterners. Bad luck! This is the second year in a row I've been on the road for the play-offs. Last year I was in Santa Barbara. Willy Wilson can't be more depressed than I am this morning.

Staring at the crooked door frame again. The moulding is badly cracked. When I switch on the ceiling light I see two different colors of white paint where they patched the worst cracks so they wouldn't show. There are two closets on the same wall as the door—one twelve-foot wall with three badly fitting doors. There isn't room between them to hang a small picture or a calendar. Nowhere in this room is there a thought for the people who live in it. The disdain is blatant. The only considerate note comes from the lightbulbs in the closets. These automatically turn on when the door opens. It is friendly being greeted by a lightbulb in a closet. But such thoughtfulness could only have come from a former tenant. How many lonely women before me have lived in this dark hole in the wall? But they weren't camping. They were surrounded by the props salvaged from years of living. A round mahogany coffee table covered with snapshots on plastic stands. Three ladies on a couch, hands clasped primly over skirt-covered knees. "Sisters," she explains. "Difficult family. Poor things, they always had to live in Alicia's shadow and she was never a gracious person." A dashing young man with a coat flung over one shoulder standing by a train. "Yes, him." She shrugs. "One day he was here and then he wasn't." "Did he ever come back," you ask. "He is so handsome." "Perhaps." She thinks but can't remember. "It is not important, *ma petite.* He is gone now, certainly." An older platinum print of a fierce looking woman holding the hand of a little girl. "*Maman*," she says and picks up the paperweight. A snowstorm of roses. Greetings from Cologne in small gold letters at the side. "One night in the railway station in that dismal city, I bought myself a real *souvenir* as normal people do. It is pretty, *n'est-ce pas?*" She pours tea from the polished brass samovar into tiny cups bearing a coat of arms. "A gift from Lord M." She smiles and turns away. It is an affecting moment and you are courteous and say nothing. You look at the walls crowded with the souvenirs of the traveling artist's life—a signed letter from Braunshveig thanking her for her help in the season gone by. You notice there is no mention of the following season. Perhaps it was still too early to plan. In a narrow wooden frame there is a fan letter from a little girl in London with flower petals pressed against the glass. A relative? "She was killed in the bombings," she answers. "She would have been a great dancer. Already she was in the third form." Rows of signed publicity photos, 8 x 10s of Liuba Tchernicheva as Zobeide. Frederick Franklin as a soaring James—"Such a nice man." A romantic head shot of Baronova in braids. A serious face with great soulful eyes looking mournfully out at the camera, "Good luck, your friend Leonid" in a tight little scrawl in the corner. A framed snapshot of a large man accompanying two ladies in mink leaving a theatre. "Spessivtseva," she says sadly. "Olga had everything but luck."

But I have no souvenirs. I never figured on furnishing my apartment. I'm only putting on a good show on Central Park West for a very short time. Marcia's paying the rent. But what if my new life were to last for a year? I would have to then, wouldn't I? Without the souvenirs of my ballerina past I couldn't get through. They would compensate me for the fatalism I would have to live with every day. My ballerina couldn't go back to California in a couple of weeks and turn in her decorous old life for the scrappy life of a California conceptualist.

I must get up but when I try I fall down again.

I'm like the birds after the rain, their feathers almost too waterlogged to get off the ground. They swoop low. Once one nearly dashed into my face. He cried with fear. I heard him. I don't have the strength to cry. Is it really only a week since I left California? I don't remember the old life anymore. I am grown senile like my mother. I will repeat the same question over and over. "How was lunch, Mother?"

"Did I have lunch?"

Think about my dogs. The sounds they make. Mozart jumps into the air with little cries when Blaise brings her food. No, no, she greets her food with short percussive barks, she whimpers when she's hoarding a rock in her mouth and showing off. She can't bark without dropping the rock and Suzy is waiting to grab it. When you sit on the porch Suzy begins her fierce basso barks. Relentless staccato rhythm, she won't let you off until you throw a rock for her. Carmichael barks only at night. No, that was poor Haydn barking on the porch at night, playing King of the Mountain to the valley. That's how we knew it was her and not Suzy—when she died I could sleep through the night for the first time in years. Yes, but sometimes I still hear that bark and wake up. Carmichael warning off the coyotes and skunks. I would lie awake trying to figure out who took over Haydn's job. Probably Mozart. There's a hysterical note. Carmichael is too lazy to care. How little I remember. What kind of person am I anyway? When the FBI gives its informants new names and sometimes even new faces and moves them to other parts of the country, they get depressed and homesick for the old lives that aren't there anymore. They can't get it together and spend their time in front of the TV set. Some of these people are gangsters, killers, but they're as faithful as David's mother, who's always wanting to go home, meaning 70 years ago to her mother and sisters in Scranton. Am I so coarse that I can take on another life so quickly and so well? I really haven't changed then from the adolsecent who had no self and became an actress so she could borrow other people's. I'm still a quick study. I only have to do something twice for it to become a habit. Maybe that's why it was so easy for me to stop smoking.

But even though I don't remember the old life much, nostalgia for it is killing me. Last night, in one of my dreams I saw a rolling green golf course with people walking sedately around, only instead of looking for golf balls, they were looking at graves.

Now I'm crying.

But that's absurd. I've never been on a golf course. I was in a cemetery only once; and when I stumbled on a foot-high stone and read *MOTHER*, I had a laughing fit and had to be forcibly removed from my grandmother's funeral.

Someone is walking around on the floor above. Her heels pick up speed with the light patter of rain. She comes to rest. I don't hear her anymore. There she is again, running quickly out of the room. Now she is at the other end of the apartment. The rain is very faint now. She has a purpose, that woman. It does me good to listen to her. But here in my hand I have the note I found last night shoved under my door.

Dear Mrs. 5G,
You probably are unaware but your high heels make a lot of noise and give me a headache. I know you will alleviate this condition and stop doing this to me.
(Signed) Mrs. 4G

I could send this note directly to Mrs. 6G overhead only I don't want to lose her. It's comforting to know that another person is close by. A door slams in the hall. My floor creaks. A police siren goes by with the menacing chant that makes me think of Anne Frank . . . I never hear voices in my house.

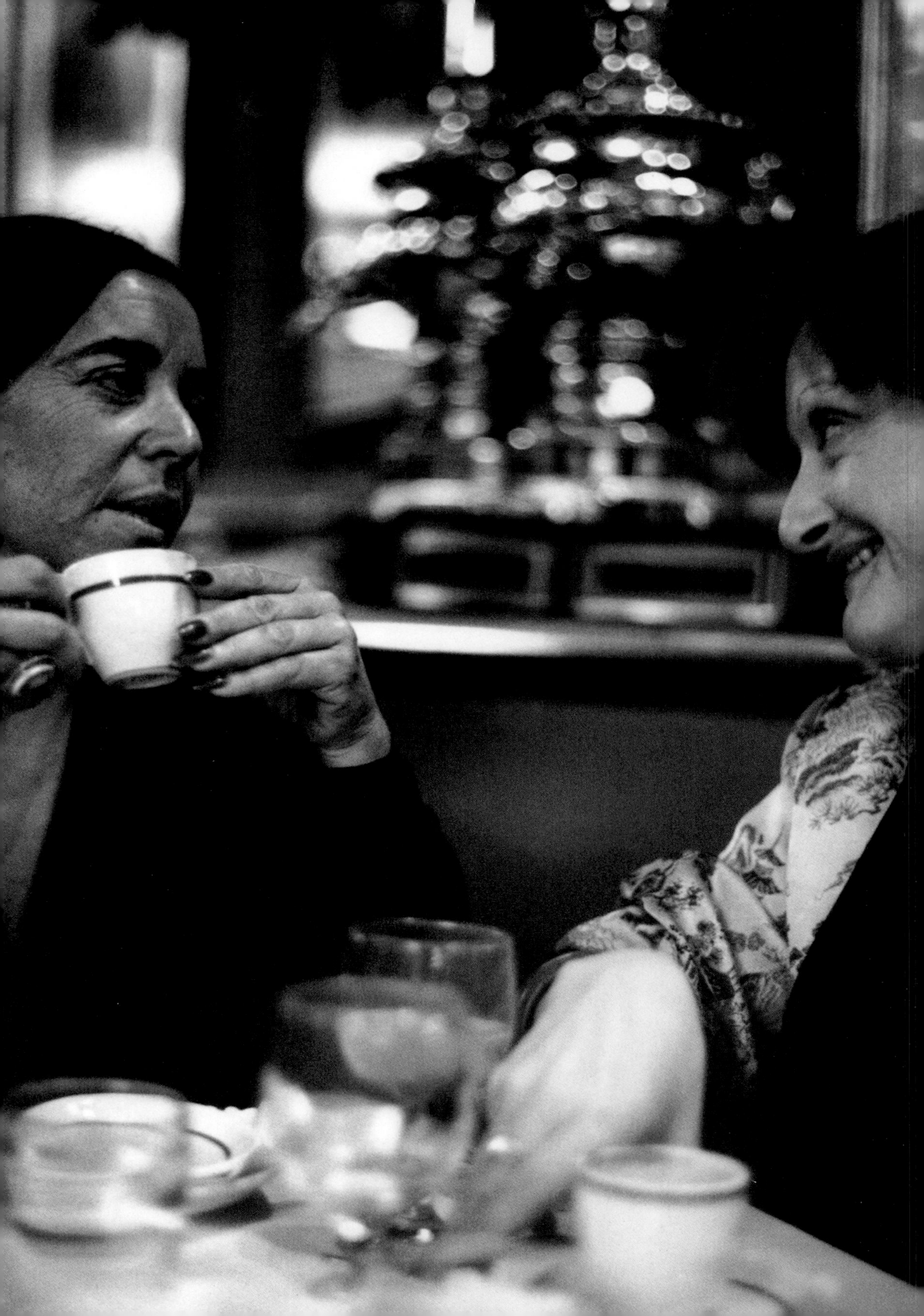

MONDAY ***October 20***

Just back from dinner with Anna. Met first at Raoul's for a drink. Curious how Antinova would feel in an expensive restaurant run by Algerian right-wingers.

Anna was late and I waited for her at the bar. The makeup had gone especially well, and observing myself in the mirror behind the bar I felt like one of those black models from *Vogue.* I sipped my drink with my head turned at different angles. Too bad the Chivas came in a clunky, square glass, but I had been embarrassed to order sherry. The most interesting pose turned out to be a partial head turn with my eyes staring mysteriously over the rim of the glass, one eyebrow arched, with what I took to be irony; but I really couldn't see too well. It was cocktail lounge lighting and I wasn't wearing my glasses.

I turned to the bartender and tried to interest him in a friendly conversation. He was a big, tightly muscled Mediterranean who looked like he spent his free hours in a bodybuilding gym. Even though business was slow he ignored my attempts at conversation. After my third try he turned his back on me and went to the other end of the bar.

I felt a hot blush on my face but I don't think anyone noticed under my dark skin. Anyway there were very few people at the bar and nobody was paying any attention. I felt like a failure. Had he read my real age? He wasn't so young himself. Who did he think he was anyway? Maybe he was a racist. He could be one of Raoul's relatives. Maybe he had tortured dark-skinned Algerians during the war.

I felt the anger start down in my stomach.

"Now calm down," I warned myself. "What if he's not a racist? What if he's only gay?"

He was one of those well-preserved, young-looking men whose age is hard to figure, who you usually place somewhere in the middle forties because people put the worst light on things. That would easily make him a candidate for action in the French-Algerian War. He looked like a mercenary, with his careful movements, that impassive closed face . . .

Suddenly, instinctively, I knew he was gay. The sort of gay for whom women don't exist. That's pretty racist, isn't it? Uh, uh, paranoia . . . I started to laugh. He heard me and looked up without the least curiosity. He made me feel like a pathetic old woman all dressed up with no place to go. I got depressed again. Since I became Antinova I've gotten entirely too dependent upon seeing myself in other people's faces not to be hurt by a blank one. Any blank one . . .

I'm insatiable for admiration. But how could I not be when I only know I'm really Antinova by the way people look at me . . .

I put down a bill for another drink. He ignored it. Nobody else at the bar had money showing. It was a long time since I sat alone at a bar. In the old days you put your money down and paid on delivery. A courtesy. But the custom must have changed. It gives me away as low class. Probably only dives still require cash on delivery. I banged the money with my fist. Hell, I come from Harlem! No white creep is going to put me down.

"Another Chivas," I demanded in a loud voice.

He took his own sweet time about it and fastidiously avoided my money when he finally brought the drink.

"You paying?" I sneered.

I was all set to have my first experience of being thrown out of a bar, when Anna rescued me. She sailed through the door bringing a blast of cold air and scented furs. She laughed when she saw me all dressed up and said she knew from my voice over the phone that something was up.

We went to some Greek restaurant "where everybody goes now." Still the same old Anna, sensitive to the smallest scene shift. But she seemed shorter than I remembered, until I realized I was wearing high heels and, for the first time since I knew her, she was wearing flat ones. She had led me all around Italy, a grand Italian dealer in furs and leather, balancing above me and everybody else in six-inch heels, while my short legs scrambled to keep up—a scruffy little American artist in jeans and sneakers. Italian men used to turn around and laugh at us in the streets. Mutt and Jeff. Sometimes I got so enraged I would give them the finger, and Anna would get scared because you don't do that to a man in Italy. He could kill you. "Let him try!" I was always on the edge of tears. The loss of my language had devastated me. I didn't know any Italian at all; and when they condescended to speak with me, it was in simplistic platitudes, because they had learned English but didn't really *know* it. I was appalled to hear myself respond in some kind of pidgin. I was helpless like a child and enraged by my impotence.

Now, years later, I leaned nonchalantly back in my seat and listened to Anna's morose conversation. The old scene is depressed, alienated. There's no good art being done anymore. No creativity.

What was this scene she was talking about? Was I part of it? She implied a sense of collusion, of belonging. But I didn't feel like that. As a matter of fact I was beginning to feel insulted being told such things at the very moment I was sitting across from her—a living artwork giving her a private showing. Wasn't I creative?

She felt there was no longer any continuity with the young, who aren't very interesting anyway, though as usual they manage to work themselves up over the silly things they are doing.

"But Anna, when I was a young artist, the older ones didn't move over to make room for me . . ."

"It's a period of reaction," she insisted.

Has she taken out a subscription to *Newsweek*? It was fascinating. Would she lecture me about 'quality' next—

"Even Alana Heiss is getting married," she finished triumphantly.

I tried to cheer her up. Italian New Image. That looked sort of lively.

"They are not sincere," she said.

But I thought it was a good thing. You know, the New Regionalism. All of us colonials getting back at the New York oppressors.

She shrugged.

"Italians will always hate themselves. It is their fate."

She and Giorgio are fixing up a new loft in the West Thirties, near where Marcia had her old one. Marcia was right. The Lower West Side is the coming chic.

Anna complained about the workmen.

"Nobody does an honest day's work anymore. There is no quality. No pride in their work."

I agreed the American worker is a goldbrick. Getting something for nothing is built into the American system. But to hear an old Art World European Leftist sound like a retired admiral from Rancho Santa Fe at her first confrontation with a real live worker seemed a little strange. I remembered a couple of kid artists who presented documentation of a restaurant where they were working, in the hope of transforming the workers' grievances into political action. "And what do you have to teach a dishwasher who's been washing dishes for twenty years," I shouted at them. "Your mothers have been doing yours for years."

Anna told me about her recent summer trip to the Greek islands with Giorgio. Her expressive mouth turned up at the corners like a gentle comic mask while her great eyes looked tragic. Anna's eyes have two expressions—tragic or cynical. "It was decadent and magical at the same time. The old culture is everywhere. In every rock. Every face."

But Italy isn't exactly New Amsterdam. I thought of the gloomy arcades of Bologna. That was surely a medieval stage set.

She snorted with contempt. With Anna it is always all or nothing. She dismissed Bologna.

"Gothic!"

Anna: "Greece is pagan. Etruscan."

Me: "Etruscan?"

Anna: "I mean Achaean. Every man is Ulysses."

Me: "And every woman, Iphigenia?"

Just like an Italian to have an inferiority complex about Greece. For me Italy was the ancient past—the Renaissance, the Middle Ages—Rome! But she had inherited it and for her it was a discotheque, a shopping center.

She looked to the Isles of Greece for glamour.

She told me of a kind of pumice stone that they use there to remove body hair. They rub it gently into the skin and the hairs come away cleanly and without pain. It is very ancient. Goes back to Cleopatra. Just like *Vogue*. The beauticians found Anna fascinating, because she hardly has any hair on her legs to begin with. She was polished smooth like marble. Greeks are hairy.

"It is very sensual," she said, "to be worked on like Cleopatra."

I told her about how my new nails made such a change in my life. How I have had to learn to accomplish the simplest actions of daily life in a different way, so that everything I do takes more time and effort.

"The result is real pleasure in my accomplishments. No action is too small to be noticed. I have a stronger sense of the physical world."

I leaned over confidentially. I knew she would understand.

"Above all there is a strong sensual streak to my new experiences. I am always watching myself, so I enjoy my movements, the feel of things. Nothing I do goes unnoticed. I am both observer and observed. I'm like a kind of Peeping Tom looking into a mirror, and it turns me on."

I was silent a while, wondering whether I should confess what came next. The temptation to share it was too great.

"I am always conscious of helplessness and dependency now," I whispered. "It is an absurdly old fashioned feminine feeling. I am fascinated by my own vulnerability, excited by my softness. What it all boils down to is that I think I've fallen in love with myself."

I took a cab back uptown. It was beginning to rain and I was glad to get one right away. At least it hadn't been a repeat of the night before, when I couldn't get a cab because nobody wanted a black passenger so late at night. I settled comfortably into the warm leather seat, prepared for a sleepy late-night drive.

The driver was a kid with a punk haircut and leather jacket. Through the windshield mirror I saw a long, bony, very pale face with dark glasses. He looked an odd type for a cab driver, but then at night there were all sorts of moonlighters and part-timers. Maybe he was a Viet Vet working his way through college.

I didn't have much time to think about it, because we began picking up speed and went though a couple of red lights to catch up with the staggered greens. We dashed between other taxis for a couple of blocks and screeched to a halt only when a cab stopped to pick up a passenger and we couldn't dart out of the way. We tapped the guy's bumper and he started yelling, but by squeezing between him and an oncoming car, we lost him. We turned onto Eighth Avenue as if it was the Indianapolis Speedway. The driver bent fiercely over the wheel, his nose thrust up against the flooded windshield, as the wiper scrambled over the glass trying to keep up with the rain. It had begun to fall heavily by then, and the streets were a blur of red and yellow lights as we flashed by. There was a truck double-parked in our lane with some people standing by the door on the street side. We headed straight for them. My driver never swerved. I closed my eyes and somehow they escaped. A fire engine came up the street, and when everyone pulled over to the side we raced ahead of it, then made a right across the slower lanes into a side street and careened down two narrow blocks to Sixth Avenue, where we picked up the traffic again.

I didn't say a word. It was pretty obvious by then that I had hit bad luck. The driver was a speed freak and my instincts told me to lay low. He must have been enjoying scaring me to death, because I caught him looking back at me in the mirror. I maintained a stony face and stared out the window. Fuck him! That lousy little amphetamine head was having his fun and I wouldn't give an inch. Damn it, would I be killed in a cab driven by a refugee from a chain and leather bar before I had the chance to finish my Antinova piece?

At Sixty-Third he made a U-turn in the middle of the street, narrowly escaping a collision with the oncoming traffic. Fortunately for us, cars drive fairly sedately down Central Park West, but we could still hear the echoes of the protesting car horns from the next block when the doorman opened the door for me.

"You're one hell of a driver," I said with just a shade of irony.

"Thanks. It's in my blood," he confessed shyly, forgetting he had deliberately tried to scare me to death. He probably got his kicks from scaring women.

I couldn't resist leading him on some more.

"Thanks," I said. "I enjoyed that a whole lot."

He beamed and gave me a military salute. He seemed totally disarmed and would probably have driven me around the city the rest of the night for free.

From the *Century* doorway I watched an elderly couple getting into the cab after me. They were congratulating themselves for getting one so quickly. There were very few cabs around at this time of the night—most of them were midtown, waiting for the theatres and clubs to let out. Should I warn them? The small portly gentleman with the dapper grey moustache and the checkered fedora wouldn't thank me, nor would his wife, trying to protect her blue-grey perm from the rain with a copy of the *New York Times.* I would only be making a problem for them—a dark lady coming out of the night to prevent them from getting into the cab they were so lucky to get. They would think I was a hysterical woman. Obviously I wasn't normal. Look how frantic I was getting. Or if I could control my anger, they might think I was a cold-hearted rich woman who was against the workers. Wasn't the cabbie a worker? And here I was heading for *The Century*—one of the class buildings on Central Park West. I could be a racist. What was a colored girl doing anyway in such a fancy building late at night? I could be a call girl maybe. Or a terrorist. Like Angela Davis. She used to dress up nice too and look what kind of a person she was. They looked like nice liberal people and I was putting them into a bind because I was black and they didn't want to let on they were afraid of me. They would end up taking the cab anyway because they needed one, and they wouldn't want to insult the cab driver, who must be innocent. After all, he has a legitimate license. The man would probably stall for time by studying the license with a great show of interest. Maybe the doormen would be dragged into it and have to vouch for me; and what could they say? "This is Madame Antinova. She's staying in the Goodman apartment for three weeks." See, what did I tell you. They would look knowingly at each other. "A prostitute." Then that bastard of a cabbie would certainly drive them home like the little old lady from Pasadena. They would all talk about me and decide I was a poor crazy woman. So many lonely people around. It isn't safe to walk the streets anymore . . .

I waved good-bye and the bastard waved back as if we were conspirators. I suppose at that moment we were. I relinquished the problem. It was theirs now, I thought, as he pulled away from the curb, leaving rubber.

TUESDAY ***October 21***

Lunch with Kim Levin in an expensive East Side restaurant. Discreet lighting. Rolled linen napkins. Hovering waiters. I would have preferred the sleepy old Art Deco Automat on West 57th. We could have eaten beans baked in a ceramic jug with a mug of strong coffee as we sat by the graceful window in the mellow light and an elderly woman sleepily bussed the tables. Outside, dancers would hurry by on their way to the rehearsal studios up the block. But the Automat isn't there anymore.

"Here's my black story," Kim said.

John drove a cab nights when he first came to America from England. He was waiting for his pilot's license to come through. One evening a black guy carrying three heavy shopping bags asked to be driven over the bridge to the Bronx. They chatted pleasantly before pulling up in a deserted street. The buildings looked empty. "They're tearing down the old neighborhood to build a city project," the man explained in disgust. "My mother's holding out to the end. Until they promise her she can move into one of the new apartments." He waved a hundred dollar bill under John's nose and said it was all he had so he yelled up to his mother to bring down a twenty. She didn't hear him so he left the bags on the back seat and went upstairs to get the money. John began to worry. An old black man shuffled up to the car. "Whatcha doin'?" he asked. "Waiting for my passenger to get the fare from his mother," John answered. The old man wheezed into a handkerchief. "What's in them grocery bags?" Garbage. Old newspapers. "They do that all the time around here, young fella!"

On our way out of the restaurant, we stole fresh strawberries from a serving tray.

Dinner in North Moore Street below Canal above Chambers at Peter and Jack's place. We drive through blocks of empty lots and partially demolished buildings to reach the solitary high rise standing like a lighthouse in a sea of rubble. "What is this place?" The cabbie whistles when the hefty black doorman helps me out of the cab. The name on the license is Israeli. "America," I answer cheerfully.

The apartment is a snug nest high above the city. Books of all colors and sizes crowd shelves assembled with wood planks and concrete blocks. Together with small paintings and prints they hide most of the stark white plasterboard walls. Scattered typing paper, sketch books, art magazines, miniature constructions, artist's books, end tables with softly lit lamps, cuddly resting places fill up the little box living room and make it look larger than it is. Jack's polished little harpsichord is settled in too. It's come all the way from California. Young couples used to have apartments like this on the Upper West Side or further up in Washington Heights, sometimes if they were lucky in the West Village or perhaps in a six story brick house on a quiet sunny block in Chelsea. The apartments were larger then; landlords were only just beginning to substitute modern kitchens and bathrooms for old fashioned space and thick walls. From the '40s on, the buildings got more meager with every decade, and the meagerer they got the more they cost. I used to see an analyst several mornings a week in the late '50s whose neighbor coughed regularly all through the session. One morning he didn't cough and I wondered if he was sick. Sometimes though, a couple was lucky—somebody died; and the energetic pair shelled out fifty dollars to the super before any of the other readers of the *New York Times* classified section heard of it, and the next day moved into a spacious apartment with a real kitchen. When they were built back in the '30s or '40s, these apartments often had sunken living rooms. I never got the hang of them and always tripped on the carpeted stairs. Like in Armand and Dolores' old place on Nineteenth Street. where I further discomforted myself by habitually sitting down on wet diapers. Sometimes the young couples were in graduate school together, but more often the wife was teaching junior high in Bedford Stuyvesant and he was a struggling young poet who slept late. The apartments were furnished with proceeds from the wedding each couple more or less submitted to. I remember one couple, Lit. Majors, he was Dr. Johnson and she was Trollope. She refused to be married by a rabbi and sit on a dais under a green arbor in a catered dining room and collect envelopes like a medieval Moroccan, but he was practical and insisted they had no other way to furnish an apartment. Did she want to live with his mother on Ocean Parkway? She gave in; and by the time the shopping and rehearsals and catering and invitations and ruffled feelings were over, the groom wanted to chuck the whole thing and elope. But she was a fierce person. "It was your idea," she reminded him grimly. "Now that I've put in all this work, I'm going to get something out of it, damn it."

I feel old and awkward and burdened with boring memories. What am I doing here celebrating a young couple's anniversary when I never knew the date of my own? Since I was a kid my attitude to celebrations and holidays has always been practical—how long is the vacation!

We are in the dinette, the euphemism landlords use for the alcove set off from the kitchen by a small partition. It's just the kind my mother always wanted but couldn't afford. Now that she's nearly seventy and retired to San Diego she has one but she doesn't cook much anymore, just sits at the table in her dinette with a deck of cards and tells her fortune.

Jack is working hard to impress me only I don't understand the message.

"Real china." She lays a decorative looking dish in front of me. "In Antinova's honor!"

To be polite I make a point of studying the floral pattern closely. I ostentatiously lift the heavy silver. This must be the real thing. Suddenly I'm back in the early '60s. A conversation with Trisha Brown. We are leaning against a parked car on Sullivan Street, trying to impress each other with our liberation from traditional "girl" things.

"And we don't use anything but stainless steel," she says proudly.

"We don't use stainless steel," I answer scornfully.

"We do," David interrupts.

"We do not," I shout. "I wouldn't be caught dead with stainless steel."

To this day Trisha probably thinks I crack my boiled eggs in the morning with a silver spoon. But the fact is, I didn't know what stainless steel was. It sounded modern and expensive. Too fancy, I was sure, for our virtuously tacky utensils.

Peter's big head of red hair flames cheerfully around his face. He wears it like a halo. He takes to marriage like a fish to water or a bird to air. How graciously he accepts the dishes Jack sets before him. It's as if he's been doing it for years. He expands before my eyes. Who would have guessed little Peter had such a talent for marriage? He should have been born married, he's wasted too much time already.

Ken beams with the proprietory air of the old family friend. The evening paper lies open on his lap so he can drop out and read when the conversation lags. He gives the impression that he comes to dinner every night. Is this why Peter treats him with affectionate exasperation? A bachelor friend must feel like a leftover to a newly wedded man. Ken is the third man but he isn't embarrassed by it. I don't think he notices. He accepts Jack's service as if it's coming to him. Same for Peter's generosity in sharing her. What else are old friends for?

He is doing an exhibition for the Woman's Inter-Art Center. It will probably be a retrospective. Everytime I've seen a show of Ken's it's been a retrospective, and he can't be more than thirty.

"Why don't you do a new piece?" I ask him. "Retrospectives are death. Look what it did to Don Judd."

"But I have a large body of work they don't know in New York," he objects. "Other people are given credit for things I did years ago."

"There's no justice in the world. There's only luck. And you've just got a piece of it. You're doing a show at the Woman's Inter-Art Center and you aren't even a woman. I call that luck!"

"But what about my old work? I can't just forget it."

"Who's reminding you? If you show it now people will say you're not original. They've seen it before."

I suggest a set of narrative drawings similar to the ones he used in the performance I saw in La Jolla. "Your drawings are terrific," I encourage him. "Besides, that funky primitive style is in fashion now. You'll look snappy. Up to date. Interesting. Young."

"But I'm not young. I've been around since I was fourteen. I was Fluxus West when I was still in high school."

The problem of encouraging children, I thought sourly. After excommunicating practically everybody from Fluxus, George was willing to take anybody else—even a child.

"Making art is dead anyway," he says. "I think being a critic is the only way to go."

Jack carries in a large serving tray. Two handsomely baked chickens lie in a bed of small white potatoes.

The husband pushes back his chair and stands up for the first time since dinner began. The wife ties a starched white apron around his waist. She hands him a gleaming cutlery knife and an ornate pair of poultry shears. They study the birds together. It is an impressive sight. A ballerina would envy the high arch of the graceful breasts. The crisp brown skins gleam in the overhead light like expensive Chinese paper.

"Good looking birds," Ken says.

We hold our collective breaths while the host places the blade delicately along the slope of one breast. He teases gently with the tip then suddenly presses firmly down. Bones crunch.

"More to the right," his wife suggests.

Host: "What part do you want?"

Everybody says: "White."

Peter gives Ken a disapproving look.

Ken shrugs apologetically.

"Well, there are two chickens," he says.

And finally I get the message. They're going to all this trouble for Antinova. Jack has a show coming up in a few weeks in Philadelphia. Still she takes the time to prepare Antinova an elegant dinner. She was your student, for God's sake. She's probably lonely here. Peter's an old fan from *Gain Ground* days in '69, when he was still an undergraduate at Columbia. Ken presented you with a dozen roses when you did *Before the Revolution* at the Kitchen, this evening is an *homage.* Like Kim this afternoon wanting to go to an elegant restaurant even though she's short of money. She wanted to *dine* with Antinova, not grab a sandwich. As a retired ballerina you should appreciate their efforts to rise to your occasion. But tonight because this youthful situation provoked unpleasant memories of the fifties when you were young and miserable, you misunderstood their sweet intentions. You are a nasty, bad tempered old woman.

I think I'm beginning to freak out. I know what I need, a good fuck, that's what. With who? David is 3,000 miles away. I couldn't make it with anyone else even if I wanted to. I can see myself camping in my shabby apartment without furniture except for the sheet covering the window—"Well?" Am I a savage? One must cover the windows!" A nice young man is staring down at my radiantly white body ending just above the nipples and a little below the elbows in a rich, sumptuous brown.

"Too much sun," I try to brazen it out. "And don't come too close please. I'm impermanent."

Later Jack lends me a pair of earrings painted with the startled face of Mme. Vigee le Brun's teenage daughter. It matches my ring.

"For Madame Antivova," she curtsies.

You have to admire her. She's a charming actress. Even now in the perverse role of wifey she carries herself with panache. And who am I to quarrel with actors? Just because I don't think too much of the play? They certainly play it with dedication and seriousness. They've done their research. But looking at Jack's delicious little face I worry about Peter. He's so incorrigibly innocent. What will happen to him if the curtain comes down?

WEDNESDAY ***October 22***

Left two blouses with the 24-hour cleaners downstairs by the side entrance. It will be easy to pick them up tomorrow when I get home. Turns out the crook who owns the place figured that one out too. $7.50 to launder two blouses! I ask the girl at the counter to repeat the price. I'm not sure I heard her right. She's a young black woman with a desperately unattractive sullen face, so dark it's hard to see her features since she deliberately holds her head down out of the light. It's embarrassing. Her bad luck incriminates me. It's not fair to have exotic blue eyes and comparatively light skin with gay touches of rouge running up to my ears, when her body is shapeless and you know that if you touched her, her skin would feel like leather. Why should she smile at me? We aren't friends.

As usual when pennies are at stake, I get cheap. I can't make up my mind whether to leave the blouses and be robbed or go to the trouble of looking for a more reasonable place.

A tall unwholesome looking white man in shirt sleeves comes out from the back, where rows of cleaned clothes packed in glistening plastic bags hang from ceiling pulleys. A shorter man with a brown hat and bulky overcoat peers nervously over his shoulder.

"You got a problem?" the tall man says.

"No," I answer, not without some amusement—he looks so bugged. "Just surprised. I'm new in the neighborhood."

I can't believe it. The bastard is actually sneering. He doesn't believe I live here at all. What did I do, come down from Harlem for the honor of overpaying him? Cool it! You have an appointment with Sean and Ida. They're waiting to see a run through of tomorrow's performance. You have no time to run around Broadway looking for a sympathetic laundry, and you certainly don't want to wash these shirts by hand. You'd have to borrow an iron too. That does it. I try to placate him with a whimsical smile. It usually works. I hold out the clothes in a gesture of peace, but he doesn't take them. He just lets them fall on the counter in front of him. They are inexpensive blouses, and after many washings the threads have become frayed and torn. With my dirty clothes lying out there on the counter, I feel exposed, naked. Dirty laundry is embarrassing enough, but to have it rejected by the laundry man is worse. My face grows hot. I'm stunned. All of a sudden these people have dragged me into a scene. The little man with the hat can't control his glee and begins to jump up and down. Is the laundry man showing off for his brother-in-law? I know the game. It's called *Step on the Shvartsa.* She's only a girl and can't hit back. I could make them sit up all right with a couple of well chosen Yiddish expletives. But I restrain myself. This is no time for self expression. I used to see men like him when I visited my father's furniture store in Harlem years ago. All along 125th Street the shop windows of the discount furniture stores displayed their gaudy merchandise under signs promising easy credit. Some were fatalists like my sweet natured father, who found himself selling furniture in a ghetto, when he would much rather have been inventing new machines. He invariably treated his customers with a natural courtesy they appreciated, even when they knew he was cheating them. My father was the best salesman on the block because he was a nice guy. But there were some like this man, miserable bastards eaten up with ulcers and bad sinuses, who blamed the customers for their own failures and enjoyed the grim game of cheating the poor as a kind of revenge. A large sale never failed to unleash a flow of contempt for the departing customer. "You should be grateful," I once told my father's partner, a second cousin who, together with his bookkeeper wife, was embezzling several hundred a month because my father was too embarrassed to confront him. "Those animals?" He spat on the floor. Now, years later, I see the same soft flesh hanging over this one's belt. Too many dinners of overcooked beef and potatoes with frozen vegetables. Too many late night tuna sandwiches on white bread and Sarah Lee cream cheese cakes. The only exercise he gets is when he can't find a parking place on the block. Traffic jams, pinochle games, breath fresheners, and cigarettes, and on Sundays bar mitzvahs with a heavily girdled wife and cranky overfed children. Every time he looks at a person he calculates his worth to the lowest common denominator. It's a particularly Jewish trait. A guest at my mother's hotel once asked David if I was his twentieth choice or closer to his tenth. This man had a theory that every man's first choice was always Elizabeth Taylor or Marilyn Monroe, but life was unjust and most men had to work their way down the list to their tenth or eleventh choice. That amiable cheerless man had worked all his life as a mailman. At my mother's hotel his small wife consumed several bowls of cold cereal together with shmaltz herring and eggs for breakfast every morning and two steaks for dinner. She was skinny and quick as a sparrow, and outlasted everybody on the dance floor, till sometime in her seventies she dropped dead one night in the middle of a *czardas.* Within a month her mailman followed her out of this world. Which means, I suppose, that given the full range of numerical possibilities, a tenth choice can occasionally give you a full house. But this man in the cleaning store never pulled a good hand.

My skin stretches tight and dry across my face. I'm turning into a wrinkled prune. My eyes are too strained to focus on anything. My lips are clamped shut. I don't think I could say anything without croaking. Why should I let this bastard inconvenience me? He has to accept my blouses. This is America, for God's sake.

"Here." I shove them at the girl without looking at her. I can't bear to see the expression on her face again. It's the same one I can feel on my own. She quickly makes out the ticket. I made her react to me anyway. She's trying to defuse the scene and get me out of there as fast as possible. OK, sister, I'm going. Out on the street I remember I didn't check for a brown ring around the collar. It doesn't matter. They'll just think I wear too much makeup. It wouldn't occur to anybody in that store that a white woman would go around passing.

At the corner I hail a cab. I need some quiet time to calm down and unravel the events in the cleaning store. But the cabbie begins to complain about his wife.

"I'm a good provider," he says. "I work overtime. My whole paycheck I give to her. So what, I keep a few extra dollars from tips. A fella needs a glass of beer with his pals, don't he?"

His voice has the gravelly tones of a heavy smoker but he whines like an overfed dog wriggling around on the carpet, making believe he's still the cute little puppy he used to be.

"A couple of bucks for a little fun now and then? Ain't a guy got the right?" He looks back at me and waits for an answer. I'm afraid we'll hit someone so I agree it doesn't sound unreasonable.

He appears satisfied and hums an old Sinatra tune, swinging his head and shoulders with the syncopated rhythm.

"You married?"

"Yes."

"You live there on Central Park West?"

"Yes."

We stop for a red light and he turns around and looks me up and down.

"You're my type," he whistles. "I could give you a good time. You know that."

He's too fat to fit into the driver's seat without jamming his stomach up against the steering wheel. We're going through the Park and when he swings around a curve he sucks in his breath so the wheel can turn.

"Hey, ya hear me?"

"Yeah, I hear you."

"Well?"

"Well, what?"

"You're my type, that's what."

His confidence is amazing, and he isn't even white, he's diabetic yellow.

"My wife is a constipated woman," he says. "That's her trouble. I can tell you're not a constipated woman."

"How can you tell?"

He throws his head back and roars with laughter.

"Lady, I been driving a cab for years. What I don't know about people . . ." He snaps his fingers. "You don't need a college degree to know what I know."

"So how do you know?"

"That's easy. You're sweet. Relaxed. You don't nag a man."

He winks at me in the windshield mirror.

"I know more about you than your mamma."

We turn onto Madison just a few blocks from the gallery.

"The traffic's bad," I say. "I'll walk from here."

His sad watery eyes plead with me.

"Sure you won't change your mind?"

I wave him away and cross the street. I can feel his eyes follow me up the block. It's not hard to guess what he's thinking. White men! Yuk!

The rehearsal was a success. Sean says the performance is magical. He wraps me in a kind of chivalric courtesy. I think he would like to throw his loden coat in the mud and escort me over it. With my long nails and deliberately feminine makeup and clothes, I must seem fragile and vulnerable to a kindhearted man. He enjoys protecting me. Since he just started working at the gallery he must think this is my natural condition. When I come in in the morning he tells me I'm beautiful. I like him to come close so we can smell my perfume together. He may have a crush on me. Probably because his wife is expecting a baby any minute and he's at loose ends. But it's nice to have a charming young man at my beck and call.

Ida and I take off for a downtown restaurant, where I order chops and mushrooms and she dallies over an artichoke. She can't get over how glamourous I am.

"Not bad for an old lady," I agree.

"Don't talk about that. I just had a birthday."

"I never notice birthdays."

"Don't be superior. This one you'd notice."

"Did you celebrate?"

"Twice. Once for the others and once for myself."

It seems Gideon and the kids made a party for her at the loft. I think Beth and Scott took charge of everything. They bored her to death. Their goodwill made her buggy. She may have felt patronized. Couldn't wait to get away from them. Their unsolicited goodness depressed her for a week. The following Sunday, the actual day of her birthday, she and Gideon went to visit her mother in the nursing home. On the way back, on an impulse, she stopped to buy large quantities of luxury foods—paté and olives, caviar and smoked fish, imported cheese and crackers, several bottles of good French red—while Gideon sat it out in the car. When they got back to the loft he went to his room to read and she started to eat her goodies. After awhile she knocked on his door and invited him to her birthday party. They sat around gorging themselves and laughing at last week's dumb party and the arrogance of children and watched TV and made love and got drunk. "What a lovely birthday," I said.

"The best one I ever had," she agreed. "And I made it for myself. It was my birthday party for myself and I invited Gideon only because I felt like it."

Ida has one of the most strangely beautiful faces I have ever seen. A thoroughgoing disdain for the world stares out of the deep brown pools that are her eyes. She pulls her dark hair back from the aristocratic face without a semblance of coquetry. She is somber, furious, and unrelievedly desperate. She rarely has anything good to say about anything. Some people find her depressing. Her dependable pessimism invigorates me.

Staying with her is one of the great pleasures of my New York trips. I hope she doesn't feel left out because I'm living alone this time around. We both miss the closeness but I'm embarrassed to say anything about it. I think she's angry with me for seeing Anna again. I keep forgetting their historically possessive rivalry, it was always so submerged, never allowed to surface. I'm still afraid to say anything that will bring it out into the open, though I enjoy being fought over.

I confess that for the last few days I have been nasty and cruel because I'm horny. I have to be a suave and worldly ballerina for tomorrow's performance and I'm worried that my sexual frustration will poison everything. I've even been doing some light flirting with Sean, who's not only much younger than me but has a poor wife waiting to give birth as well. Now if that isn't the pits, what is! I couldn't have an affair even if I wanted to, because I'm two-toned. "It's like going to bed with Queeg Queeg, for God's sake!"

"Masturbate."

I couldn't. I never learned how. I haven't done it since I was a little kid. I used to perform such a complicated set of symbolic actions I get tired thinking about them. They embarrass me. I need to relax, calm down, not scare myself.

"Don't be a hypocrite," she dismisses my arguments. "What do you think women do who live alone? Do you think you're the only sexy woman in the world?"

It's now several hours later. I did it! For Art!

I was so scared I'd fuck up tomorrow's performance that I actually forced myself to do it, even though it was only a chore at first, something that had to be done for business reasons. I wasn't helped by my long nails. My fingers were pretty useless but the knuckles worked fine. I got tired somewhere along the way, but I persevered and ran it out like a jogger. Pretty soon I was home free. It became loose and easy, not scary at all. It's been over thirty-five years since I made love to myself, so the event took on the mysterious nature of ritual. It felt somehow spiritual. Like I was making connections. I was even in touch with the little girl I used to be. She stood by the bed, a friendly presence, though I was simpler than she had been, more directly sexual, less literary. "What ever are you doing, Big Eleanor?" she marveled. "You were too technological, dear," I explained. "Grown-ups are simpler, less prone to exaggeration." She sniffed and put her nose in the air. "It seems to me you are insufficiently intellectual about this." I gave her a pitying look. My breath was coming hard and fast now. "They call it love, honey. You wouldn't know anything about it." But she smiled happily just the same when it was over. She was very young. What do you expect from a virgin? So this is what Pavlova must have been doing all those lonely years on the road when people wondered about her and took guesses. They said she wasn't sexual, that she sublimated in her art. And all the time she was deceiving them with a secret lover. It's probably how Markova could stand traveling around the world year after year with that teasing faggot she traveled with. First Madame would consume a box of miraculous French chocolates and then she would retire to her silken sheets. All over the world, in hotel rooms and in sleeping cars, ballerinas are making love. *Mes amies,* I embrace you all, a thousand kisses . . .

Good night.

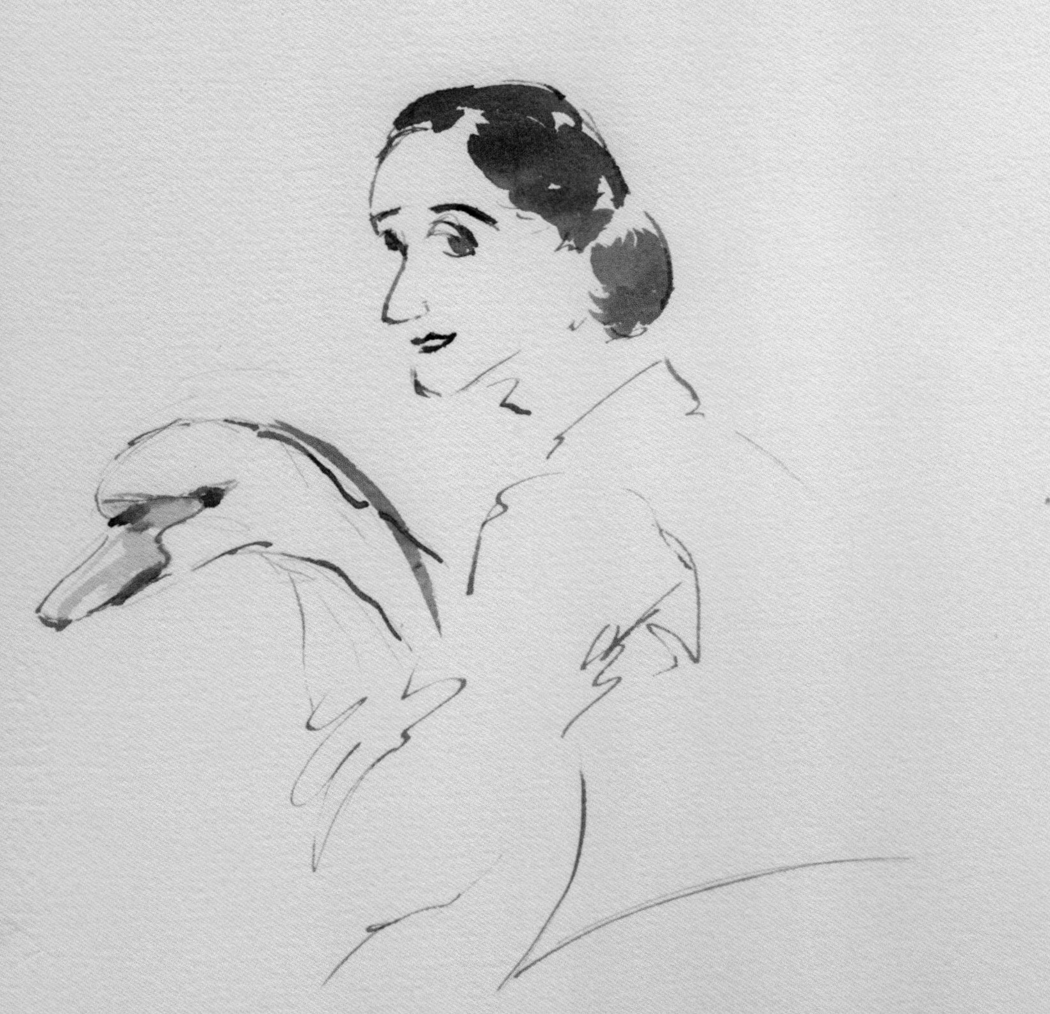

THURSDAY ***October 23***

The Antinova performance has a standard visiting artist format. Antinova chats with the audience about her life, art, friends and enemies, growing old, whatever comes into her head. She reads a chapter from her soon to be published *Memoirs* and shows slides of the work she did with the *Ballets Russes* back in the '20s. I have to be "up"— witty, catty, self-congratulatory, worldly, as a retired ballerina from the sophisticated Diaghilev company would be. By the time the performance ends, though, I'm revealed as a lonely old woman, whose art has been ignored by history and whose friends have died, leaving her ship-wrecked in an alien time. "Sometimes one feels as if one's memories are borrowed from a book," she says. "How can they be real if nobody else shares them?"

Tonight was the first performance and I was in state of grace. I scintillated. I was witty, sophisticated, light as a feather. I charmed the audience shamelessly. I knew I had this one even before I went on. I was so cool I forgot my usual rituals. I didn't kneel before the window where I could see some bit of sky and pray to it for a good show. It's true that for less important performances I don't kneel, I pray standing up. I'm less precise then, merely muttering "God be with me" rather than an all out entreaty with clasped hands, like "Please God, let me knock 'em dead!" This is practical. I don't want to use up my credit on a performance that doesn't count. You can't be a pig about this. He would feel used and exploited to be called upon in Calgary or Kansas City and probably take it out on me later in Chicago or London where it would hurt. But surely a New York performance is worth the full *spiel* on bent knees! I can't believe I had the nerve to forego it. And I don't think anybody told me to break a leg before going on either. This often happens on the road where I'm surrounded by civilians who don't know any better, but then I always ask somebody to wish it on me. This must be the first time I forgot, since that day, years ago, when I went to L.A. to video-tape *The Little Match Girl Ballet* and Yvonne Rainer, who was visiting, told me to break a leg. It seemed like the last thing in the world a friend would say to a ballerina. "Why are you saying such a nasty thing?" I cried. "That's what we say in the theatre," she shrugged, looking embarrassed.

But I learn fast. I've been a professional ever since.

Even Janet Kardon couldn't depress me. When she congratulated me after the performance I forgot that she'd left me out of her Biennale show of drawings by performance artists. It didn't matter that her show was undistinguished, I didn't like being left out. By rights, I shouldn't have been. Since she spent the evening surrounded by my drawings I figured she was punished enough. She looked very glamourous, not at all like the nervous bourgeois lady I met back in '76 at an earlier Biennale. She used to look like a docent. Now she looked snappy and competent, with that peculiar glitter the new fashions confer upon a woman of a certain age. "You look beautiful," I said with real pleasure. I meant it. She was surprised. The art world doesn't normally give away free compliments. "You do too," she

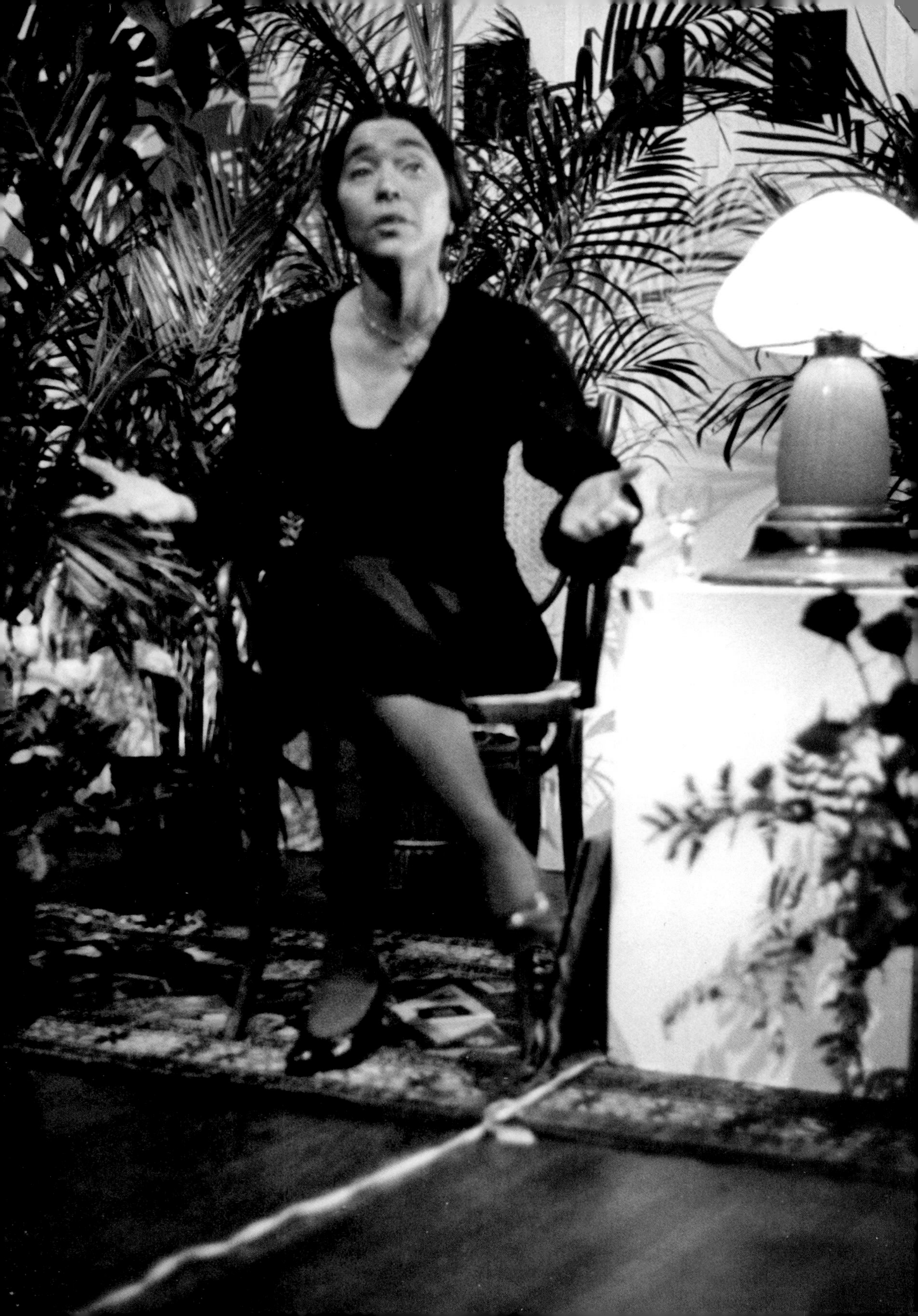

said uncertainly. I acknowledged the truth of this by a gracious movement of my head. The art world is pretty small. I'll get her later when the chance comes up.

We went to dinner at a Thai restaurant on 6th Avenue. Pat Baxter and Ed Schlossberg, Jeff Weinstein, Carrie, Ida, Marcia and Bill. Jeff had raved about the restaurant in the *Village Voice*, and there was a xerox of his review taped onto the front door, where you couldn't miss it. The last customers were leaving when we came in, but the handsome Thai waiters were delighted to see us even though it was after hours. They hovered around our table.

"Aren't they nice," Jeff whispered. "They're so polite. Not like Jewish waiters."

"That's because you're the food critic for the *Village Voice*," I reminded him.

He was shocked.

"Oh, no! The restaurants don't know what I look like. I'm very careful about that. When I go on cable I wear a mask."

Carrie asked if I would wear long nails when I got back to California.

I got huffy. The question seemed so absurd.

"Of course not," I snapped. "I'm an artist."

Carrie is down as usual. So is Pat. In her case it's Ed, I'm sure of it. She should have known better than to work for such a good looking boss. She should have taken the job with Stefanotti, she would have been safe. I don't think any of them want to be out tonight. They're just keeping me company because they know I have to eat after a show. Only Jeff is happy. He comes alive in restaurants.

A far cry from the days when he lived in Del Mar with Melvin and they were both so broke they stole food from the neighborhood market on 15th Street. They got away with it for a couple of years, until they got careless and the old man who owned the place caught them and called the police. "They had been watching us for some time," he told the others who didn't know the story. "We were too confident by then. That last time the police were waiting for us when we walked out the door. It was very embarrassing. People would stop with their shopping carts, trying to hear what was going on. The worst of it was the old man felt so bad about it. He had seen us around the store for years. He used to say hello to me at the post office. Now he couldn't know if we had been stealing off him that long, and the thought made him sick."

"What happened?" someone asked.

"Melvin convinced him we were starving graduate students. We were Jewish too. So he didn't press charges and we arranged to come in each week and pay him $2.

"How much did you finally pay him?"

"Nothing! I was too embarrassed to show my face. I never went back."

(I remember Maria collapsing into paroxysms of shame when her husband was arrested for drunk driving. She hid in the house with the lights turned off until they released him. He had to hitch home because she was too ashamed to come pick him up.)

Jeff says what he likes best is eating a different national cuisine every night. One night Greek, the next maybe Lebanese. Some Venezuelan a few days later. Next week Haitian, followed by Pakistani or Vietnamese. There are a lot of refugees who come to New York to open restaurants. They have big families so they never have to hire help. They're not bothered by union wages. They cut down on personal expenses. The whole family eats in the restaurant. If there are kids they come in after school to help out and stay off the streets.

"Do they make it?"

"Some do. They come and go. I try to visit them all."

What if the food is lousy? How does he feel about screwing a family business with a bad review? To whom does he owe his allegiance, the middle class readers of the *Village Voice*, some of whom are his friends, or El Salvadoran refugees?

"Last week I slaughtered Luchow's," he said.

"Are those Germans still around?"

What was that boyfriend's name? The sweet blonde one who worked as a host at Luchow's? We met in a scene class at Berghof's, where we worked on *The Cherry Orchard* together. He was a dull actor, too committed to sincerity to ever get off the ground. Once I pinched him hard on the ass to get some action out of him. It was like pulling teeth to get him "up." I suspected him of being a closet case, but we were both lonely and between things, and for a couple of months were good for each other. Going with him was like coming in out of the rain. The rain stopped as soon as I went in, but when I went back outside it really poured. I couldn't get used to his working hours—six nights a week, including weekends. In those days a girl hid at home on Saturday night if she didn't have a date. Going out alone was sad, but going out with a girlfriend was an advertisement for failure. One night he felt sorry for me and invited me to dinner at the restaurant while he was on duty. He showed me to a small table against the wall where he had placed some white flowers in a cut glass vase. He was nervous and shy to have me there. I was scared too. The place was Heavy German, all brass and polished wood. Giant chandeliers gleamed down over the dining rooms like watchful birds. Sitting there in the sumptuous dimness I could believe I was in a Glackens painting, heavy brown and gold with a discreet varnish covering big men with cigars and ladies of the night. The entire evening was a Post-Impressionist blur because I left my glasses at home. I didn't want to look too intellectual—they might guess I was Jewish and my friend would be embarrassed. The boss and his young wife lived upstairs in an expensive apartment fitted out with heavy antique furniture and dark oil paintings, but they ate their meals at the center table in the main dining room, where they spied on the waiters and waved to the regular customers. Later the blonde wife told me what a nice young man my friend was. Since she was my age I thought she was awfully pushy, but I held my peace for the sake of my friend. Everybody fussed over me as if I was a bride. The red faced waiters patted me tenderly with their free hands as they weaved by balancing large silver trays on their shoulders. Once a waiter brought me a thick cookie with kummel seeds in the shape of a heart. It was the size of a small plate and was a special present from the pastry chef, whose broad face beamed at me through the window of the revolving door, his high white hat dancing up and down to show approval. Their attentions confused me. I didn't know my boyfriend was so popular. He was sure each week at Luchow's was his last and they were scheming to fire him. He had to maintain extreme vigilance not to fall into the traps his enemies set for him. I became depressed. Here I thought I had finally found a nice wholesome guy and he was turning out to be just as crazy as everybody else. "It was a good restaurant in the days of John Sloan," I said.

FRIDAY ***October 24***

Antsy today. Always crazy before a performance, but living alone is also beginning to get me down. If I'd been staying with Ida we would have brooded over recent insults and injustices. Till late into the night we would drink herb tea and one-up each other with tales of woe. I don't know if other professions have such a recurrent need for confession and complaint. Maybe we're too sensitive. Or paranoid. But we carry such a heavy load of wrongs we would collapse if we didn't lay them down sometimes. A few years ago at Alex Smith's opening at the Mandeville gallery, Alex and Chris and I all stood around with gloomy faces while she went on about how nasty Jane Livingston had been to her the week before during the installation of her piece at the Corcoran. So I told my Jane Livingston story and Chris told his. I was just getting around to Maurice Tuchman when we were interrupted. We promised ourselves an all day gripe someday, just the three of us. "We'll have pizza and wine." Alex did get down to San Diego again when she taught a painting class for us and we had two delicious hours over enchiladas and tacos at Fidel's. Later, Chris and I met in Washington for the sculpture convention and we griped in a bar in Baltimore, while Max Neuhaus nursed his drink and beamed like Buddha. But the truth is I never feel much better afterwards. On the other hand, I don't feel worse either. And for a short time I can imagine I'm taking charge of my life, stamping out the bad guys and showing up their evil ways. But it's been several weeks now since I've shared my griefs. They're poisoning me. I had planned on rehearsing at home but couldn't stay put, so I rushed off to the gallery. The weather has been turning all morning. Fierce rains are predicted by tonight. But Ron and Frayda hadn't turned the lamps on in the darkening office where they were working peacefully when I barged in. "Everybody has pieces of me," I shouted. "There isn't a single image that can contain me. I'm doomed by my own complexity. The art world is too stupid to understand me. I'm lost. Doomed!" I liked that word and repeated it several times. "Doomed! Doomed!" "Sit down," Frayda said. "I'll get you a cup of tea." "The show is wonderful," Ron said. "Everybody loves it." "Who? Tell me who! Name one important person. I am surrounded by enemies." "Ingrid Sischy isn't against you," Ron protested. "Has Artforum ever done an article on me?" I shook my finger accusingly. "Tell me. I dare you to answer." Ron shrugged off Artforum. "Nobody takes them seriously. A fashion magazine." "But Dennis has had five articles already. Vito has been on the cover of Art in America twice. What are they, fashion plates? Only Eleanor is despised." I was just about to prove how it was all Martha Wilson's fault when I read the shock and worry on their kind faces. Why am I doing this to my friends? They aren't artists. They won't break in with their own horror story. "Mea culpa," I shouted, rushing off into the street. It was only one o'clock. I had the afternoon to kill. A light rain was beginning to fall and the wind was coming up. The sky looked mean. An empty cab stopped at the corner of Madison for a red light. I jumped in. "Rains predicted for tomorrow," the cabbie said cheerfully. "I'm taking the day off. Whenever it rains I take the day off." Great! I wish I could take the day off. There won't be an audience if it rains. Nonsense! Just a couple of years ago several hundred people trudged through a snowstorm to watch you perform. But this performance is not open to the public. Invited guests think a lot of themselves. My fans are only the rank and file. Why did we keep the performances secret? Why didn't we advertise? Because the gallery is small, because the salon atmosphere would be ruined by crowds, because Antinvova needs an intimate atmosphere. I know, I know, but fuck Antinova. I—Antin—can't perform before a small group. It's humiliating. And I blame the ones who come for those who didn't. I'm always counting the house.

"Is something wrong, Miss?" the cabbie asked. "Why are you holding your head in your hands and groaning?"

With the storm gathering outside, the apartment is darker than usual. I change to leotards. Maybe a workout on the parquet floor in the living room will cool me off. There's an urban glamour to this empty room even with the quilt over the window. A good place to do a full *barre*—my back needs one too—I've only been doing perfunctory warm-ups since I got here. But I can't keep my mind on it. Out of class the routine is boring enough, but today it's like putting on a straitjacket. With some nervousness, I try improvising. I never dance anymore. Ever since I became a ballerina I've been into self-improvement. I won't strike a pose or do a *temps* unless it does me good. Ballerinas are like that. So now I hum a nocturne from *Les Sylphides,* and getting a good grip on my lower back, glide across the floor doing *ports de bras* in all directions, bending forward, back, to the sides, my arms floating around my head. The music carries me in little gusts across the room. A couple of cat hops and grasshopper steps, and with a wink of my leg I spring lightly onto the couch, where, alas, my feet sink ingloriously into the cushions, so I soar back down to the floor again and canter away. Beating a stamp with little feet, I gambol and preen; but a *pirouette en dehors* from a perhaps overly-deep fourth lands me on my butt because I turned my head and shoulders too quickly. To cover my disgrace I bend languorously over my front leg like the dying swan and pretend I meant to be there on the floor all along. I haven't danced like this since elementary school, when I would drag my mother in from the kitchen so she could admire me dance to our worn-out 78 of *The Waltz of the Flowers.* On Sundays she would show me off to Uncle Irving and Aunt Goldie, and I "danced ballet" for them too after my three-year-old *wunderkind* sister played the piano. They would sing a melody and she would play it back for them with all the right notes because she had perfect pitch. Uncle Irving scratched his ass and laughed like a hyena whenever she played his tunes. He played the guitar and fancied himself something of a folk singer, and he would try to catch her with unlikely transpositions but her ears didn't miss a trick. It was like magic. She always won. Banking slightly to the left I dipped into an *arabesque fondu,* brought the left leg from behind to the side and *devant* and turned once *en pose en dehors* on half toe, ending in *fondu* on the left foot, the right *sur le cou defied devant* continuing smoothly into a *développé devant* while still in *fondu* and stepping smartly into *arabesque* from the *développé.* With a minor inflection of the leg I began to articulate the curve of the finale. Tears sprang into my voice. My rich dark contralto swings into a sweet upper register as I bound into a set of *cabrioles.* Like the birds on the bouganvillea bush back home, as long as I don't have to carry a tune I'm such a lovely singer. The music and the dance float into each other but I hesitate. There is too much expressiveness here for an empty room. By tonight I'll be wasted. There'll be nothing left for the audience. I'm a professional. I can't throw it away. I hover uncertainly on half toe, like a hummingbird with too many hibiscus blossoms to choose from. But who am I kidding?

I can't stop now. It's like trying to call off an orgasm that's already started. I erupt into the closing fanfare. I spin. I dive. I lift. I am a snow leopard on an elan or a lynx upon an antelope as I command the stage with a mighty double *pirouette*, fingers strutting above my head and Riabouchinska eyes flashing. Time freezes. I am a still photo waiting for history. "Brava. Bravissima." One man shouts before the others. He is always the first, this man. His passion cannot be controlled. He is in love with me. They are all in love with me. I offer myself in an ever deepening set of bows to the *cognoscenti* on the couch. "*Merci, merci.*" The *hauteur* of the *artiste* is gone. "*Mon ame se pame de tendresse.*" Such adoration is humbling. The egotism of audiences is a terrible thing. They are ravaging me with their love. Have mercy. I must escape. I hide in the bathroom. When I dare to emerge they are gone. There is only the dusty room, very dark now, with an old green couch covered with the pages of last Sunday's *Times.* I throw myself on the pages. They crackle. I'm washed out. I think I sleep but maybe it's that half sleep, half waking, when thoughts flit through your head like silverfish and then they're gone.

The phone rings. Mother calling from California. She's crying.

"Why did you leave me?" she weeps.

I hear her through a veil. It's raining on the phone.

"Mother, it's a bad connection."

"All you think about is yourself."

"Mother, I'm doing a show."

"My daughters have deserted me."

"I'm doing my job, Mother."

The petulant voice goes on. I have to break into the complaints or there'll be no end to them.

"Hey, Mother, know who I thought of today? Uncle Irving and Aunt Goldie."

"He was a cruel man," she says. "Didn't he die?"

"No. Goldie left him. He lives in Florida with another woman."

"I thought he was dead."

"Uncle Willie is dead."

Her voice is uncertain.

"Willie?"

"Gertie's husband. You know, Lorraine's father."

"Poor Lorraine. She died."

"It was a long time ago, Mother."

"Such a nice girl. Who did you say her father was?"

"Willie. Uncle Willie."

Her voice is sad and defeated.

"I don't remember," she says.

Growing old for my mother is the daily erasure of history as her relatives and friends disappear forever, no longer recoverable by the mention of a name, a relation. Uncle Willie, Aunt Francis, Butch, Eric, Rissa. If she puts a pot of water up to boil she forgets it's there. If she smells the burning plastic of the handles she'll pick it up and throw it into the sink. Her fingers get red from the burn but she doesn't feel it. And even this is not certain. Some days are better than others. On these days she recognizes more parts of the world. She holds a more or less reasonable conversation. Doesn't ask the same question over and over. Soon her eyes become suspicious and shrewd. Mother is finding herself. It is the signal to warn her psychiatrist. An attack of madness may be on the way. "I danced to *Waltz of the Flowers* today, Mother."

"Ah, Tschaikovsky." She begins to sing. She still has a sweet pretty soprano like a young girl's. She used to love Lily Pons. The Russian melody sings through the rain falling through our bad connection. Some things stay. Maybe they're the important ones.

"Good-bye, Mother. I have to do my show now."

"Good-bye, dear. Thank you for calling."

The private performance this afternoon left me soft and vulnerable for the evening one. My pathos was stunning. People had tears in their eyes. I thought of Markova. "I would like to share my *Giselle* with the young dancers. There is so much I know. But they do not come to me." And Alicia is a legend. Poor Antinova has nobody but me.

At the end when the lights go on I hustle the embarrassed crowd, offering myself for salons and parties and hawking signed copies of *Before the Revolution.* This time I actually sold some. While I was signing a copy Ron came up and asked if Irving Sandler could have a gift copy for his little daughter. Irving is my friend. His eyes show how moved he has been by the performance. The child stands at his side, thrilled to be so close to a famous ballerina. She devours me with her serious, little girl eyes.

"I am an *artiste*." I smile politely. "I do not give away my works. The fee is small. I will be pleased to autograph the book for you."

I put Irving's $10 in my purse and write a pretty dedication for his daughter, assuaging my guilt by writing Antinova clearly so she can read it instead of my usual scrawl. But I could kill Ron for insulting me. How could he ask me to do such a thing? Does he think I'm kidding?

SATURDAY ***October 25***

Rain again today. Small crowd for the evening performance. Only about 40 or 50 people show up—among them Barbara, Lynn, Martina, Joey—and their dates! Waiting around in the back office for the place to fill up I drank more sherry than I should have, but it was depressing to work so hard just to make art for the employees of the Ronald Feldman Gallery. Where was the art world? I didn't see any critics when I spied through the narrow slit in the door. Robert Pincus-Witten had promised to come but hadn't. John Perreault wasn't there. Nor Betsy Baker or Ingrid Sischy. I must not be fashionable anymore. That really spooked me and I poured another glass of sherry. Have to be careful. A tipsy ballerina is charming but a drunken one is gross. This is real sherry from *Jerez de la Frontera* and it has some punch—a fragrant dry wine that sweetens the spirits when it goes down. It isn't working though, as I stare morosely out at the elderly little people slowly filling up the seats. Who are they? Sean has to put out a lot of chairs tonight. There are a lot of people who can't sit on the floor. They look like Ronald Feldman's relatives. They could be collectors. Collectors look like uncles. When I go into my hustle at the end I'll look helplessly at the plump cheerful gentleman with the neat grey moustache and round glasses who looks like my father in Florida. He could hire me to give a talk at his grandson's bar mitzvah. But the petite wife with the carefully drawn fish mouth and the missing forehead covered with sculpted blonde bangs won't let him do it. I'm in luck. He's with that younger man who's just arriving, the one removing the newspaper from the reserved seat. The ring of relatives around the room reminds me of Lita Hornick's annual Park Avenue bash when she invites Morty's relatives to slum with the *mishugena* poets she publishes. When I finally go on I'm a quivering wreck. The tears roll down my face, threatening my color, as I recall the dirty white swans in the *Bois de Boulogne* when I lived in the small hotel with the white column off the *Pont de Saint-Cloud.* And when I considered the stupidity and narrowness of the world of art, I was overcome by a wave of sorrow and loss for the world that might have been. I choked and had to wait before going on. By the time the house lights came up and I began hustling my books and offering my services, I couldn't distinguish my patron from the other sweet faced Jewish gentlemen looking so trustfully up at me.

As usual I make myself available in the foyer. People are distressed. Most try not to meet my eyes and make a quick exit. Some are crying. They look a little afraid of me. An Israeli artist asks if I will be around in two weeks when his mother flies in from Haifa. She would understand me, he says. "Alas, I will not be in town then." I murmur regrets at not meeting his mother. Ron introduces me to a young couple. The woman pats my shoulder sympathetically. Later he tells me they are the architectural group—SITE. "They were shocked that you had to sell yourself to rich people's parties," he giggles. "They wanted to know where I found you." "Russian War Relief," I tell him. "Maybe they'll contribute." Pierre Restany kissed my hand and confessed he was falling in love with me. I protested. "But,

Pierre, you are always falling in love." A suave Argentinian artist in an Italian suit gave me his card and invited me to a party. "The important people will be there. It will be useful." "When?" I asked. "I'm very tired." "Tuesday." "I'll come." "This is the second night I have been here," explains a short, swarthy middle-aged man introducing me to a young Italian woman in halting English. "Last time I did not understand. Now I understand." They go off smiling.

We left soon after. The rain was letting up but I was cold with only my embroidered shawl for cover so we went to an Italian place a few blocks east of the gallery. It was dark and expensive, the tables crowded close together the way they are in chic ethnic restaurants. Ron was in a meditative mood. He talked a lot about Joseph Beuys. How when he was arranging the Guggenheim show they walked together in Central Park, lunching on frankfurters and knishes, and talked to the poor sad beasts in the zoo, and watched the evening come up over the rowboats on the lake. Together with Frayda they sat on the rock promontories hanging over the narrow walk paths and the three of them talked about things and hoped for rabbits to come by. They fed peanuts to the squirrels and Ron described the great man squatting comfortably on his haunches, the fedora flopping over one side of his long melancholy face, as he whispered little German love words to the squirrels. They darted up to him and ate the peanuts out of his hands. They licked his fingers. "They didn't lick his fingers," I protested. "They did. He has a way with animals." And all the time that the people at the Guggenheim and the Modern were wheeling and dealing, the great man walked innocently with Ron and Frayda in the warm spring sun. "A simple man," Ron said. I could see a tall lanky man in a fedora, suspenders holding up the old-fashioned shapeless trousers, moving slowly through Central Park, followed by squirrels, rabbits, pigeons, starlings, and sedately bringing up the rear, all the stray dogs, their tails wagging proudly as they marched several abreast, the alley cats walking with confidence between the legs of the dogs, and the kittens scuttling under the cats. German shepherds, Dobermans, and boxers walking democratically with dachshunds and pugs. A pregnant one-eyed Siamese sits serenely on the noble back of a Saint Bernard. Under the regal flanks of a Great Dane swoop the little swallows and other chirping things. The man in the fedora slowly rises up on his toes, his arms make a great embracing arc and he begins to dance. All the creatures, great and small, bound and gambol, imitating his movements like little children in school. He takes off his shoes and gives them to a shabby old man on Social Security sitting on a park bench. "Bless you, my son," the old man calls out. The man in the fedora blows kisses to the right and the left, as people on all sides unleash their pets, and the rich dogs join the poor dogs and the ranks of the little army swell from the wooden trellis of 72nd Street all the way up to the decaying walls of 110th . . .

Later, the empty apartment depressed me and I changed into jeans and sneakers and went down to the all night newsstand on 57th Street to pick up a copy of the Sunday *Times.* I felt young and scrappy in my own clothes again and came on like a dancer out of a chorus line. Not that there was anyone around to notice. Broadway above 57th was dead as a doornail. But there was a spicy spring smell in the still-wet streets. Some trees must have gotten confused and come out blooming after the rains. I flirted with some ugly guys with bad complexions in the little all night market near the Art Students League. Back home I didn't fall asleep for hours and lay around reading the paper. Kansas City lost to the Yankees. The big city boys intimidated them. Too bad . . .

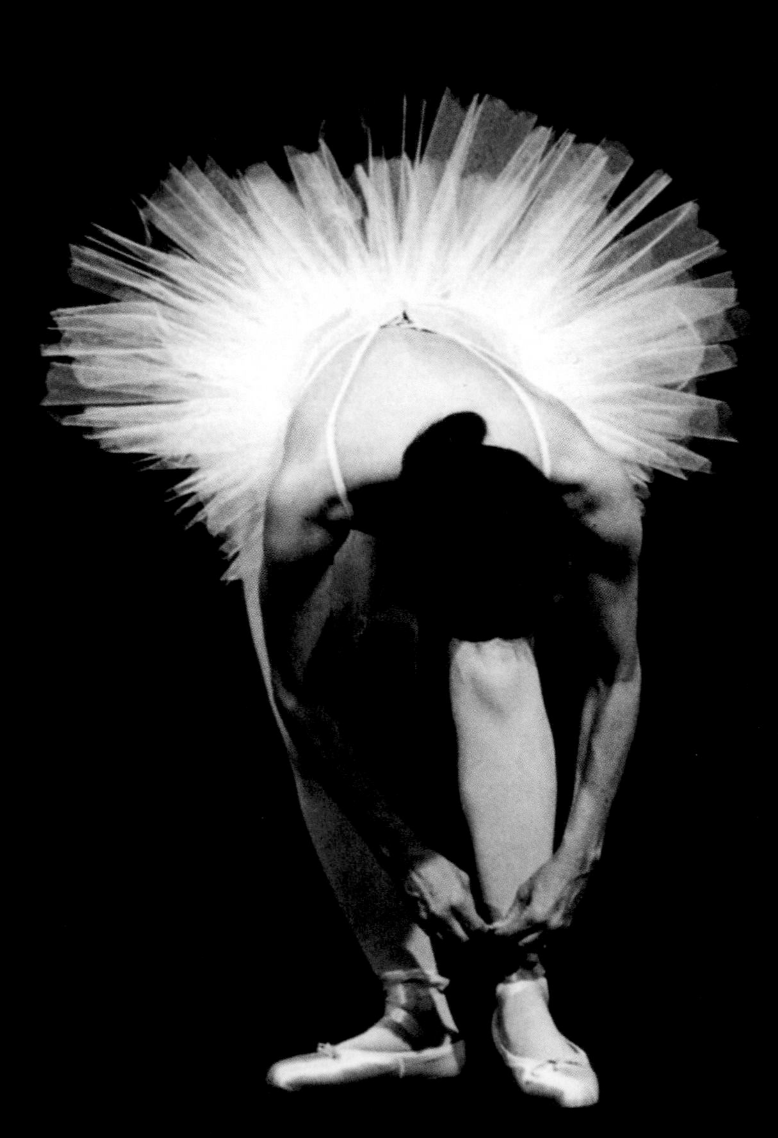

SUNDAY ***October 26***

Fell apart today and stayed home, I had no heart to go out into the world. Being a glamourous woman is a job and I needed a day off. But this presented some problems. Without my dark face I couldn't be seen by the *Century* staff or my game was up. But I also couldn't afford to waste the day entirely. I had to get down to the basement to do some laundry—I was running out of clean tights.

Like all Central Park buildings that had seen better days, *The Century* held on to old class distinctions. Service people making deliveries entered the building from the basement, where they took a freight elevator operated by a fat and indolent man whose heavy flesh seemed to have grown around his squat wooden stool. He had nothing else to do all day but stare sleepily at the passengers. On the other hand, the tenants and their visitors rode the private, automatically operated elevators, but these stopped at the lobby floor and didn't go down to the basement at all. To do my laundry, I would have to ring for the freight.

The old magician's trick of leading their attention to the wrong spot—that's the way to go.

I threw the dirty clothes along with sheets and towels into some pillow cases, and from under the sink in the kitchen collected several half filled boxes of detergent, an empty Clorox bottle, and an unopened box of Borax. For good measure, I grabbed the Woolite and mineral bath salts from the windowsill in the bathroom and went back to the kitchen for Ajax and Calgon dishwashing detergent. A laundry bag went under each arm, along with boxes and plastic bottles, with the third bag balanced precariously on top, where it covered my face. I had already tried to pull on a pair of leather gloves to hide my white hands, but my nails were too long and I couldn't get them on; so I stuffed my hands into the sleeves of my ski jacket. My wrists and arms held the load together, along with a good deal of help from my face, which I pressed down into the soft center of the topmost bag. When I staggered into the elevator there was no way the operator could see me, except for my sneakers and the bottoms of my jeans. I couldn't see him either. I was one big bundle.

About halfway down, one of the detergent boxes began sliding down, and when I tried to hold onto it with my elbow, it sprang a leak at the bottom and began to trail a thin stream of white powder.

Man: "That detergent is spilling." (shocked voice)

Me: "Please hurry. (groan) This laundry is too heavy for me."

When I staggered out to safety, trailing powder behind me, he slammed the gate and took the car up, expressing his disgust with a sequence of percussions.

I didn't want to wait around for the cycle to finish, since people would certainly be coming down with their wash. Besides I had shopping to do at the Gristede's Market on the corner, and I couldn't face the elevator man again without my camouflage. It would blow my cover and he would probably wag his finger at me and order me to clean up the mess I had made on his floor. I felt like a disobedient child. I wonder if that wasn't the way people felt trying to elude the Gestapo. It's hard to feel confident and grown-up when you're trying to escape. The scale of everyday things changes. Proportions are different. Small objects become large. They crowd your headspace so your usual concerns have no room anymore. Before you know it you're a child again—and a bad one, too, because you're making a nuisance of yourself.

I searched the damp corridors for the service exit to the outside. There were lots of doors, but most were locked and the others were empty rooms. It was eerie opening doors not knowing what you would find. New York is a harbor town and its basements belong to one of the largest rat populations in the world. Just last year a secretary had been attacked by rats in Wall Street in broad daylight. What if a gang of rats waited for me behind the next door? It was possible. I could hear shuffling noises on all sides of me.

The corridors were poorly lit, usually by a single bulb hanging from a chain. By the time I reached the end of a hallway there was very little light left. God, what would happen if the power failed? How would I retrace my steps to the elevator? But what good would the elevator do me if the power went out? I would be at the mercy of everything. What if a mad elevator man hung around down here masturbating in dark corners? If a woman ran past him would he improvise? Recently a young flutist from the Met had been killed backstage by a stagehand, who threw her down an elevator shaft. Some of these corridors led into cul de sacs where my body could lie unsuspected for days in a dark corner. I was nearly hysterical, rushing around opening doors I thought I had already checked out. But there were so few landmarks I couldn't be sure. I blundered onto a staircase behind one of the doors and started up. The door slammed shut behind me leaving me in total darkness, but I held on to the bannister and groped my way up the steep steps out into the light.

I came out into the front part of the lobby where the elderly Jewish ladies sit with their shopping bags and watch the people coming into the building. Fortunately there was a strong wind coming in from the Hudson—it had rattled my windows all morning, and I hid my guilty white face in the hood of my ski jacket.

At Gristede's the friendly black girl I had chatted with earlier in the week gave me my change without so much as a glance. I was scared she might recognize my long nails: but either white fingers took precedence over nails or, what was more likely, my nails were more distinctive to me than they were to anyone else.

It's evening now and I'm depressed. My depression came upon me slowly, as I felt the silence of the apartment close in on me along with the deepening darkness. Time to turn on some lights and get out the French bread and sherry. I'll eat the new caviar I bought at Gristede's. That should cheer me up, but I wish they would get the black kind for a change. I like it better. What a turnabout from my usual diet! I'm still disgusted by white bread, but here in New York I'm taking full advantage of the ambiguous nature of French bread, though I noticed this morning it's making me constipated. The European spas of the '20s used to make a big thing of enemas. All his life Stravinsky enjoyed talking about his bowels and daily enemas. Probably it was the rich food.

MONDAY ***October 27***

Photographed Antinova around town today. Worked with Mary Swift, who shot some pretty pictures of my King performance in Washington last year. Her work has a wistful romanticism which suits Antinova. Then, too, she seemed solid—a competent person. She wouldn't be intimidated by waiters or petty officials who didn't want their patron's picture taken. There's a hit-and-run aspect to the kind of shooting I planned to do and you have to be something of a guerrilla to get away with it. But I had only met Mary once before—in Washington—and I miscalculated. The improvisatory nature of our work disturbed her.

I had hoped the city would speak to me of Antinova. I figured if I went to her places she would be there and I would be her. When we arrived at a place I searched for her—through a window, out the door, around the corner. I walked into the scene and played it for both of us, while Mary tried to photograph the action as it rolled. But not every place was right for the kind of romantic encounter I imagined. I made a list of promising places. Places for a native, not a tourist. Picturesque places though not necessarily famous. Genteel, cultured, sometimes expensive places, filled with atmosphere—Antinova would lunch at the Russian Tea Room not the Four Seasons. But there were problems. Lincoln Center looks like a bank in Kansas City. And though Carnegie Hall has style, most of it is hidden away in the auditorium under the great dome or on the wide carpeted stairways winding down from the balconies. I remembered as a child the best part of Philharmonic matinees was moving down the stairs with the crowd, the final applause still ringing in our ears. Row after row of signed photographs of performing artists behind thin gilt frames lined the walls all the way up to the immense ceilings. Photos of glamourous ladies with tweezed eyebrows and stern young men with curls standing up over high, intellectual brows. Plump tenors in exuberant tuxedos and expansive divas under diamond tiaras. Here and there, a platinum haired Brunhilde dreaming behind sculpted plaits. I had hoped to get tickets for a recital by some young unknown. We could have sneaked some good shots of Antinova attending an old friend's concert. The young violinist becomes an old cellist. It is his annual recital. Every year the crowd becomes sparser. The mailing list shorter. Mostly they are the old man's students now. There are not too many of these anymore. The best ones go to Juilliard. They want a degree. Antinova sits next to an old couple. There are so few of us left. She studies the program. The melancholy tones of Saint-Saëns sigh through the hall. The heart turns over. The years slip away. It is 1925 again. How full toned the young artist was then. How beautiful we all were, children of paradise. A discreet tear slides down Antinova's cheek—the one on the side where Mary Swift crouches behind a column. She is changing cameras now. She moves further back to get a wider view. I don't think we would have been caught. There couldn't be many ushers on a weekday afternoon. The artist would cut costs as much as possible. His friends would approve of photographers. They are young. There was no scheduled concert and I didn't even try to get in. I wasn't about to waste hours hassling

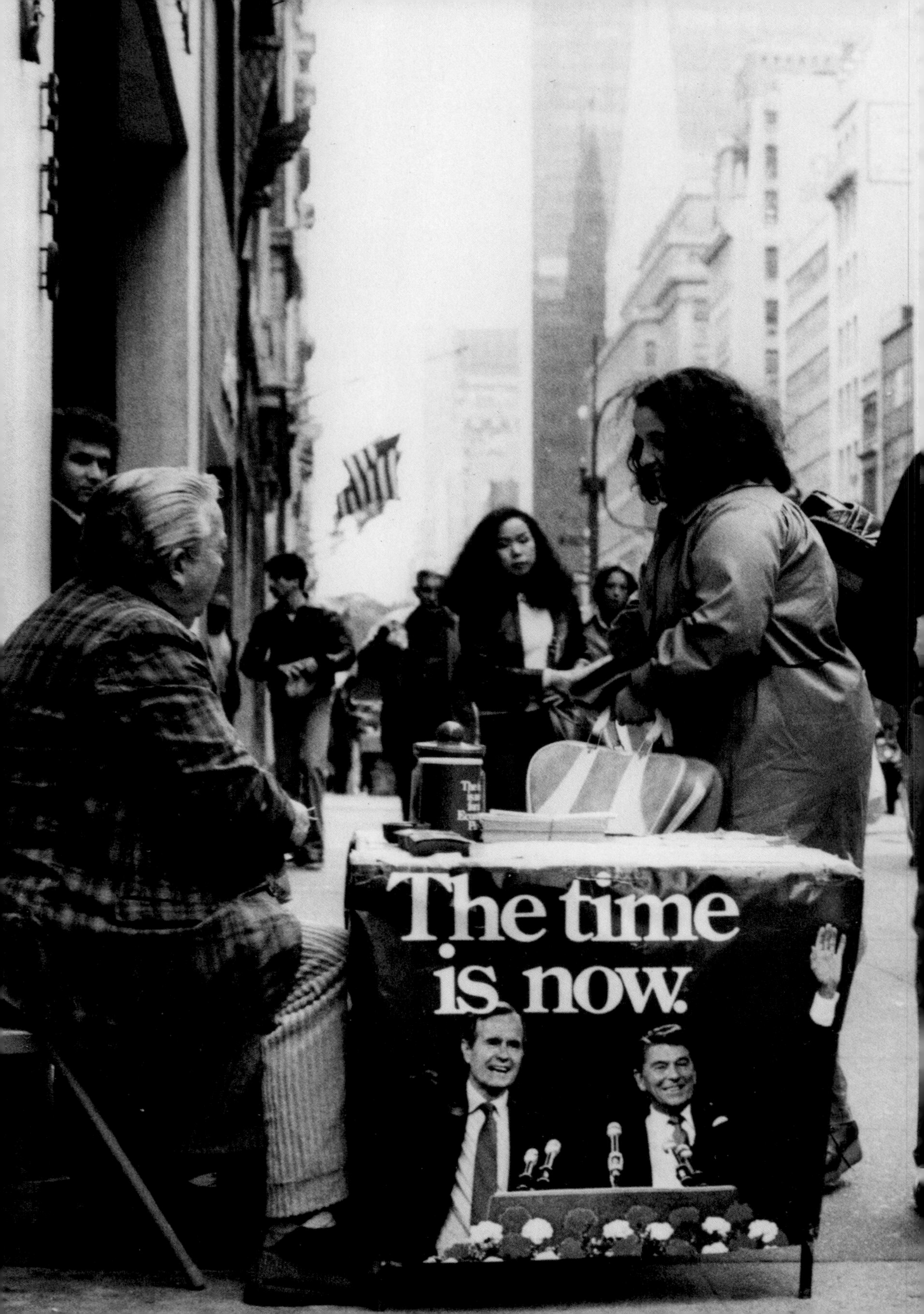

The time
is now.

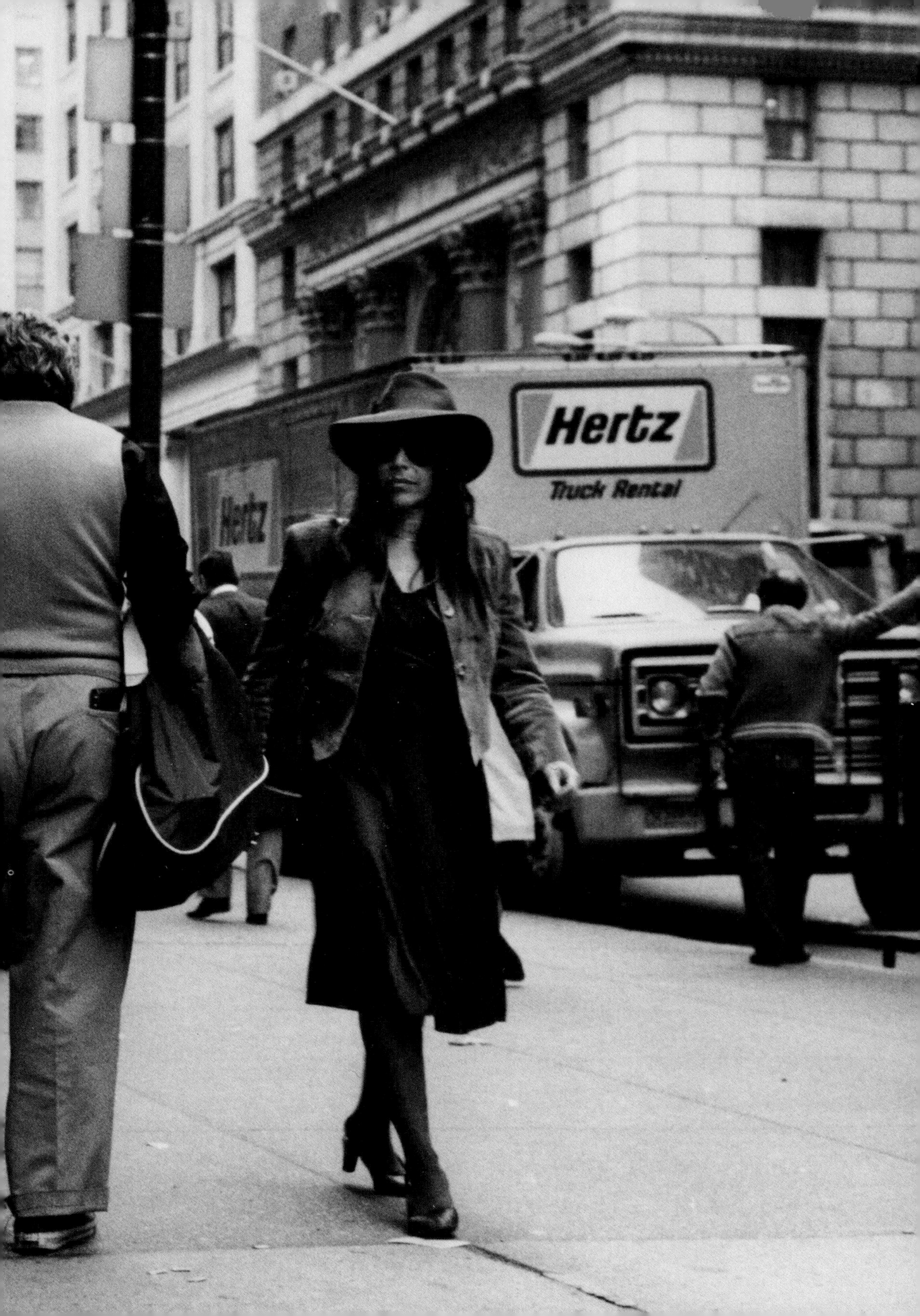
Hertz
Truck Rental
Hertz

with bad tempered box office attendants and their snotty supervisors. No place, with the exception of the Russian Tea Room, was indispensable. I would not set up and design every image the way I did for *Angel of Mercy* and *100 BOOTS.* Instead of the pregnant moment—the passing fancy. City life is always presenting itself and falling away. Like riding in a bus moving slowly through traffic. You're moving but so are the three people you were idly framing a moment ago. All go off in different directions. You drop the others and watch the woman walking in your window. That's Antinova. Then the bus picks up speed and she's gone. Or you're stalled and she crosses the street. Maybe you pick her up again in the window across the aisle. "Excuse me." The fat lady waits for you to tighten your knees so she can pass. You slide into her window seat. It's warm and a little sticky. When you look up again Antinova is gone.

But all day I suffered from an identity crisis. It started this morning with a bad set of openers. First, there were my new voluminous purple slacks. I'd admired a model in *Vogue* wearing short trousers and high heels and I shortened my pants so they wouldn't cover my ankles. How could I be such a fool? Have I already forgotten how years ago when I was having my hair cut I asked for a style worn by a model in *Harper's Bazaar*? Dark hair flowed out of her head like a Gothic heroine. The hairdresser threw the magazine to the floor. "That's not a haircut, it's a photograph." He cut my hair short like Jean Seberg. "This is how you should look." But how else could I catch up in provincial San Diego? I wasn't going to sit in Balboa Park and watch the girls go by. They might be pretty, but they wouldn't be stylish. In the mirror this morning, I knew I'd goofed. The slacks were absurd. I was a midget wearing castoffs. Bony ankles shipwrecked between two-inch heels and the deep purple sea. The next piece of bad luck was my new expensive suede jacket. The padded shoulders removed most of my neck. The camera would cheerfully slice off the rest. At the last minute I switched to my beat-up green velvet Grenadier jacket. It has a certain 18th-century look. Shabby bohemianism was more in character than the silhouette of a linebacker. Mary was getting antsy. I was taking hours. I clamped the purple fedora onto my head. "Break a leg," I prayed and sailed off. Downstairs a dark shabby woman with enormous eyes stood in the mirror. It took a second to recognize myself. "Like a cleaning lady," I thought dismally. "I look like the maids going home at 5 o'clock." On black-and-white film the skin has to be pretty dark to get out of the light range. So this morning I went darker for the camera. I had to use more makeup than usual and it was difficult to blend the tones evenly. I made something of a mess of it. I was splotchy in places. I looked old too. The excess paint settled into my wrinkles. They crisscrossed my face like a vengeful magic marker. The camera would linger over every one of them. I usually look younger than I am because my face never sits still long enough for people to notice my wrinkles. My charm depends upon expressiveness. But the camera resists mobility. It will freeze me forever into a wizened mummy. But there was no going back. I didn't have the heart to wash it off and start over. I would have fallen into bed and pulled the covers over my head and never come out. Mary would have been lost before I reached the door. She was waiting to bolt. The improvisatory nature of our shooting was getting to her. I gritted my teeth. "I will jump into a story as it offers itself," I encouraged her. "All you have to do is follow me." I struggled to talk confidently. My depression was getting heavier by the minute. I could hardly keep moving. My brave blackness was sinking into failure and shame. I took Mary by the elbow and steered her through the quiet restful recesses of the park. There weren't too many people here to see our misery. "Look, Mary," I said, "I will join that man over there under the big tree and throw peanuts to the pigeons as he does. Be sure and get both of us and the birds too." I talked with the man for half an hour. His son is an artist. Paints and shows in a gallery on Madison Avenue He teaches in the Midwest. It is very hard to make it, his son says. You need pull. The man doesn't understand his son's paintings. They are abstracts. He likes realistic work. He is a retired schoolteacher. He comes to feed the birds every day. I am retired too. From the ballet. The Russian ballet. He adores the ballet, though opera is his favorite. He sings a few bars of an aria. *Vesti la Giuba,* he explains. "My favorite." Mary is taking pictures all the time. I motion to her to change sides. My hand is getting tired of throwing peanuts. I have to pick up the ones that aren't eaten and throw them again. I can't keep asking the man for more peanuts. He is running out too. Mary is finished. I shake hands with my friend. He makes a peace sign. "Long live art," he says. Mary and I walk down the dark scraggly path between rock formations and out into the open lawns. "Was it too dark in there for you?" I asked her. "Speckled," she says. "Did I look too old? I hope you got my good profile." "You worry too much," she says. "Don't you want to look natural?" "Yes, but I am frightened by the camera." "But you're always in front of cameras." "Yes, but I've grown so old. I saw myself in a store window before we turned into the park." "But Antinova is old." "Yes, but I'm not." "But you're Antinova." "Yes." I was wretched. Back to the apartment to change for lunch. Afterwards, Anna met us at the Russian Tea Room, magnificent in a flowered frock. It was pretty late—about 3 o'clock—but people were still lined up behind braided ropes in the dark front room. They offered us seating upstairs but we preferred a table in the back where chandeliers and samovars glittered in the mirrored walls. "There will be a long wait," the hostess said disapprovingly. We had exceeded our limits. Who were we to have preferences? "We'll wait," I agreed humbly. We did. Longer than we should have. People were being seated on all sides of us. We thought some of them came after we did. Action was called for. A bribe was in order. It is how things are done in aristocratic circles. I have learned this from the autobiographies of the Russian dancers. But I am an American. I have no experience with such things. There was both a head waiter and a hostess. Whose was the worthier palm? Mary Swift settled the matter. She got bored and began to shoot. At the first pop of flashbulbs, conversation ceased. The tinkle of moving crockery and silver stopped. The hostess converged on us flanked by three big waiters. I stepped in front of Mary whose mouth hung open, the perennial American tourist who just put her foot in it.

"My, my," I sang out smiling fiercely and waving my hands graciously in all directions. "It is nothing. A foolish mistake. We are only practicing. There is no film in the camera."

Who would use flashbulbs without film? Luckily we had fallen into such grave sin the staff lost their wits and didn't ask.

"Our guests are important people."

The hostess was outraged and demanded punishment. But the crime was without precedent. She didn't know what to do about it. Now was the time for finesse. I slipped a $10 bill into my hand and tried to shake hers. She looked down at my groping fingers and ostentatiously removed her own. The money remained in my palm but her voice became more conciliatory.

"Earl Wilson comes every afternoon," she whispered portentously, pointing vaguely in the direction of the back room. "He writes his daily column here. He must not be distracted."

"It is my friend." I look at Mary. "She is too enthusiastic. I too am an important person. In certain circles, of course. For years, I have longed to visit the Russian Tea Room." I shake my head in a grave manner. "It is important that we are here."

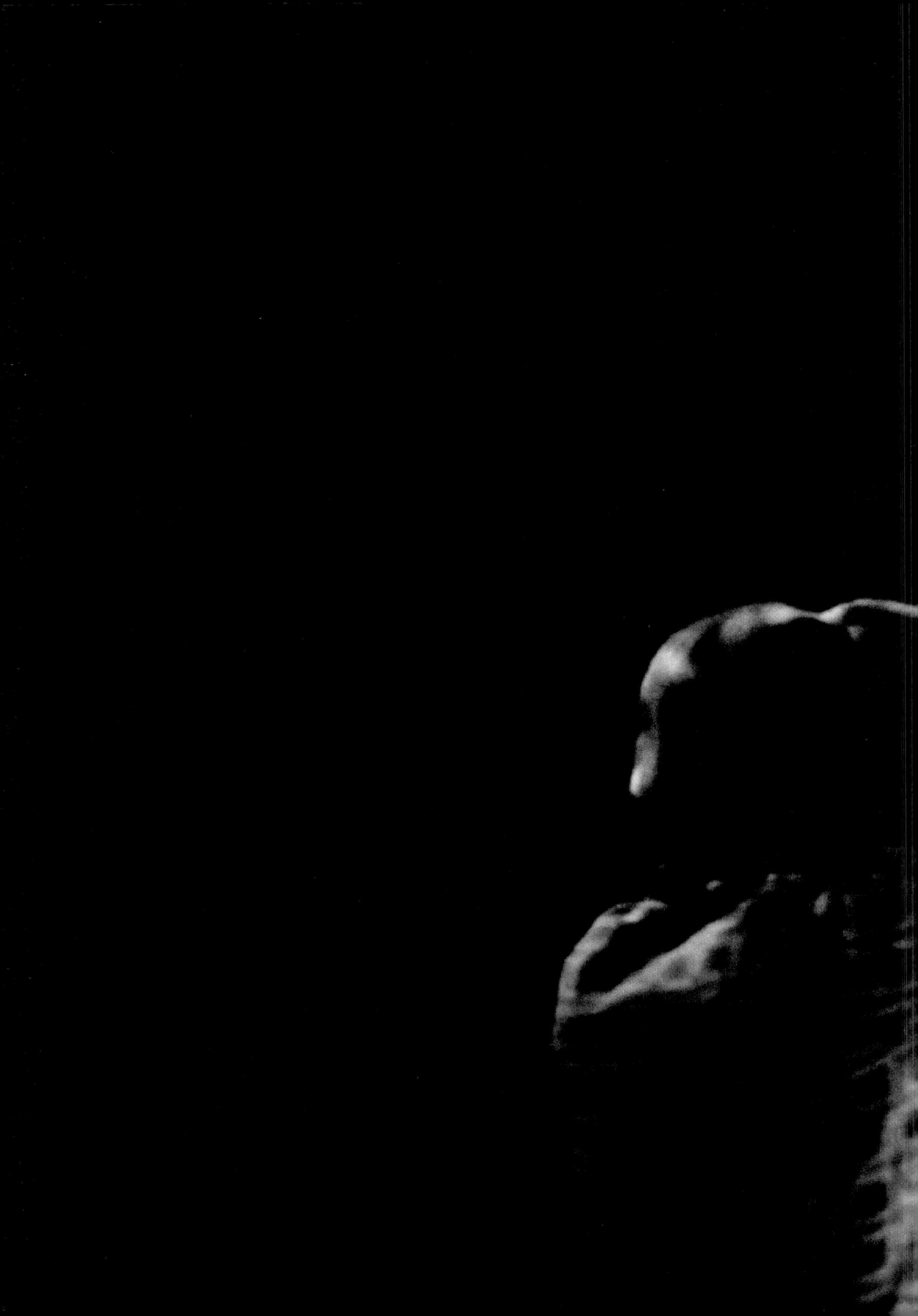

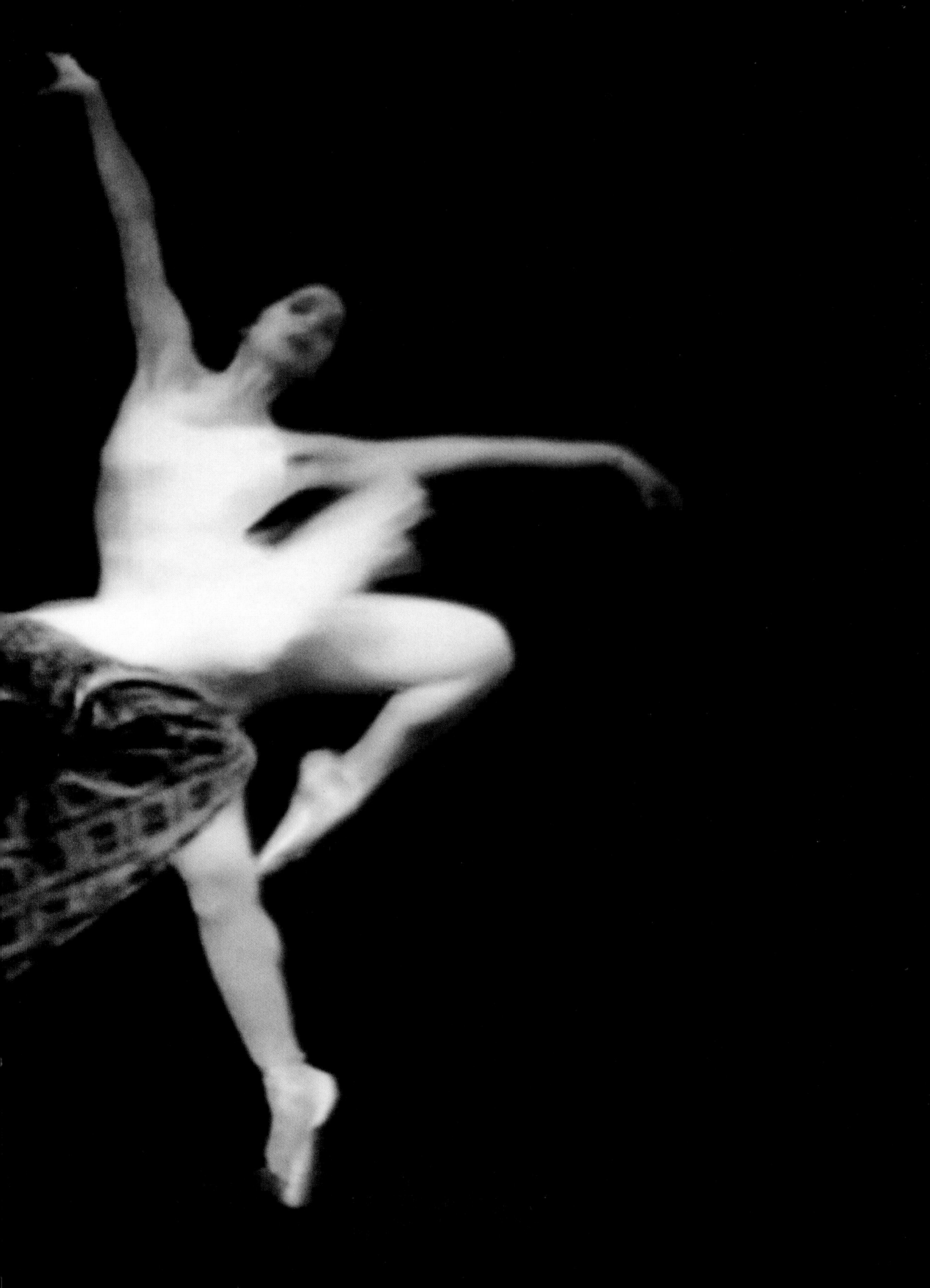

I wore my black silk performance dress. Back in the early '30s the jet and rhinestones had been hand sewn into Art Deco flower patterns. My nails were long and manicured. My ancestry was as indefinable as hers.

Anna stepped in with a sweeping Italian gesture. She looked sternly at Mary.

"She does not understand," she said impatiently. It was apparent to any sensible person that the culprit should have remained on the back of a horse somewhere on Long Island. Such people can be dangerous. Anna sniffed with just a hint of disdain.

"An American."

That settled it. Anna was a Princess and Mary was a Daughter of Industry. The little old one with the suspicious racial coloring and the face of a monkey was less certain but she talked well. The hostess was a woman of the world. She shrugged her shoulders. There was no accounting for tastes. She drifted away. The bribe remained. A sweaty reproach in my hand. When the head waiter led us to a nice table in the back, I gave it to him.

Later, when most of the diners have left and the waiters are preparing for dinner, we shoot discreetly in our little corner. Mary moves in tight. She is careful not to offend. The staff wear a somewhat aggrieved look but go about their business as if we aren't there. When we leave, I slip the hostess a $5 bill as I had seen a departing couple do earlier. It disappears neatly into the pocket of her skirt. She is a lady and accepts gifts.

"We must not intrude on the privacy of our guests," she says. "You understand."

I wave aside the memory of the unfortunate incident.

"I am Antinova, the dancer," I introduce myself. "I hear a slight accent. Are you Russian?"

"I was born in Singapore." She evades my question.

I nod knowingly. Singapore. Stopover for White Russian aristocrats fleeing the Revolution with diamonds in their curtain rods. A sink of intrigue. Up close she has a vaguely Eurasian look. She is small, tough, no longer young. We have much to say to each other.

"Visit us again," she entreats. "We will look after you well."

She shakes our hands warmly—even Mary's—and we cross the threshold of Old Russia into the cold glare of the late afternoon sun.

TUESDAY ***October 28***

Barbara and Brian have a studio duplex in the West 60s. A piano in one corner piled high with manuscripts and books. Barbara's flower drawing and Brian's geometries float on the floor. I whisk the papers off a chair to make a place for myself, adding them to the orderly piles on the floor which grow with every visitor. Some are already tall as tables. They will remain there forever. A palette with glamourous bits of color rests on an orange crate. A worn portfolio leans against the side. Brushes stand up in a chipped coffee mug. A day-old chrysanthemum in a vase. A fine skin of dust covers everything. It settles down over me. Barbara paints with the drawing pad on her lap and talks about her book. The genteel bohemianism takes me back to the days when I was an unemployed actress and modeled for a living. Eugene Speicher's studio was very much like this. Only he had been an orderly man who divided his year into two equal parts—six months of flower painting and six months of portrait commissions. After the flower periods he always had trouble getting his hand back at painting heads and he would hire models to sit for him until he loosened up again. I was surprised to see how pearly his portrait of me was. Of course, he was a flatterer. That's why he was so successful. But the flattery wasn't obtrusive. It was in the opalescent skin, the charming mouth, the vulnerable curve of the cheek. It was my face—he merely added adjectives. I stood at his shoulder when he put down the brush and we admired the painting together. "You're wasting your time," Mrs. Speicher called down from the balcony. She was a nasty woman in a starched housedress who carefully calculated my $3.50 an hour and watched suspiciously when I broke the pose to go to the bathroom. Mr. Speicher sighed, picked up a palette rag and flicked it across the still wet paint. "What are you doing?" I wailed. "Yes, it was a nice one," he agreed. "So why did you destroy it?" It was a small canvas. It took only a couple of moves across the surface and the image was gone. "I am doing Mrs. Whitney next week," he shrugged. "She will pay me a great deal of money. You, you pay me nothing." "So what? Sell it to somebody who wants a picture of a pretty girl." Mrs. Speicher shouted impatiently. "Why do you talk to her? You are wasting your time." "Extra Speichers on the market bring down my price," he explained patiently. "So keep it for yourself then," I persisted. He shook his head. I never modeled for him again. Mrs. Speicher would call. "Where are you, you? Come tomorrow. " But it bothered me to work for him after that. I didn't mind incompetents painting useless pictures. They couldn't help themselves. I used to model three hours on Sunday mornings for a rich accountant who worked diligently on a single painting for several months. When winter ended he stretched a new canvas and started on the spring one. A painting a season. He did the best he could. I never felt I was wasting my time. It was a job like any other. Better than most beause it left my mind free. I could rehearse the roles I was doing for class. But Speicher was something else. I left him to Mrs. Whitney. They deserved each other.

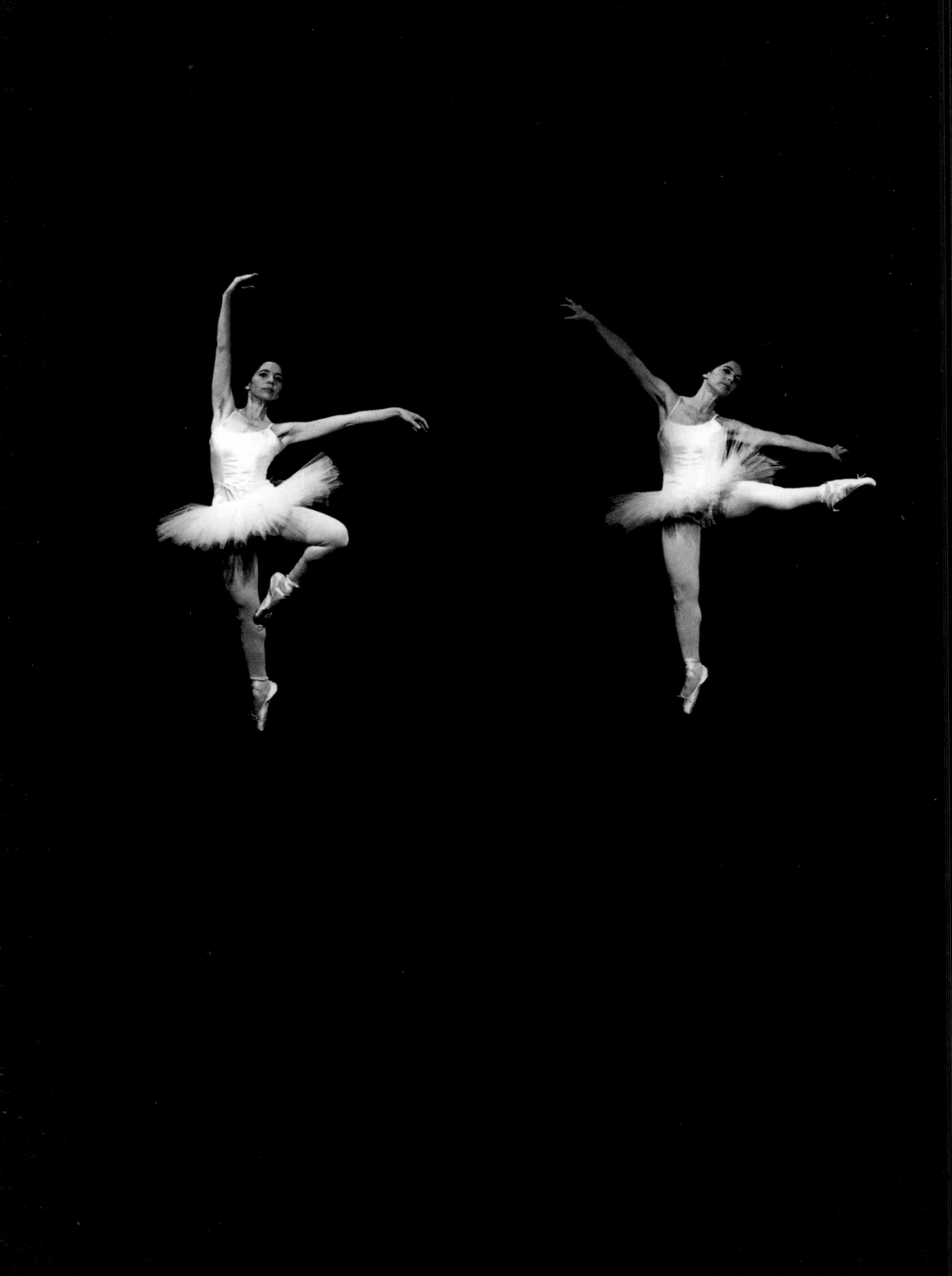

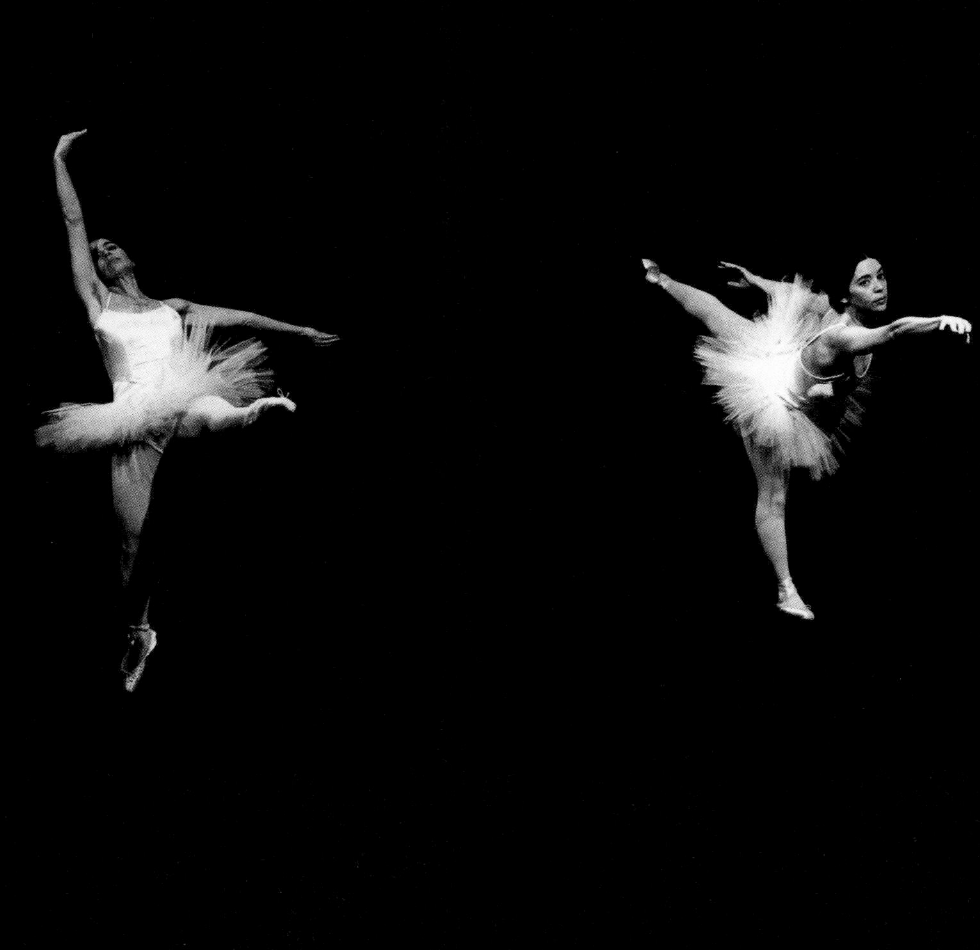

"Eleanora."

I look up expectantly. Vanessa Bell leans over the railing of the balcony.

"Come look at the pictures."

My eyes adjust to the somnolent light. It's only Mary checking out the angles from above. I sigh and go up to have a look. "We should get some good pictures," she says. She hums a little tune. She is happy here. So am I. After all, Lopokova left the Diaghilev Ballet to marry Lord Keynes and live in Bloomsbury. Barbara's place is the closest I'll ever get to it.

The little poodle jumps up to be petted. He barks with delight. Guests belong to him. We are captives. Who would be so base as to refuse him? "But you will work for a living this afternoon, little beast," I whisper into his silky ears. "You must pretend to be my dog for the camera." There are yellow streaks on the underside of his coat. He is growing old, little Flannie. He would be poor Clarkie's age. I hope he's a better actor. Clark flopped in his first performance. And I only took him up to San Francisco with me because he was so devastated when he was left behind. The beautician bathed and brushed him till his fur puffed out with the exuberance of cotton candy. She tied green ribbons behind his ears and his narrow fox face went mad with pleasure. A cocker-Pomeranian mix, he had the profound vanity of the very small dog. He must have loved me very much to stay with me when I never combed him or trimmed his nails. Instead of bathing him I picked the fleas out of his coat and crushed them between my fingers. His silky red fur was matted and scraggly. He deserved better of life. He was a Ballerina's dog and a King's dog too, but he hid in shame at the lumberyard when a well groomed Afghan trotted by. He should have been Markova's dog. He would have sat on a satin pillow and worn a jewelled collar. Poor Clarkie only wore a string around his neck. When I stopped paying for dog licenses he didn't even have that anymore. Yet he followed me wherever I went. I told him everything. He would sit next to me in the car and listen sympathetically to my complaints about the art world. For almost ten years he was my shadow. But an independent little bastard always. If someone he didn't like made too much of him, he snapped and drew blood. When he was cross, his fox nose wrinkled up and his nostrils flared. He became the nastiest son of a bitch. But how proud he was when I carried him, powdered and pampered, into the Palace of the Legion of Honor to do the performance. The King had been scheduled to appear but the Ballerina came instead. She wore a white satin *tutu* and *pointe* shoes. The guards rushed over. "We are doing a performance in there." I pointed across the Great Hall where a crowd of people could be seen. "They are waiting for us." "Sorry. No dogs allowed," they said. "Don't be ridiculous." I picked up speed until I was almost running. "He's in the show." They ran after me but I got there first. The sight of all those people smiling expectantly at our entrance intimidated them and they backed off. Clark couldn't resist some triumphant barks. He was such a ham. But when it counted he turned out to be a flop. I was doing improvisations in those days and I expected him to respond with his usual war games when I shook my cane at him. But instead of circling around me threatening to attack with frenzied barks and growls, he retreated into the audience and sold himself for love. He spent the afternoon being stroked and petted by strangers. He ignored the well-known cues. He refused to play the part he played every day of his life in a play he had invented himself. "The show must go on, you creep," I hissed at him and went into the audience to get him. That 15-pound lump of stubborness went heavy as a ton. When I tried to make him stand up, his legs gave way and he slid back down. But that was a long time ago, Clark. I don't care if you were a lousy actor. I wasn't so good myself in those days. I wish you were here with me now. If my shepherds hadn't accidently killed you when you strayed into one of their melees you would be with me now. This is a role you could play so well. The beautician would make you beautiful again and you would prance down Central Park West at the end of a rhinestone leash. In my lonely bed you would lie in my arms and lick my face when I was sad. You would be proud to belong to such a glamourous lady. I would take you everywhere. You would never be lonely. Not like the poor dog in the hotel in Washington. He barked all evening till I couldn't stand it anymore. "I can't sleep," I complained to the clerk at the desk. "We are very sorry, ma'am," he apologized. "The dog belongs to one of the ballerinas dancing tonight at the Kennedy Center. I will see that she takes him with her to the theatre tomorrow." I was shocked. "Oh, no," I said, backing away. "I don't really care at all. It's fine. Don't bother." "But you should not be disturbed," he said. "It will not happen again." "I want it to happen again," I shouted, making a dash for the elevator. "I forbid you to say one word, do you hear?"

When you are on the road your furry animal is an emblem of affection. He warms your soul and your cold cold flesh. The hotel room isn't strange anymore. You can't wait to return. A dish of bonbons. A ruff of powdered sugar. Loving chocolates. A sweet feast . . .

Barbara is talking about her recent sufferings. Her book came out last year and is a great success. She tells me she's been sick ever since. Bedridden part of the time. She worked on that book for nine years. When it went out into the world she was bereft. "It was like giving birth," she said in a wondering voice. I recognize the postpartum depression.

I always get it after a show. I'll get it when I go back home. You pay for your life. Your art. Your work. The good things in life are never free.

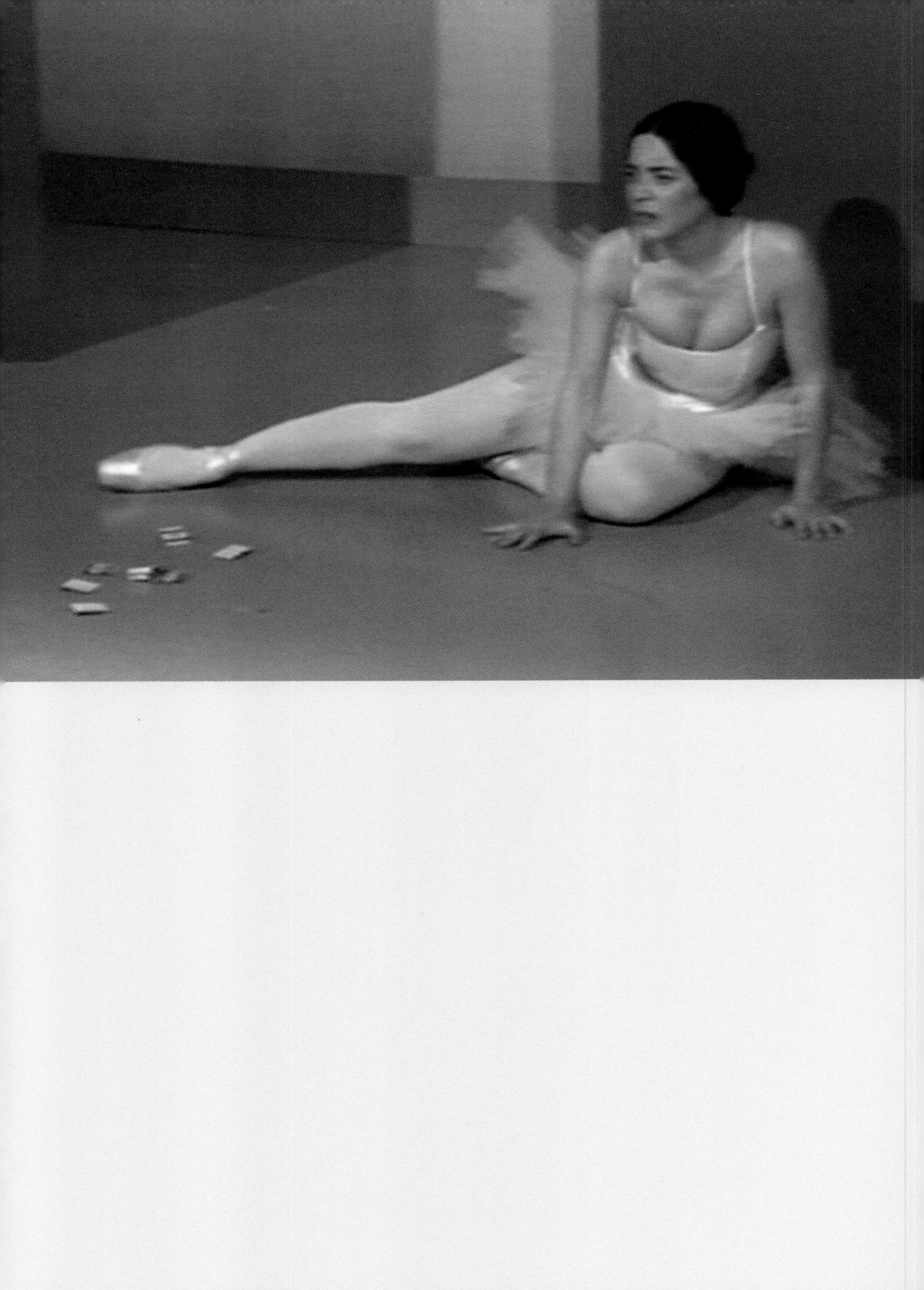

WEDNESDAY ***October 29***

The final performance tonight. I spend the day moving through the dark apartment like a ghost. I'm bored and depressed. Good thing it will all be over the day after tomorrow. I'm sick and tired of this city. Time to go home. My friends will be glad to see me go. They have busy lives to live and I'm like a tourist with too much time on my hands. I never could see what Doug Heubler and John Baldessari saw in going on the road. Doug still speaks wistfully of his days as an itinerant artist in Europe. I remember meeting up with a slight and unencumbered Dan Graham in London just in from Turin or some such place. Being outsiders freed them in some way. Maybe they were hemmed in at home and broke out on the road. Sort of a salesman syndrome. But I'm never moored safely to the world, not even at home. I get lost at the drop of a hat. Being on the road too long is dangerous for me. It gets harder to navigate when the scenery changes.

I phone Ida but I'm in for a surprise. Her voice is low and fierce. There are tears behind it. "How could you have used Anna in your pictures," she rages. "The woman is a witch. A discredited person." I'm so surprised that for a minute I don't understand what she's saying. What pictures? Then I remember. The Russian Tea Room. "But I forgot about it already," I say. "That went Monday." What is all this about? "You've given her a credibility she doesn't deserve," Ida went on. The hurt goes thick in her voice. Oh God, the old sorrows again. I explain that Anna was superb typecasting. "They would never refuse her a table at the Russian Tea Room. I'm just a *parvenu.* She was my ace in the hole." But this is only part of the reason. I can't tell Ida that being Antinova brought about a reconciliation with Anna, not for the sake of the present but the past. It was Anna, years ago, who rescued me from the depression of my stupid Museum of Modern Art show, which nobody came to see because *100 BOOTS* was an outsider like me, and she took me off to Europe where she promised me great things. So she couldn't pull it off. So I ended up crying into a transatlantic phone in Cologne, stared at by uncomprehending migrant workers from Greece. She did the best she could. She was playing it by ear herself. Anna is my past.

I can't discard her without losing myself as well. Being Antinova lets me see that for the first time. Let's not go over the old ground again. "Ida, you are a successful artist. You have the gallery you want. You show in Europe. You sell works. She's not doing much of anything. What the hell do you care if I take some pictures with her? I'm not *Interview Magazine*." But the past is seething all around us. Kirk Douglas stretched out on the ropes. It is his last fight. His whole life unrolls before his eyes between the count of three and ten. "You're out," the referee shouts. I blew it. I should have used Ida in the pictures. She would have been great. She has Russian *intelligentsia* eyes brooding in old photographs. She is the sister of Dostoyevsky's Possessed Woman. She could have come to Carnegie Hall with me for the old man's concert. We would have sat in the reading room of *Goethe House* beneath the bust of the Great Man. We could have had our tea leaves read by a gypsy woman on 20th Street. A dozen other lost possibilities run through my head. She would have inspired me. I would have ignored my self doubts to make a dazzling frame for her. She was the best typecasting of all and I blew it. I feel like screaming. I con her into an uneasy truce and hang up shaking.

I dial Marcia's number. I'm jumpy now. I need help. Maybe she can pick up a *brie* and join me for lunch. But her voice is rushed. She's in a meeting. She has to make up her mind whether to join a ceramic commune or go it alone.

This is the last straw.

"What the hell is a ceramic commune?" I shout.

"A group of women who share a kiln. Should I set up one of my own in the loft or should I join them?

"Do you like them?"

"I don't know them."

"So why would you join them?"

"I get depressed by myself. They might be good for me."

I hang up. I am surrounded by irrelevance. Tonight is my final performance and nobody gives a shit.

I call California.

After ten unanswered rings I hang up and call school.

"Hello, Nancy. Is David there?"

"He's in class. How are you? When are you coming back?"

"Never," I shout and slam down the phone. That should jolt them. Nobody thinks of me at all. If I don't do something soon I'll explode.

Emily left a bottle of crimson nail polish in the bathroom. I'll do my toenails. That's a nice private act. She must have had the bottle a long time. The stuff is thick like goo. I'd better file the nails down first. I haven't trimmed them in years. They're kind of like claws. The big toes are almost as long as my fingernails; the job takes an hour because I'm afraid of spilling the polish on myself and spoiling Madame Jolie's manicure. By the time I finish there are drops of color hardening on my feet and legs. There's no remover so I'll have to wear them like beauty spots under my stockings until I get back to California. I dangle my legs over the arm of the chair to dry and watch TV. Itzhak Perlman plays a Mozart violin concerto over Channel 13. His spoiled petulant face embraces the curves of the violin with voluptuous passion. He's making love to it in public. Nobody says he's self-indulgent or perverted. And the people clap at the end. He's a genius, they say. A genius can do anything. When my mother tried to stop me from dropping out of college, I reminded her, "Pavlova didn't go to college. Bernhardt didn't go to college." "But you aren't Pavlova," my mother shrieked, pulling my ears in exasperation. "How do you know?" I rushed out of the room screaming, "I'm young yet." I pour a glass of sherry and consider the problem of when Pavlova became Pavlova. She couldn't have always been Pavlova. My stomach is rumbling. I wish I had some caviar. I could ring down to the doormen. Ask them to pick up some groceries at Gristede's. But they would only tell me to go fuck myself. They know I'm not Pavlova. Brooding over my misfortunes, I watch Perlman make love to his violin.

The phone rings.

"I hear you're never coming back," David says cheerfully. "Where ya going?"

Gently I lower the phone back onto its cradle. I won't be dragged down by lowlifes. I am surrounded by peasants. It is always so with original spirits. Duse used to rage against the pettiness of her fellows. “The theatre can only be saved by exiling the actors,” she insisted. “They destroy all that is noble and great.”

By the time I reached the gallery in the evening, I was making extravagant gestures and flowing in several directions at once. Pincus-Witten and his friend appeared. I gave them my hand to kiss. So it took the final performance to bring you out. Better late than never. I owe you a lot, Grey Bobby, and you don’t even know it. You gave me that copy of Karsavina’s *Memoirs* a couple of years ago, and from out of your miserable handwriting “Graf Bobby” became the lame *balletomane* and sweater manufacturer Bobby Duff, 8th Earl of Fife, who whimsically introduced himself to me at the stage door in Cannes so many years ago; “My friends call me Grey Bobby. I have led a very lonely life.” For the last time I hid in Ron’s office and counted the house. I was very close to tears. After tomorrow I won’t be Antinova anymore. Or will I? Can I turn it on and off like a light switch? When Eleonora Duse did her first Juliet at the age of fourteen she rose still trembling from her coffin and wandered through the streets of Verona for hours. Her father followed her. He respected her silence and did not talk. The life she had assumed on stage was still fixed in her facial muscles. It was a living mask. Fear gripped her. Perhaps she was lost forever. Taken over by the mask . . . A lot of New Wave kids were coming in. Small startled faces under ruffs and crests. Here and there one painted white with rice powder and a deep red mouth like an asterisk. Stray quarks with pointed Spock ears and black holes for eyes. Waves of heat surged through me. My final performance will be done for the little galactic masters. Proceed, Madame Antinova, and I sailed out into the darkened room. Small serious faces looked up at me with total confidence. Belief shone in their eyes. Not a hint of shame or suspicion. I couldn’t resist tweaking the ears of a tall Venusian Viceroy sitting on the aisle. “Listen,” I could tell him. “There are wishes, lies, and dreams and the greatest of these are lies.” This was a lie, of course. But he wouldn’t care. He adored witches and longed to be ravished by dreams. You could see it in his eyes as he tenderly covered his ear with his hand, holding the warmth of my shadow as I passed. I took my time and considered my audience. Every night the artist must stand before another door. What key will unlock this one? I leaned forward and took them into my confidence. Laughing softly, I gossiped about my lost comrades. What’s a little gossip among friends? They can’t hear me anyway. They’re gone, every one. The confessions tumbled out of my mouth. When words wouldn’t come, my eyes spoke for me. “I am unlucky. I have always been unlucky.” With a shrug I dimissed fortune. Duse, now, was lucky. All her life she had the master key to unlock doors. But one night in Pittsburgh she stood before the last door and it wouldn’t open. An icy rain fell, mixed with sleet. She knocked at the stage door but it was locked. Nobody came to open it for a long time. When they did, she shivered with cold. Her teeth chattered so much she couldn’t talk. But she compelled her feverish body to obey her and *La Porta Chiusa* went on as scheduled. She had never acted so magnificently. “There was an aura about her,” they said later. “Something uncanny.” It was her last performance. She died of pleurisy and pneumonia in her hotel room a few days later. And if the door had opened, what then? When you walk through the room is always empty. It is very cold. Snow freezes the tops of mountains. “Quick, my Swan costume,” Pavlova called out on her deathbed. The people are waiting to see me die. Later I drank too much and got confused. I lost my wine glass. A boy in white trousers and a white shirt and shoes rushed impulsively to my aid. I was touched and only with an effort stopped myself from embracing him. He blushed at his boldness. The young Jean-Louis Barrault was not more beautiful.

Later, the *Ristorante Eleonora Duse* with Geoff Hendricks and Brian Buczak. A touristy affair with nightclub lighting and an *a la carte* menu sandwiched into a fake leather binder. It was the kind of place your rich uncle would take you to celebrate your high school graduation, and after dinner he would give you a watch and ask when you were getting married. But we sat under a large print of Eleonora Duse and the remaining walls were hung with prints of the theatres in the different cities she had played. The *Ristorante Eleonora Duse* might cater to the after-theatre crowd from Kansas, but Geoff and Brian were doing their best.

"We adore Duse," Geoff said.

He described her old home in Asolo. A winding steep hill, hardly any road. "It was that narrow." Geoff put his hands together in prayer. The tiled porch hung out over the mountains. It hadn't fallen for centuries. Way below you could see the Veneto plains. And the Adriatic sparkling behind a mountain range. "You feel like you're in a ship. All you can see in front of you is blue. You could be floating on the Adriatic."

You can't float on the Adriatic. I tried it one night during the Festival of the *Reden-tore.* Great Catherine wheels celebrated over Venice. We got tired and took the bus to the Adriatic. We left our clothes on the sand and waded out naked. It was warm like a bathtub. The water reached to my knees. It never got higher. I could walk over to Yugoslavia. When I lay down to float, I rested on the sand.

"Her house is a shrine," Geoff said. "A lot of *fascisti* material around. She was Mussolini's mistress."

I didn't think so. She would have been old by then. She died in 1925. But to Geoff it doesn't matter. Age doesn't count when you're talking about the Gods. Her first performance was in the 1860s as Little Cossette in *Les Misérables.* She was five years old. They told her to cry so the audience would like her. The little girl was amazed. "Why would people get pleasure out of seeing a child cry?" she asked her mother. Her mother was dying of tuberculosis and had other things on her mind. There is no record of her answer. But her daughter continued to measure success in tears, her own and her audiences'. "I cried very well today," she would say. "The audience was very moved. Not a dry eye in the house." She was a lot like Pavlova if you think about it. When the Dying Swan fluttered around the stage even the hearts of Brazilian dictators wept. On her birthday, Casals stood in the wings and accompanied her. The golden cello sang out over the weeping audience. On stage, the helpless bird sank to the floor. The tears of Rio poured over the well-fed faces. They washed over the glittering gems. They cleansed the sparkling medals. Later the people showered the stage with flowers, diamonds, champagne, in an orgy of adoration and self-abasement. The artist went to a restaurant and ate several steaks and tried not to be depressed.

The waiter couldn't keep his eyes off me. He was obviously fascinated. A dark handsome kid from the Dominican Republic.

"Via Florida," he said and winked at me.

I hoped the darkness hid my wrinkles.

"He's sweet on you," Marcia giggled when he went to get our pasta.

I was cool.

"A *landsman*," I said.

Over the indifferent food we talked about the last days of George Maciunas.

"He was short of money," Geoff said. He would buy unlabeled food cans at 2¢ apiece. He preferred it that way because he never knew what the day would bring.

"Peas, beans, tomatoes . . . frankfurters . . ."

"Frankfurters? In a can?"

"You can get anything in a can. Every day was an adventure."

"What if he got onions?"

Geoff shrugged. "You win a few. You lose a few."

He used to wear a white suit and spend the day lying on a mattress in the living room. Every day he asked his mother which was the right tie. He had seven—one for each day of the week—but he was color blind.

When we were paying the bill, the waiter asked me where I was from.

When I said Russia he didn't believe me.

Everybody said I really was from Russia and he laughed at us.

"I'll bet." He said it in a voice that sounded like it would wag its finger at me, if voices had fingers.

"Well, I do live in California now," I admitted.

He stopped laughing and gave me a sharp look.

When we left he was at the bar talking to somebody. It was late and business was light.

"Good-bye," I called out as we passed.

But my blackness had turned into a suntan. He didn't even bother to look up.

THURSDAY ***October 30***

Lunch at Barbara Cavaliere's down in the financial district. She made an omelette for me while we talked. John Boone, the young artist she lives with, hung around for a while. He told me about a new print series he's planning to do. Like his performance works, these too are all about money. He's been thinking of getting a job on Wall Street as an executive trainee so he can be closer to money. He needs a job anyway. We can't live on *Arts Magazine* paychecks, Barbara laughed. But would they let him quit when the training period was over, I asked. He looked surprised. Why would he do that? He wants to work with money, doesn't he? It's his art form. I was impressed. This guy is planning a life performance that might take his whole life. I remembered an old boyfriend years ago asking me, quick, what do people want most? I had no idea. He shook his head. Not money. Not sex. It's power. At the root of everything is the will to power. Of course, he was a Catholic and something of an idealist. John Boone gives me the feeling he'd like to sit in a room with lots of green paper money and count it out into little piles. Artists are like that. But he does make a good impression. Dark, handsome, a serious face. He'd have to change his pants though. Too tight. Looks a bit of a dandy. How would he come across in wide pants with creases and cuffs? He shakes my hand firmly. Gives me a straightforward look. His eyes are sober but progressive. This man is moving. Up. "Pretty good, huh?" he inquires with satisfaction. He's practicing to be a corporate executive. "You'll pass." I agreed. But he isn't so sure about that. There's the age factor. He's been out of college for a couple of years. He may not be young enough for the best brokerage firms. The correct thing is to be recruited out of college. What has he been doing for the last few years? It would sound irresponsible when he told them. You can do it, Barbara encouraged him. There's only a difference of a year or two. He agreed that they might find the fact that he was an artist interesting. Gives him a touch of class. Barbara thought so too. She should know. She used to be married to a banker. That really surprised me. You don't look like a banker's wife, I said. She shrugged. A neighborhood branch in Queens. He sat behind a formica desk and advised elderly widows and spinsters on their deposits and transfers. He bowled once a week. Mowed the lawn after church. Coached the bank's Little League team. The '50s unrolled before our eyes. Barbara warmed to her story. Frame bungalows in Hempstead. Wall-to-wall carpeting. Lights twinkling on and off on the Christmas tree through the picture window while the house slept. Bankers are like everybody else. But my notions are more romantic. Bankers are silver-haired gentlemen behind mahogany desks in wood-panelled offices high above the city. Secretaries move softly over thick, muffled carpets offering bourbon glasses on sculpted silver trays, while the great men exchange currencies over the telephone with Swiss financiers, German industrialists, adenoidal City men in London, agitated Bourse men in Paris. South African diamond mines rise and fall between shots of Southern Comfort. Gold rains down over the city. Oil flows through the valleys. Plutonium sinks into the sea.

Disgraced soybeans pile up on the lawns of America. But I was wrong. More likely he's out checking whether the real estate in an undeveloped area with a septic tank system constitutes a mortgage risk. He's not likely to have a sleek mistress out of Vassar who only differs from his wife by being twenty years younger. Instead he tried unsuccessfully to hold onto the one he had by beating her up when she went to college. What was a good Italian wife doing in a school anyway except to attend a PTA meeting. He was shrewd. Suspected the worst. A pants chaser, no doubt. I became indignant. What a bastard. Did she get revenge? What happened? Barbara shrugged. "I just left. He made it rough but I had no choice. My teenage son chose to stay behind." I was angrier than she was. I demanded justice but she figured she was lucky to get out. Her tone was whimsical, ironic. John drifted away, the *Wall Street Journal* under his arm. "Got to study up on puts and calls." We settled down to more talk. Once or twice she remembered about the interview we were supposed to do. We should get on with it, she said without enthusiasm. But she drifted back to her life story. She never got to turn on the tape recorder. Her pretty, tough, good-natured New York Italian face never stopped smiling. Her voice was rich and robust. If the story caused her pain, you couldn't tell. I don't think it did. She seemed to be entertaining it as a fiction which happened to belong to her only remotely, in an offhand way. She was mildly curious but hardly desperate. I wondered why she was telling me about herself and to whom she was talking. Was it Antinova or Antin sitting in this darkening room where dusk was beginning to fall? I began to lose sense of who I was. Soon I lost the sense of where I was. Italians are natural actors. There isn't one who couldn't do *Tosca* if they trained her early enough. Surrounded by shadows, Barbara glowed with an ethnic vitality not even life could kill. We drank mugs of good coffee and several glasses of red wine. Then John came back and I sort of drifted down the stairs to find a cab. It's dangerous down here at night, he called down and came after me. The traffic was backed up for blocks. He grabbed a stalled cab and helped me in. The leather seat felt cool and soft against my head. In the cab next to us a distinguished looking man was reading the *Wall Street Journal* while methodically picking his nose. Without looking up from the paper he sucked his finger. I wondered if his driver was watching in the mirror. He must be thinking how gross the upper crust was. They turn into pigs when nobody's looking. What must they do at home?

"So. Are we going to stand here forever? Where the hell are we going?" My driver glared at me through his rear view mirror.

"Nowhere yet," I laughed, gesturing at the stalled traffic. "Relax. We've got plenty of time yet."

The remaining daylight glowed purple. The red and yellow lights of the cars shimmered in the evening haze

The driver turned around to shout at me.

"What the hell? Are you wise-assing me! I said, 'Where are you going?'"

Jesus. Another nut. Maybe I should slip out the door. But the meter was down already.

"Spring Street Bar," I said in a conciliatory tone. "Corner of Spring and Greene."

"Spring and Greene," he mimicked. "Jesus Christ! Spring and Greene. Where the hell is Spring and Greene?"

"It's downtown Soho," I said very slowly. I was getting mad myself. "Just drive and I'll tell you how to get there."

"You'll what?" he yelled. "Now you're telling me how to drive! I don't need nobody to tell me how to drive."

He was purple with rage. The veins stood out in his neck and his brow was twitching.

"So drive your way," I said. "Just leave me alone."

He was mumbling to himself and his hands were shaking on the wheel. It would be smart to butter him up. We could crash if he didn't cool down.

"Oh come on," I said in as friendly a voice as I could. "Cut it out. I'm sorry if you had a bad day. It wasn't my fault. Why take it out on me?"

"Jesus Christ," he yelled, turning around again. He made a fist at me. "If I wasn't driving, I would knock you down for that. What the hell do I care about you?"

"OK, OK. Have it your way. I'm only making conversation."

With difficulty I managed to keep my voice cool but I was beginning to have an irresistible urge to smash his face with my bag. There were a lot of makeup bottles in it and he would feel it. "Just drive and I won't say another word."

"Just drive," he mimicked in a falsetto. "The 'lady' says 'just drive.'" He dripped sarcasm. "Yes, ma'am. No, ma'am." He swung around again. "Listen bitch. Don't tell me what to do."

I sat back in my seat. This was the final straw. I felt like I had lost a battle. I was defeated. My last night as Antinova and I'd probably be murdered. And who would the papers say died? By the time they were through explaining whose two-toned bloody body they found, the citizens of New York would figure I was up to no good and deserved what I got. Unfortunately, I had locked the door. Maybe if I tried to inch the knob up I could sneak out. Throw him a dollar to pay for the meter and run. My fingers inched up to the knob while I looked out the other window as if I were interested in the view. I didn't want to make him suspicious. Shit! The plastic top came off the knob and I couldn't pull it up under the best of circumstances. I tried to slide towards the other door.

He swung around.

"What you got up your sleeve, bitch?"

"I'm just changing my position," I said. "It's uncomfortable to sit in one position all the time."

He was grumbling to himself. Oh Jesus, I think I'm going to faint. At the same time I was in a state of rage. The bastard. The lousy filthy bastard. What does he hate so much about me? My blackness? My femaleness? Both conditions are so damn ambiguous. Instead of blaming him I'm looking for clues in myself. Trying to make myself invisible so I won't make him angrier.

The cars were moving slowly and the snarl was untangling. Well we'd find out soon enough if I was on my way to Soho or a candidate for the garbage dump under the Williamsburg Bridge.

I closed my eyes to try and steady myself. Along with rage, I was scared. My heart was pumping so fast I could get a heart attack. Maybe I should take a valium. But it would slow my reflexes down and put me off my guard. This man was a murderous bastard and it would be more dangerous to take him for something else. When I opened my eyes again we seemed to be moving uptown at a brisk speed. It seemed like we were going towards Soho. I tried to make myself as invisible as possible. I wouldn't even let myself breathe deeply, even though I was short of breath and needed to fill my lungs. I had been taking such short rapid breaths I didn't fill my lungs enough. I was dizzy from lack of oxygen. But we were getting closer to Spring. I was sure now. Unless the man was an unbelievable sadist and was only planning on riding past the Spring Street Bar to crack me up entirely, he might let me off where I wanted to go. It occurred to me suddenly that I would have to pay him. A ludicrous thought. Did he regularly do this number to scare women into leaving him all their money in their relief to get away alive? Rather than count the bills I wanted more than anything to leap out of the car when it came to a stop. Take whatever you want. Thank you for not killing me. But when I felt that I might get away with my life my rage became as violent as my fear. The one thing I knew was that I didn't want to leave that motherfucker a tip. I made a show of taking out my wallet and reaching for a lot of bills. The cab stopped at the corner of Spring and Greene. I was prepared. The fare came to $3.90. I was through the door like a light and turned back to thrust four dollar bills into his hand.

"Keep the change," I shouted and bolted.

He began cursing when I ran into the side door of the Spring Street Bar. Inside it was dark and crowded. I hid in the ladies' room in case he was coming to get me. Later, I slipped out and called Ida from the wall phone. She came right down and we celebrated my last supper as Antinova.

RECOLLECTIONS OF MY LIFE WITH DIAGHILEV

1919-1929

by

ELEANORA ANTINOVA

Illustrated

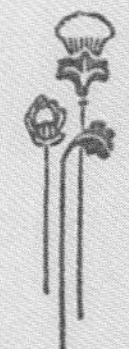

Black Stone Press
San Francisco

FRIDAY ***October 31***

When I woke up this morning my first thought was wow! I don't have to put on make-up anymore. I can lie around in bed doing nothing for as long as I feel like it. I'll go out to breakfast. Poached eggs on toasted English muffin, home fries, side order of bacon, black coffee. All I have to do is slip into jeans and sneakers. No more wiggling into tights and twisting around to snap my bra with recalcitrant fingers. But going down in the elevator I got nervous. What would the doormen say? They had been courteous and I had deceived them. What sort of number was I pulling? Who was this not-so-young white hippie coming out of our house as if it were hers? Maybe they won't recognize me. But then won't they ask who I am? No way! Not on a busy weekday morning. They aren't all that vigilant. I lost my nerve and slipped out the side door where there's only one doorman, who never notices me. This morning he was deep in conversation with an elderly tenant gripping a Zabar's shopping bag. It was a magnificent autumn day. The sun was warm. The air had a zip to it. Breakfast gave me heartburn. By the time I got to the gallery I needed ginger ale to settle my stomach. Ron wanted me to sign the photographs for the limited edition of the *Memoirs*. I should have signed them yesterday. What's come over me today? I never feel like a fraud signing Antinova. I am Antinova. There is no other. But today something's wrong. Is it a hoax? Yesterday it wasn't. I could dash off the signature like that, rip through my theatrical Russian *A* over to the *t* in a single bravura stroke. But here's the same *A*—cramped and timid—it doesn't spill out over the page, the poor thing's looking for a place to hide. The cross line doesn't make it as far as the *t*. I have to deliberately make the line longer by faking a single stroke. I sit in Ron's office trying not to look at the show out there in the gallery. Some of the drawings are alright, I guess. Why do I make these pictures? They embarrass me. Why can't I be like everybody else? I'm a freak. An outsider. I never do the right thing. Dan Graham will never love me. Hey, I better get out of here before my bugginess explodes. It's only the usual after-the-show blues. I said goodbye and beat a retreat. They're glad to see me go. It's time. I walk down Madison for a while. It was grim. I've become the invisible woman. Not one black person has seen me all day. They walk by me as if I wasn't there. They're not snubbing me. They're just not seeing me. I stared morosely into the eyes of a black man with a big Afro like a dark halo around his head. Zero. You're just another white woman and the big city is full of us. Face it. We all look alike. I'm drummed out. Dropped. Lost. Insulted, too. Angry, even. Who are they to treat me like that? Racists! Fuck them! But I can't help missing the silent approving glances of the black men. I even miss the calculating scrutiny of the black women. They were both acknowledgments. Wordless greetings. I've lost my people. Overnight. Like that. Back at the house, I packed and sat around for a while, too alienated to go out and be the *Shadow* again. How did Lamont Cranston take it when his friends looked through him as if he were glass? I was getting anxious just sitting around for two hours waiting for Marcia to drive me to the airport, so I went around the corner to the *Ballet Shop* on Broadway. I'd noticed it earlier in the week but Antinova was ashamed to browse like a lowly fan. "I am not a *balletomane*," she said disdainfully. But it turned out she was a silly snob, because there were several young dancers there. I knew they were dancers by the way they talked. Dancers are always trying to cheer each other up. To them animation is a professional idea. They come on like gangbusters, probably to keep from crying. After hours of enforced silence, they talk the way other workers take coffee breaks. A note of hysteria creeps into the rising voices. They talk about engagements and spoiled chances, long shots that didn't pay off, the latest chiropractor and lingering injuries. Dancers are paranoid people. It is a nasty life. "All right, kids," the young man at the counter calls out when they get too loud. "This isn't Grand Central Station, you know." They giggle and part. The door opens. Shrieks of greeting. It starts up all over again. The store is a dark, intimate little place with a dry old smell. Surprising, the amount of ballet trivia it holds. Colored photographs of the ABT stars, cocktail table books, practice records, porcelain toe shoes, bronze reproductions of Degas dancers, Nureyev T-shirts, postcards, sheet music. They must do a brisk business with the Lincoln Center matinee crowd. There were a couple of shelves of secondhand books. Only a few date back far enough to be interesting. A biography of a recital dancer from the '30s—Doris Myles—has a detailed description of backstage at the *Théâtre du Châtelet,* where Diaghilev had several seasons. Among the newer books, a *Dance Horizons* reprint by Irma Duncan. While waiting to pay I noticed some framed photographs on the wall behind the cash register. Autographed portraits, some full shots in costume on *pointe,* contemporary stuff. It's hard to tell one from the other. They all look alike, quick, athletic, and dashing off into important positions. One was different. An older photograph, slightly faded, a profile shot of a woman with a magnificent aquiline nose and a neck like a column. Strings of beads and pearls crisscross through her long dark plaits. A tiered helmet—or is it a turban—sweeps down over her forehead almost to where the dark somnolent eyes look off into the distance. Detached, exquisitely poised, she sits in a salmon pink silk mat, set in a carved neoclassical gold frame. A signature floats inside a smaller window cut into the mat a few inches below the picture. I couldn't make out the name but the face looked familiar. I felt that agitation you feel when you're on the verge of a discovery and you're afraid to give way to the excitement because you might be disappointed.

In a deliberately unconcerned voice I asked the young man how much the old photograph behind him cost.

He looked blank.

"Beats me. Nobody ever asked before."

A thin older man with steel frame glasses who looked like the owner of a hardware store spoke over the young man's shoulder.

"$150," he said and took it down for me to see.

It sat warm and friendly in my hand. A fine dust covered the surface. I might have been the first person to handle it in over a decade. My thumping heart was right . . . *from Lubov Tchernicheva* . . . in airy graceful letters, more French than Russian. My mother still writes like that. The signature of a hand schooled before the First World War. The letters rose and sank in equal lengths. There might have been a ruled line holding them up, but there wasn't. The pleasure of making letters with a light pen dipped into an ink bottle. Ballpoint pens could only have been invented during the age of the typewriter. Up close I saw the photograph was a standard publicity shot, the size of a postcard, screened in the '30s with rather rich velvety tones already turning brown. I studied the arrogant face. They always said she was beautiful and regal. You could see why the young Sokolova was a little afraid of her. "She was a Queen. One of the few left from the early days. She didn't mix with us. She was of the inner circle."

"It's a very fine frame," the young man encouraged me. "Real period."

I turned the picture over to give myself time to think. It was a lot of money. And what did I care for frames? The young salesman could think of no other reason to buy it. Poor Lubov. She was my teacher in *Before the Revolution.* I painted a life-size masonite cut-out of her. When Allan Kaprow saw me working on it in my studio he acknowledged her undeniable *ambience.* "This is a French person." There was a faded tab pasted on the back of the frame. $125.

I showed it to the young man.

"Well, I don't know," he said uncertainly. "That's an old price. You can see it's faded." He appealed to me as one reasonable person to another. "Inflation, you know."

"Ask your boss," I said.

"$125," the boss agreed. He knew a gift horse when he saw one.

"I'll take it," I said.

The young man looked surprised.

"You will?"

While ringing up the sale he tried to make me feel good by telling me how lucky I was.

"She's one of the old ballerinas, you know. Firebird. You can tell by the Moorish costume."

"No," I said. "Zobeide. The Favorite Wife from *Scheherezade*."

"Oh, is she?" He looked vague. "I don't really know the story ballets."

"Sure," I said. "You like the Bach ones. *Concerto Barocco*." He was pleased.

"How did you know?"

I shrugged.

"They're athletic. They're young. They're American."

"Do you know her?" He indicated the picture.

"She was my teacher."

It came out unexpectedly. I was as surprised as he.

"Oh." He looked impressed and a little puzzled.

"In a manner of speaking," I started to explain. But what could I say? I held my ground. "In her later years," I concluded lamely.

"Do you know Madame Danilova?" he asked. "The School of American Ballet. I've never had her, of course. Master Class for ballerinas. The girls say she's something else." He thrust his hands up over his head and made a bored snooty face. "In the old style, but gives them a touch of class which is necessary, you know."

"I saw her dance years ago. When I was a little girl. My mother used to take me to see the *Ballets Russes.* I saw them all—Markova, Dolin, Massine . . . Eglevsky, Baronova, Toumanova . . ."

"I saw Tallchief, once," he said eagerly. "She was very tall . . ."

"Tchernicheva was also tall. For her day . . . Who was the partner who complained of the massacre scene from *Scheherezade*, 'when she died I got out of the way fast'?"

He whistled with admiration.

"You know a lot. Are you a historian?"

Yesterday I would have been insulted. "I am a ballerina," I would have said in a huffy voice. But today I am only tired and sad. I ask him to wrap *Madame's* picture separately, instead of throwing it in with the books as he is doing.

I watch him wrap my present to myself.

"No, I'm a restorer," I say.

"Of paintings?"

"No. I restore histories. You could say I replace the lost . . . the missing . . . and those that should have been . . ."

"Sounds like fun. What do they call you?"

I took my present and my books and turned to leave.

"A fool," I grinned.

The young man laughed.

"Aren't we all?" he called out as I went out the door into the chilly sun.

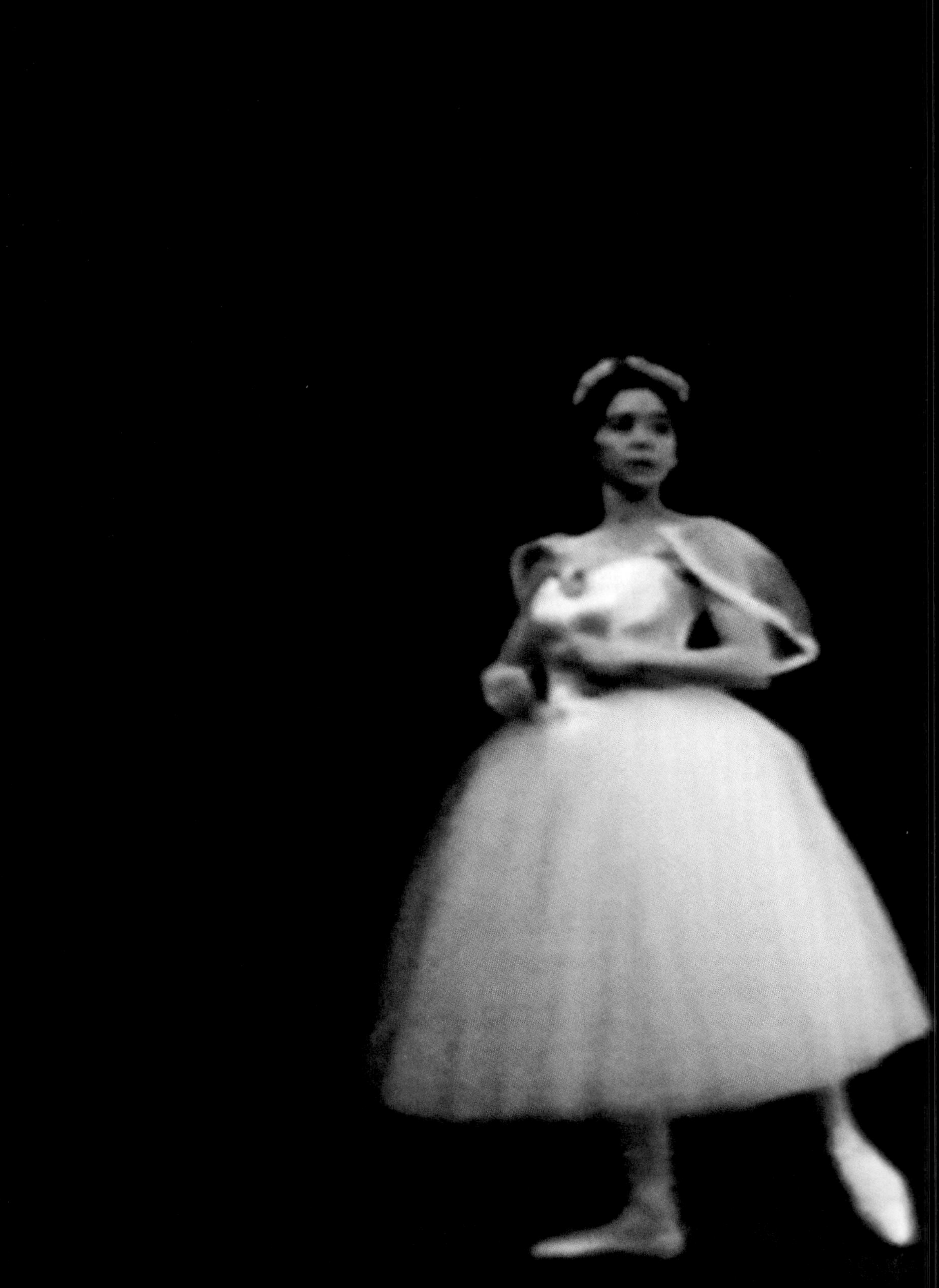

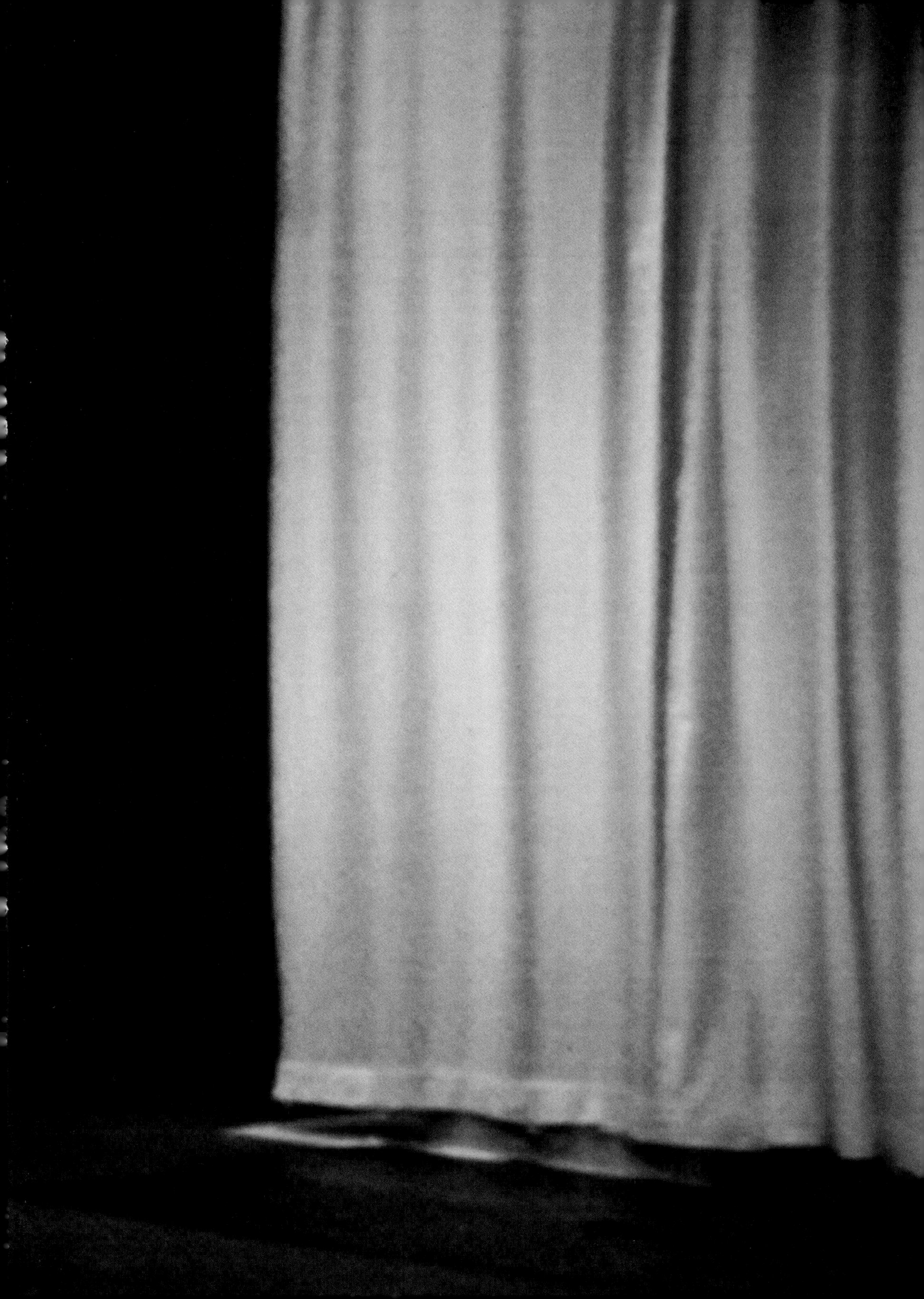

IMAGE CREDITS

Dust jacket front
Eleanor Antin, Portrait of Antinova in her dressing room, 1986, mixed media performance/installation, courtesy of Ronald Feldman Fine Arts, New York

Dust jacket back
Eleanor Antin, *The Two Eleanors*, 1973, photograph, courtesy of Ronald Feldman Fine Arts, New York

Embossing on cover board
Eleanor Antin, *Antinova and the dying swans*, 1975, ink on paper, courtesy of Ronald Feldman Fine Arts, New York

Endpapers (front)
Eleanor Antin, *The Two Eleanors*, 1973, photograph, courtesy of Ronald Feldman Fine Arts, New York

Frontispiece
Eleanor Antin, *Antinova in a Grand Jete*, 1975, ink on paper, courtesy of Ronald Feldman Fine Arts, New York

9
Eleanor Antin, *Antinova at the Ginger Man, October 1980, New York City*, 1980, photograph, courtesy of Ronald Feldman Fine Arts, New York

19
Eleanor Antin, *L'Esclave* from *Recollections of My Life with Diaghilev*, pose 6, 1976/77, photograph, courtesy of Ronald Feldman Fine Arts, New York

20
Eleanor Antin, *Ghost Ballroom #1* from *Before The Revolution*,1975, pen, ink, watercolor on paper, courtesy of Diane Rosenstein Gallery, Los Angeles

25
Eleanor Antin, Drawing from *Recollections of My Life with Diaghilev*, 1974–78, pen, ink, watercolor on paper, courtesy of Ronald Feldman Fine Arts, New York

26
Eleanor Antin, Drawing from *Recollections of My Life with Diaghilev*, 1974–78, pen, ink, watercolor on paper, courtesy Ronald Feldman Fine Arts, New York

33
Eleanor Antin, Drawing from *Recollections of My Life with Diaghilev*, 1974–78, pen, ink, watercolor on paper, courtesy of Ronald Feldman Fine Arts, New York

34
Eleanor Antin, Drawing from *Recollections of My Life with Diaghilev*, 1974–78, pen, ink, watercolor on paper, courtesy of Ronald Feldman Fine Arts, New York

44
Eleanor Antin, Drawing from *Recollections of My Life with Diaghilev*, 1974–78, pen, ink, watercolor on paper, courtesy of Ronald Feldman Fine Arts, New York

45
Eleanor Antin, Drawing from "Recollections of My Life with Diaghilev", 1974–78, pen, ink, watercolor on paper, courtesy of Ronald Feldman Fine Arts, New York

47
Eleanor Antin, *Places, please*, 1975, ink on paper, courtesy of Ronald Feldman Fine Arts, New York

48
Eleanor Antin, Antinova's Costume Drawings from *Before the Revolution*, Maid No. 3, 1976–78, pen, ink, watercolor on paper, courtesy of Ronald Feldman Fine Arts, New York

51
Eleanor Antin, Drawing from *Recollections of My Life with Diaghilev*, 1974–78, pen, ink, watercolor on paper, courtesy of Ronald Feldman Fine Arts, New York

52
Eleanor Antin, *Paris Life* from *Recollections of My Life with Diaghilev*, 1974–78, pen, ink, watercolor on paper, courtesy of Ronald Feldman Fine Arts, New York

55
Eleanor Antin, *The Ballerina and the Poet*, 1986, film still, *From the Archives of Modern Art*, courtesy of Electronic Arts Intermix and Ronald Feldman Fine Arts, New York

58–59
Eleanor Antin, *Ballerina and the Bum*, 1974, film still, courtesy of Electronic Arts Intermix, New York

63
Eleanor Antin, Drawing from *Recollections of My Life with Diaghilev*, 1974–78, pen, ink, watercolor on paper, courtesy of Ronald Feldman Fine Arts, New York

68–69
Eleanor Antin, *Hymn to the Sea*, 1986, film still, *From the Archives of Modern Art*, courtesy of Electronic Arts Intermix, New York

71
Eleanor Antin, Antinova's Costume Drawings from *Before the Revolution*, Soldier No. 3, 1976–78, pen, ink, watercolor on paper, courtesy of Ronald Feldman Fine Arts, New York

75
Eleanor Antin, Antinova's Costume Drawings from *Before the Revolution*, Sans Culotte No. 3, 1976–78, pen, ink, watercolor on paper, courtesy of Ronald Feldman Fine Arts, New York

79
Eleanor Antin, Antinova in *The Last Night of Rasputin*, 1989, 16mm film, film still, courtesy of Milestone Film and Video, New Jersey

80
Eleanor Antin, Antinova in *The Last Night of Rasputin*, 1989, 16mm film, film still, courtesy of Milestone Film and Video, New Jersey

84–85
Eleanor Antin, Antinova in *The Last Night of Rasputin*, 1989, 16mm film, film still, courtesy of Milestone Film and Video, New Jersey

89
Eleanor Antin, *Pocahontas* from *Recollections of My Life with Diaghilev*, pose 1, 1976/77, tinted silver gelatin photograph, courtesy of Ronald Feldman Fine Arts, New York

92
Eleanor Antin, *The Hebrews* from *Recollections of My Life with Diaghilev*, pose 2, 1976/77, tinted silver gelatin photograph, courtesy of Ronald Feldman Fine Arts, New York

93
Eleanor Antin, *Prisoner of Persia* from *Recollections of My Life with Diaghilev*, pose 2, 1976/77, tinted silver gelatin photograph, courtesy of Ronald Feldman Fine Arts, New York

97
Eleanor Antin, Antinova and her vaudeville partner Orlando in *In a Bazaar in Bangalore*, film still, *From the Archives of Modern Art*, courtesy of Electronic Arts Intermix, New York

99
Eleanor Antin, Antinova in *Swan Lake*, with James Tackett, film still, *From the Archives of Modern Art*, courtesy of Electronic Arts Intermix, New York

100
Eleanor Antin, Antinova in *Help! I'm in Seattle*, 1986, photograph, courtesy of Ronald Feldman Fine Arts, New York

103
Eleanor Antin, Antin as Antinova in *Before the Revolution*, premiere performance at The Kitchen, New York, 1979, photograph, courtesy of Ronald Feldman Fine Arts, New York

105
Eleanor Antin, Antinova as Marie Antoinette in *Before the Revolution* from *Recollections of My Life with Diaghilev*, pose 2, 1976–77, photograph, courtesy of Ronald Feldman Fine Arts, New York

108–109
Eleanor Antin, *Torn Ribbon*, 1973, photograph, courtesy of Ronald Feldman Fine Arts, New York

112–113
Eleanor Antin, Portrait of Antinova in her dressing room, 1986, mixed media performance/installation, courtesy of Ronald Feldman Fine Arts, New York

116
Eleanor Antin, Antin performing as Antinova, 1981, photograph, courtesy of Ronald Feldman Fine Arts, New York

128–129
Eleanor Antin, Antin as Antinova visiting her friends, 1981, photograph, courtesy of Ronald Feldman Fine Arts, New York, and Diane Rosenstein Gallery, Los Angeles

134
Eleanor Antin, *Recollections of My Life with Diaghilev*, installation/performance photograph, 1980, courtesy of Ronald Feldman Fine Arts, New York

146–147
Eleanor Antin, *Loves of a Ballerina*, installation photograph, 1986, courtesy of Ronald Feldman Fine Arts, New York

152
Eleanor Antin, Antin as Antinova with Anna Canepa at the Russian Tea Room, New York, 1980, photograph, courtesy of Ronald Feldman Fine Arts, New York

167
Eleanor Antin, *Pavlova and her favorite swan*, 1976, pen, ink, watercolor, courtesy of Ronald Feldman Fine Arts, New York

169
Eleanor Antin, Antin as Antinova reading from *Recollections of My Life with Diaghilev*,1980, photograph, courtesy of Ronald Feldman Fine Arts, New York

178
Eleanor Antin, *Torn Ribbon #2*, 1973, photograph, courtesy of Ronald Feldman Fine Arts, New York

182–183
Eleanor Antin, Antin as Antinova in New York, 1980, photograph, courtesy of Ronald Feldman Fine Arts, New York, and Diane Rosenstein Gallery, Los Angeles

186–187
Eleanor Antin, *Caught in the Act*, with Phil Steinmetz, 1973, film still, courtesy of Electronic Arts Intermix and Ronald Feldman Fine Arts, New York

190–191
Eleanor Antin, *Caught in the Act*, from *Choreographies*, 1973, silver gelatin photograph, courtesy of Ronald Feldman Fine Arts, New York

194
Eleanor Antin, *The Little Match Girl Ballet*, 1976, film still, courtesy of Electronic Arts Intermix, New York

195
Eleanor Antin, Antinova in *The Little Match Girl Ballet*, 1976, film still, courtesy of Electronic Arts Intermix and Ronald Feldman Fine Arts, New York

204
Eleanor Antin, Cover from *Recollections of My Life with Diaghilev*, 1974–78, limited artist's exhibition edition, Black Stone Press, San Francisco

210
Eleanor Antin, *Caught in the Act*, waiting to go on, 1973, film still, courtesy of Ronald Feldman Fine Arts, New York

Endpapers (back)
Eleanor Antin, *Love's Shadow*, with Luke Theodore Morrison, 1986, film still, from *The Archives of Modern Art*, courtesy of Electronic Arts Intermix and Ronald Feldman Fine Arts, New York

Published by:
Hirmer Verlag
Nymphenburger Strasse 84
80636 Munich, Germany

Written by Eleanor Antin

Concept: Eleanor Antin
Hirmer project management: Rainer Arnold
Layout and typesetting: Petra Lüer / WIGEL, Munich

Copyediting: Jonty Tiplady
Additional text editing: Lynn Schuette
Proofreading: Rita Forbes
Pre-press and repro: Reproline Genceller, Munich
Printing and binding: Passavia Druckservice, Passau, Germany
Paper: Luxo Art Samt New 150 g/sqm
Printed in Germany

Bibliographic information published by the
Deutsche Nationalbibliothek

The Deutsche Nationalbibliothek lists this publication in the Deutsche Nationalbibliografie; detailed bibliographic data is available on the Internet at http://www.dnb.de.

ISBN 978-3-7774-2538-2

www.hirmerpublishers.com

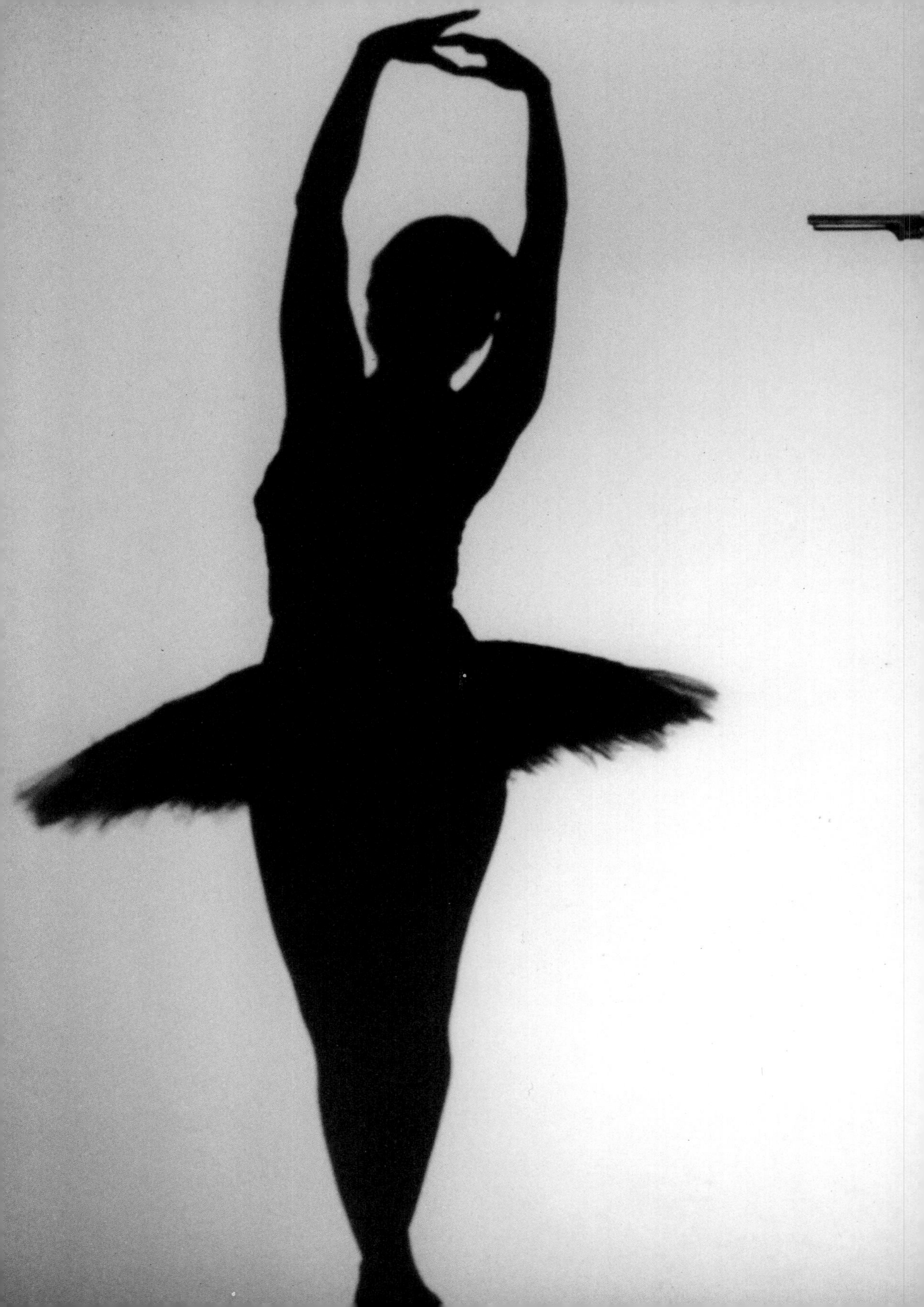